# ONE TO GROW ON

## Will Carlson

*Greenhouse Grower*
*Editors*

Meister Publishing Company, Publishers
Willoughby, Ohio

Meister Publishing Company
37733 Euclid Avenue
Willoughby, Ohio 44094
www.meisternet.com

ISBN 1-892829-07-X

*First edition*

This book is gratefully dedicated to *all* my students:

- 1,500 undergraduate students at Michigan State University (MSU);
  - 40 graduate students at MSU;
- 30,000 students in Extension courses from the United States, Canada, and around the world; and
- all those who have read my columns over the past 30 years in *American Vegetable Grower* and *Greenhouse Grower*.

I hope you have all found One To Grow On!

# Contents

## TAKING CARE OF BUSINESS

## CULTIVATING EMPLOYEES

## CONNECTING WITH CUSTOMERS

MARKETING YOUR PRODUCTS

# Editors' Preface

Growers knew Will Carlson long before they met him, especially those outside the state of Michigan. They got to know him the same way most of us did – by reading his enormously popular column first in *American Vegetable Grower* (*AVG*) and later on in *Greenhouse Grower* (*GG*).

Even when he debuted with his first column, "Bedding Plants," in *AVG* in February 1973, he was already a recognizable floriculture figure. He had wit. He had insight. He had style. And he captured the essence of the industry and put it into words like no one else.

Thirty years after Meister Publishing introduced Will Carlson to the floriculture world in the pages of *AVG*, he remains an institution with his column "One To Grow On" in *GG*. While his retirement in September 2002 marked the end of an illustrious career as horticulture professor and floriculture extension specialist at Michigan State University, his commentary remains a staple in "One To Grow On" in *GG*.

Whether appearing in *AVG* or *GG*, Will's columns consistently have set a standard of excellence, not just for Meister Publishing, but for that elite group of writers in floriculture nationwide who lay claim to the envied title of "columnist."

Most of them can't touch Will. That is why over a period of time we became so deeply puzzled by a simple question: Why haven't we published a collection of Will Carlson's columns? With Will now fully retired from university life, the answer became quite clear that the timing was never completely right to take on such a huge project – until now. You are holding the result.

It is high time we show off one of floriculture's stars. He is, after all, an unsurpassed craftsman. He also happens to have provided floriculture with a true, always informative, and often moving chronicle of greenhouse life over the last three decades. His writing style captures a hybrid skill that most others in the industry don't possess: production expertise coupled with a keen sense of business management. It's this combination that has helped growers, both large and small, transform their operations into profitable enterprises.

We have published this book because there were so many others who believed sincerely that it was a must-do project for floriculture. Among them: Barbara Carlson, Will's wife for more than 40 years, who has been a big part of his success and mother of his two sons. Sandy Draheim, who spent endless hours in Grand Haven, MI, organizing, collating, and proofreading archives of Will's columns. The *Greenhouse Grower* editorial staff, who have translated and converted volumes of Will's hand-written scribbles from paper to electronic documents. Dick Meister, chairman and editor-at-large at Meister Publishing, who has provided essential guidance in Will's role with Meister Publishing and who has been his long-time friend and confidant... The list could go on. But this book already has been far too long in coming. Let's not delay it any further.

Just one final point: Any determination of "best" is by its nature subjective. These, then, are just a few of our favorites. In re-reading thousands of his columns as we made these choices, we were cheered by the thought that we could randomly pick any of them and still have what could honestly be called the best.

Will Carlson is always at his best. Enjoy reading him. We did. We do.

*— Greenhouse Grower Editors*

# Introduction

When I got started in this business, I was bold – or naive – enough to drive a VW into a Cadillac operation and tell them how to make money. Lots of things have changed. The VW is only one of them. The overall objective is still – and always will be – helping our industry to grow and be profitable.

Throughout the past 30 years, I have had the privilege of sharing my thoughts and ideas with thousands of people who are part of the greenhouse industry in my column, "One To Grow On." Of course, the column has evolved over the years, as has the industry – and, if you look at the pictures of me that have accompanied the column, so have I!

*Will credits his wife, Barbara, for a big part of his successful career.*

When the column was first published in 1973, *Greenhouse Grower* didn't exist. The column appeared in *American Vegetable Grower*. I was a relative youngster, who didn't have a lot of experience in writing, but who had lots of ideas on how to grow the bedding plant industry. Thank goodness for my wife, Barbara, and my wonderful editors over the years, including, Edna Gould, Charlotte Sine, Jane Lieberth, Robyn Dill, Delilah Onofrey, Matt Hopkins, and Laura Henne.

During that first decade (1973-1983), the industry came to focus more and more on greenhouse crops, and, in 1983, *Greenhouse Grower* was born. As the industry has grown over the years, so has the magazine. "One To Grow On" now reaches nearly 25,000 subscribers across the United States and around the world.

When retiring after more than 35 years as a university professor, researcher and extension specialist, I appreciated this opportunity to revisit the more than 350 columns that have been published and select those shared in this book. In choosing which to include, my attention was drawn to the title of the column that appeared in *AVG* in February 1979 – "Plants Aren't the Problem – People Are." Upon reflection, people may not be the problem, but they are the challenge – and the opportunity!

Treat a bench of 100 geraniums the same and you will have the same results, for better or worse. Treat 100 people the same and the results will be very different! The articles in this book were selected, not to explain how to grow plants, but to help the reader understand how to grow people and a business.

Over the years many people have influenced and enriched my life. Foremost has been my wife, Barbara. Few people have the tremendous variety of skills she draws upon every day to support me personally and professionally. She provides the core of our family life from financial management to child raising to gourmet cook and superb hostess. She has worked tirelessly to help me develop many of my projects, including Bedding Plants, Inc., as well as sharing insights for many of my extension presentations, magazine articles, reports, and talks.

Our sons, Will and Wayne, have been a source of great joy for Barbara and me. As a parent, I hope that I have been an inspiration to my children. I can truthfully say that Will and Wayne have inspired me. Will is the executive director of the Flower Promotion Organization. He challenges me to think globally and to always be looking for the next opportunity to support and grow the industry. Wayne is a computer consultant specializing in logistic management software. He has been diligent in trying to bring his dad into the world of computer technology. Both are married and have blessed Barbara and me with grandchildren: Wayne and Danette and our granddaughter, Riley; Will and Mary and our three step grandchildren, Laura, George, and John.

I have been fortunate to have wonderful support from my extended family. My brothers, Victor and Robert, and my sister Dorothy, and their families have been a great source of help and inspiration to me.

Michigan State University (MSU) has been a great place to work and grow over the years. I have had many opportunities to interact with wonderful colleagues, excellent graduate and undergraduate students, a dedicated staff, and supportive administrators. My floriculture colleagues at the East Lansing campus and at other land grant institutions across the country, as well as with the Cooperative Extension Service, have been a strong source of support and guidance for my efforts. Industry personnel, including growers, allied trades people, trade associations, educators, publishers, and consumers from garden clubs to service organizations to individual gardeners, have helped provide material that I've used in my columns.

There is no way for me to recognize and thank all of the people who have influenced and enriched my life here. But, I would like to tell you a story about two of them.

The first is my mother, Marie Karoline Jensen Carlson. One of my fondest memories of my mother is the day I asked for a two-wheel bicycle. I asked, "Mom, can I have a bicycle?" "Certainly," she replied. "Where is the money?" I asked. "That's your problem," she answered. She believed that you could have anything you wanted as long as you were willing to work for it.

Funny thing, one of my mentors at MSU, John Carew, shared the same philosophy. Whenever I came up with an idea for a new project, John would say, "That's a wonderful idea! Go ahead and do it!" I would ask, "Where's the money?" He would respond, "That's your problem!" And with his help, my own commitment and creativity, and the support of my family and colleagues, I was able to make it happen.

This book would not have been developed were it not for the encouragement of Meister Publishing Co., most notably Richard Meister, chairman; Gary Fitzgerald, president; William J. Miller II, executive vice president; Charlotte Sine, editor-in-chief; Delilah Onofrey, group editor; and Matt Hopkins, business manager. Together, we came up with the concept for this project during dinner at the Fitzgerald home in the summer of 2002.

I am grateful to Matt Hopkins who became the project manager and developed the action plan for the book's development, editing and production. Sandy Draheim, another MSU extension retiree and the wife of one of my extension colleagues, helped me select the articles and provided input into the format.

As one of my first employers always said, "Be happy, but not content!" Even if you are on the right track, you can get run over if you stand still. I hope you will find these columns add to your knowledge of trends in the industry, some of the legendary leaders who have contributed to its growth, how you can become a leader, get started in business, develop a business strategy, cultivate employees, connect with customers, and market your products. The goal is to help you successfully grow your plants, your people, and your business!

In the following pages, you will find the wisdom of many people that I have been fortunate to have met, worked with, and lived with, in the case of my mother and Barbara. There are also things I learned from people that I have never met, who have influenced my life and contributed to the knowledge and stories that have been shared with *Greenhouse Grower* readers. These are the authors of books and articles, which have sparked ideas and kindled discussions.

As I reflect on my life of more than 60 years, I realize there are two ways that I learn. First, real life experiences – visiting and interacting with people – have made great contributions to my knowledge. Second, reading about what others have learned on their life journeys has expanded my horizons far beyond what could be experienced personally. Many of the columns you will find in the pages that follow take the ideas that others have shared and put them into the context of the greenhouse industry.

Many of the articles included are based on conversations with people whom I've helped build their businesses and the floriculture industry in the United States and Canada. While I am proud of my accomplishments, I hope to continue to learn and grow in my retirement. I want the same for everyone who reads this book. To help in this effort, you will find a list of books that build on what is included here. Some have provided the inspirations for "One To Grow On" columns. Others have been recommended to me by experts in leadership education and business planning.

My wish for myself, for you the reader and for our industry is that we "keep on growing," and that there is always "One More To Grow On!"

# ONE TO
# GROW ON

# THE EVOLUTION OF AN INDUSTRY

In the 30 years I have been writing my columns in *American Vegetable Grower* and *Greenhouse Grower*, one of the questions I was asked frequently is "How big is the industry?" When I first addressed the question in September 1977, a survey of growers in 25 states reported fewer than 20 million flats of flowers grown in less than 32 million square feet of production space with a total wholesale value of $61 million.* The most recent column responding to this question in September 2000 reported floriculture's value worldwide as $22 billion annually, led by the United States with $4.9 billion.

The evolution of floriculture has not only been reflected in dollars and cents or square feet of production space. I have witnessed tremendous changes in all aspects of the industry – moving from pencil and paper to computers, glass to plastic, mineral soil to soilless media, hand-seeded flats to containers with plugs, and the introduction of thousands of new varieties and cultivars.

The floriculture industry needs to build on its past successes, learn from difficult experiences, and move forward with strategic vision into the 21st century. Following is a selection of columns in which I share some thoughts on how the industry has evolved over the years and provide keys to how it can continue to grow in the future.

*Flowers and Foliage Plants Production and Sales, 1975-76, Intentions for 1977, USDA Statistical Reporting Service, Special Circular 6-1.

# 'Past Is Prologue' For Greenhouse Industry

*An overview of the bedding plant industry in the*
*United States from colonial times to the 1980s.*

At the end of 1983, it seems appropriate to review our beginnings and look ahead to our challenging future.

The bedding plant industry in the United States. began when the colonial settlers brought seeds or cuttings from Europe. The early major flower growing areas were around major population centers like Philadelphia, New York, and Boston.

Early gardens, like the Williamsburg Palace Gardens, were focal points of early plantings, but would be a far cry from today's colorful bedding plant displays. In the late 1780s, there were actually advertisements for such items as geraniums and marigolds to gardeners in the Philadelphia area. Shortly before and after the Civil War, bedding plants were common in the South. Plantings primarily consisted of alternatha, ageratum, and fibrous begonias.

The modern bedding plant industry started just after World War II. In the late 1940s, the typical operation sold seedlings in units or flats of 100. Retailers would break apart these units, and cut out the plants to sell to the consumer. By 1949, the industry was valued at $16.9 million.

The first significant improvement in the industry was the introduction of $F_1$ hybrids. In 1950, Scottie Sinclair of Bodger Seed Co. developed the first open-pollinated petunia, 'Fire Chief.' This was followed in 1952 by the introduction of a coral salmon grandiflora variety called 'Ballerina,' bred by Charlie Weddle. He and Claude Hope then started Pan American Seed Co. One of their first joint efforts was the development in 1953 of the $F_1$ multiflora red petunia, 'Comanche.'

In the 1950s, the plastic flat was also introduced. More and more growers began to use plastic flats or inserts as wood became more expensive and the 100-unit flat became cumbersome. Because growers wanted to sell fewer than 100 plants to each customer, the flats were broken down into 12 inserts in one flat; the smaller units were called baskets or "pills."

From 1950-53, many companies were working on developing the plastic flat, including several in Michigan. They included Alma Plastics Co., which worked closely with Post Gardens in Battle Creek and Leonard Bettinger in Toledo, OH; Lustruf, which was led at that time by Fred Blackmore; and East Jordan Plastic Co., led by Ken Diver.

Reports vary, but growers probably first started using plastic flats in 1956. From the information I can find, Leonard Bettinger was one of the first bedding plant growers to convert all his production from the wooden flats to the plastic ones. Coverings for greenhouses changed with the introduction of plastics, too.

But new varieties and plastics weren't the only reason for the spurt in growth of the industry. An increasing number of housing starts and an increasing population were also partially responsible. The value of the industry in 1959 was estimated at $32.8 million and by 1969, it would double in value to $61.6 million.

In the late 1960s and early '70s, the most significant changes occurred in breeding and mechanization. In 1966, Dr. Richard Craig of Penn State University developed the first geranium from seed, 'Nittany Lion Red.' Soon after, Dr. Lowell Ewart, then with Harris Seed Co., introduced the Moreton hybrids, and Jack Kline with Pan American Seed Co. developed the Carefree series. All had an impact on the industry.

But it wasn't until the mid-1970s that we started to see a tremendous increase in production of geraniums from seed. This was mostly due to the introduction of Sprinter varieties from Goldsmith Seeds. When Sprinter was developed, there were a total of 10 to 20 million seed geraniums sold each year; today there are more than 100 million sold.

The introduction of seeders and transplanters has highlighted the 1970s. The early 1980s saw the wide acceptance of vacuum seeders on the market, and now this equipment has seen wide commercial use. The use of the plug has taken time to develop, but it does mean reducing the amount of energy required to produce a crop, and a quick turnaround time so that finished flats can be shipped, replanted, and in flower in a short period of time. In 1979, the industry was valued at roughly $150 million, and a conservative estimate of the 1983 industry is $250-$350 million.

With continued growth, we have the responsibility to increase sales;

this is the area of most concern to growers now. In order for the bedding plant industry to continue to survive and grow at the rate we have enjoyed over the past 35 years, it will be necessary to develop the time and effort in marketing the product to increase sales.

I am hopeful the decade from 1989-1999 will be remembered as the marketing decade in bedding plants, when we begin to develop sophisticated techniques to sell more plants to the consumer.

*– December 1983*

## Megatrends In Floriculture

*How do changes in the floriculture industry relate to the perspectives shared by social forecaster John Naisbitt in his book Megatrends?*

Recently, I reread the best-selling book *Megatrends*. The author, John Naisbitt, is a social forecaster, speaker, and adviser to many of America's leading corporations. He is also chairman of the Naisbitt Group, a research and consulting firm based in Washington, DC.

Naisbitt identifies eight "mega-trends" that have altered both business and the overall manner in which our society operates. Looking at what's happened to floriculture in the last 10 years, I see that he is right on target.

### The Information Age

Naisbitt condenses the history of the United States into three categories: farmer, laborer, and clerk. In other words, we started as an agricultural society and have now become an informational society.

In the early 1800s, 90% of our people were employed in agriculture and produced 100% of our food. Today, 3% are employed in agriculture and produce 120% of our food. There are now more people employed at universities than on farms.

The agricultural society gave way to the industrial society in the early 1900s, when we learned to mass produce products. The industrial society evolved to become the informational society in the late 1950s.

The new wealth is no longer agricultural or industrial – it is in the know-how brought about by information. Our society has now learned to mass produce information in the same way it mass produces automobiles. Naisbitt states the new source of power is not money in the hands of a few, but information in the hands of many.

### The Floriculture Gap

In spite of these changes, many of us in floriculture are operating in the agricultural or industrial mind set. We want our two- and four-year schools to turn out technicians who specialize in small, specific areas. Yet

I believe the horticultural specialist of yesterday will be replaced by a generalist who can adapt.

For example, 10 years ago a greenhouse operator needed to know little about computers. Today's mechanized greenhouse systems require computer knowledge. The successful grower processes new information and adapts.

People still say to me, "Just give me someone who knows how to grow plants; I'll do the rest." In this information age, knowing how to grow plants is not a static process. We must ask for well-educated employees and then give them the latest information about plants so they can produce the best crop possible.

In both our society and our industry, more information is becoming available at a faster rate. Naisbitt indicates in 1984, 6,000 to 7,000 scientific articles were written each day. At this rate, the volume of technical information would double every 5½ years. With today's new information systems and increased number of scientists, this volume of data now doubles every two years.

This situation threatens to drown us with information while leaving us high and dry when it comes to knowledge. Our children are graduating from high school and college less prepared to deal with the new era than we were. Test scores in basic skills such as math, science, and verbal ability are lower than they were 10 years ago.

In our business, as in any other, the one who has the information first can use it to competitive advantage. This is what has motivated firms to send employees all over the world looking for innovations and trying to beat the "information float" – the gap between the innovation and their firm's awareness of it.

If the amount of information produced doubles every two years, it goes without saying that we must continue to learn to keep up with our industry. New equipment and methods are surfacing every day, each requiring new training for faster information processing.

### It's Happening At MSU

We've experienced a dramatic example of this phenomenon at Michigan State University (MSU). The concept of graphical tracking was developed in 1986, field tested in 1987, and commercially implemented in 1988. The first year, our computers took about an hour to develop a graph from a grower's data and the mail took a few days more to deliver the information. Today, the graph can be constructed in less than five minutes and then faxed back to the grower in another five minutes.

At MSU, we have also developed the Spartan Ornamental Network (SON) to help reduce this information float. It used to take six months to a year to develop, print, and distribute an extension bulletin. SON distributes the same information in less than half the time. SON also disseminates new research findings within minutes, rather than the weeks or months previously required.

### The Human Factor

The human side of high technology is also very important. Naisbitt contends that the increasing use of high-tech methods creates a corresponding increase in the need for people to meet and discuss the problems and opportunities generated by such technology.

Despite technological advances, I don't see us getting to a point where human beings are eliminated from the growing process. The more we are surrounded by high technology, the greater our need for the human touch. It will be a long time before a machine can duplicate the skills of a human being.

I predict that this human touch, operating within the information age, will make floriculture more exciting in the next 10 years than it has been in the past 100.

*– December 1988*

# What Is A Greenhouse?

*How the industry answers this question is important for a variety of reasons – political, financial, and personal.*

The experts have defined a greenhouse in various ways:

*"A greenhouse has one purpose to provide and maintain the environment that will result in optimum crop production or maximum profit. This includes an environment for work efficiency as well as for crop growth."*
– Robert Aldrich and John Bartok, *Greenhouse Engineering*

*"The term greenhouse refers in the U.S. to a structure covered with a transparent material for the purpose of admitting natural light for plant growth. These structures are usually heated artificially and differ from other growing structures such as cold frames and hot beds in that they are sufficiently high to permit a person to work from within. The European definition differs in that the structure receives little or no artificial heat. The term glasshouse is used in Europe for an artificially heated structure."*
– Paul Nelson, *Greenhouse Operation and Management*

*"A greenhouse is a structure covered with transparent material that utilizes solar radiant energy to grow plants. The majority of greenhouses have heating, ventilating, and cooling equipment for temperature control."*
– John Mastalerz, *The Greenhouse Environment*

My personal definition is:
*"A greenhouse is a specialized plant growing facility."*

I favor a basic definition because the details can change. Greenhouses can either be large enough for people to work inside or they can be automated so people don't need to work inside. Computerized HID lighting, heating, ventilating, and cooling equipment can control the environment based on plant models. Greenhouses can either be transparent to admit natural light or be opaque and use artificial light. With new technology, the variations are endless, so don't lose sight of the central definition – a specialized plant growing facility.

### Why It's Important

This fits with the definitions of other specialized enterprises where agricultural commodities are produced, such as a milking parlor or a chicken ranch.

Such a central definition is important when lawyers or tax assessors get involved, trying to label a greenhouse as an industrial, rather than an agricultural operation. In their effort to get as many dollars as possible, tax collectors are tempted to disregard the long-standing tradition of our agricultural ties.

It is critical to our industry that we are viewed in an agricultural context. Remember, floriculture represents more than 10% of agricultural production and is mentioned in the 1990 Farm Bill. The Society of American Florists (SAF) was chartered by Congress more than 100 years ago as part of agriculture and is still recognized as such. The fact that state governments allow us to buy farm license plates for our vehicles proves they consider us agriculture. A township tax collector has no right to say we are not agriculture.

If your operation is ever labeled industrial, contact SAF or the Professional Plant Growers Association for the documentation you need to make your case.

### It's Merely A Tool

Beyond the definitions, classifications, and legalities, understand that a greenhouse is just a tool. When people call and say, "What kind of a greenhouse should I build?" my answer always is, "What do you want to do with it?"

As with any tool, the answer depends on the use. Don't get so caught up in the tool that you forget what it is for. You must know what you want to do with your greenhouse and have a practical plan to make it happen.

I knew a man who quit his job at General Motors and bought a greenhouse. He came to my office and said he had 10,000 square feet of greenhouse space and needed to make $50,000 to replace the salary he had earned at GM. He was disappointed when I told him it couldn't be done.

Others have come to me to discuss hydroponic, organic, or vegetable production in the Midwest. The ideas sound great, but without planning and research into the costs and the market, the chances of success are small. Many have attempted it, but few have succeeded.

People's expectations often exceed reality. They don't know the capabilities and limitations of the greenhouse tool they are using. They haven't done their homework and planned exactly what they are going to do with their tools before they purchase them.

### Its Value Is Relative

The greenhouse itself is a direct reflection of the people operating it. A clean, well-organized greenhouse is a sign of good management, just as a poorly maintained, disorganized one is a sign of poor management. A greenhouse can be a valuable tool to produce plants and make a profit or it can be a clumsy tool with which to produce inferior plants and lose a great deal of money. I've seen both happen.

It's difficult to place a value on a greenhouse. In a bankruptcy auction, one will go for less than it would cost to build. It's easy to figure out how much it costs to build, but it's not easy to estimate the value of the entire operation. With a plan and skilled employees, a greenhouse can be worth far more than its construction value. If a grower is poor or the plan doesn't exist, it can be worth far less than its construction value.

If you want to investigate the planning and potential of the greenhouse business, get a copy of the book *Greenhouse Engineering* by Aldrich and Bartok. It gives practical information for those starting in business as well as information for existing business design, construction, control systems, and energy conservation.

*– December 1991*

# Floriculture: High Tech, High Touch

*Technical, human resource, and creative skills have evolved in floriculture out of necessity during the 1980s.*

There are three areas of management that lead to a successful business: technical skills, human resource skills, and creative skills. Let's look at how floriculture ranks in each.

### Technical Skills

High technology has arrived in floriculture. Over the last 10 years, production has undergone tremendous change. A grower who left floriculture 10 years ago would be hard pressed to step in and produce a crop today using all the new mechanization and technology available.

For example, plug production has revolutionized the scheduling of bedding plants. Ten years ago, petunias took eight to 12 weeks to produce from seed in the Northern United States. Today, they require only four weeks to flower, when grown from the proper plug. Plugs have replaced seeds in most greenhouses. They have turned both eight- to 10-week impatiens and 10- to 12-week vinca into 17-day crops.

New findings on plug storage are continuing the revolution. Plug storage allows us to maximize the germination and plug-growing areas. Once the plugs reach the right stage, they can be stored under proper conditions for two weeks to four months until it's time to grow them on. This is like depositing plugs in the bank and making a withdrawal the day you need them.

Today, 200,000 flats can be produced in the same amount of time and space that produced only 100,000 flats 10 years ago. Plug technology has doubled our capacity.

In addition, greenhouses have become more sophisticated, turning into computer-controlled caretakers of our plants. They check and adjust temperatures and light intensity, and water automatically. Today's high-tech growers can wake up in the morning, call the greenhouse's computer, and have an entire two- or three-acre greenhouse watered automatically while they drink a cup of coffee and read the paper.

Greenhouse computers have another use: Computer models of plants' developmental cycles are fast becoming a practical reality. Using computer-assisted growing, a grower can enter basic facts, such as the date planted and height of the plant, and the computer can predict the final height and days to flower. This enables the grower to spot problems early and make any necessary cultural adjustments to produce a finished plant according to desired specifications. This "Care System" will be marketed for commercial use on poinsettias this year.

Mechanization has made big changes in plant-handling procedures, too. Conveyors, carts, and centralized loading have greatly increased efficiency. Ten years ago it may have taken all day to fill two or three semi-trailer trucks with plants. Today, 10 to 15 trucks can be loaded during the same time with the same labor.

Floriculture certainly has experienced a renaissance in the area of technical skills. Research continues to help the grower produce a high-quality product in a shorter period of time. Most of our research and grower interest has been in the technical area.

### Human Resource Skills

To take full advantage of the technological advances available to our industry, we have to realize what the increased speed and volume of production capacity mean to the people working on the crop. When you talk with growers at the end of the season, most are tired and worn-out. Many can't keep up the pace.

Perhaps it's time to become "high touch" as well as "high tech." Most growers get technical training in college, but few have taken the time to school themselves in human resource management. They may read research on plant technology, but they don't read the recent research on dealing with people. We assume growers will pick up those skills on the job or through trial and error, and the result is many growers go through more employees than plants.

What makes people management more difficult than plant management is while most plants will respond the same way when exposed to a similar set of circumstances, people exposed to a similar set of circumstances will vary greatly in their behavior.

### Develop Your People Skills

Labor is still the largest single cost of production, and, therefore, warrants a great deal of time and attention. Here are some ways to develop the human resource aspects of floriculture:

**1. Recruitment.** Know what you want the person to do. Ask yourself if there is someone in your business who can handle this position or if you will have to search outside.

**2. Selection.** Choose the best individual for the job. Match employees' personality types to the type of work they will be doing. Knowing how to select the right individual will be a key to a successful business.

**3. Training.** This is the process of developing qualities in people that will make them more productive in your organization.

**4. Performance Appraisals.** It's important to let people know how they are doing, how they can improve in weak areas, and to affirm and praise them in areas in which they excel.

Most greenhouse owners do little or no training of new employees and never give a formal evaluation of their performance. When workers are unsure about what they're doing and how they're doing, you can be sure they're not doing their best.

If you can't "grow employees," your business will never grow. Some growers are so lacking in human resource skills that they consciously limit their growth by refusing to hire "outside help."

### Creative Skills

Some say one must be born with creative skills, yet many of these skills can be developed from one's experiences. A manager must answer many questions to assess the total business environment and determine how the business will survive:

• What is the competition doing? What new government rules and regulations will affect the business? What does the customer want?

• What new technology is coming on line? How will this affect production and marketing? What new cultivars and products are being introduced? What mechanization is available and how can we use it?

• What will happen in international trade? How will this affect our business? What about the new competition? Where is our niche? Do we still offer the same old products? Has the demand for them increased?

• What happens if the weather is bad?

Top managers must spend a great deal of time considering all these external factors. Only by successfully evaluating the total external environment will they be successful in the business. Let me give you a few examples:

• **Carnation growers in Michigan.** In 1966, there were 20 carnation growers in Michigan. We held meetings and talked about how to grow more flowers per square foot, but our technology could not compete with Colorado, California, and, finally, Colombia. The last Michigan carnation grower stopped production in 1988. We couldn't compete. Extreme factors such as foreign competition and environmental conditions killed this industry.

• **Cutting chrysanthemum growers in the North.** The cost of energy increased, light intensity was low, the need for excellent plant protection against pests and diseases was high, and there was chrysanthemum stunt. As a result of these factors, competitively priced chrysanthemum cuttings could only be produced in Southern areas, and few Northern mum cutting producers survived. Only a few new cultivars have been produced recently. Total chrysanthemum sales are flat. What is their future?

• **Small retail florists.** Chain stores now do more than 50% of the retail florist business. 800 numbers are advertising and wire services are fighting for survival. This is an extremely competitive market, and many small retail florists are marginal or dying. Who will survive?

• **Bedding plant growers.** In 1960, this was the smallest part of the market. In 1990, it was the largest growth area. There are many new operations getting into the business. When will the saturation point be reached? With increased technology and volume of production, bedding plant growers will soon be to the point where they can grow more than they can sell.

• **Perennial growers.** This is a growth area that is still growing. New technology and research on scheduling will revolutionize perennial production. The trend will be away from field production and into the greenhouse where this industry will be "bedding plant-ified." In 1970, we predicted all bedding plants could be grown in 10 weeks or less. I believe by the year 2000, all major perennials will be produced in 20 weeks or less.

### Be Prepared

Top management needs the creative skills to assess all factors affecting business – internal and external – and to position the business to survive and grow. Floriculture is high-tech so everyone in the industry needs technical skills. As people move up in the organization, however, they will also need human resource and creative skills.

Those who can add these skills to their technical expertise will be the valued employees or owners of profitable businesses.

*– August 1993*

# Where Is The Vision?

## Revisiting a vision identified for the bedding plant industry in 1969 lets us see what has become reality.

If you get into strategic planning, people will always ask you: "What is your vision of the future?" or "Where do you want your business to be five, 10, or even 25 years from now?" Any successful business or venture needs to have a vision to survive.

I'd like to give an example of a vision held by a group of bedding plant growers and researchers in 1969 at Michigan State University (MSU). MSU's Agricultural Experiment Station's publication, *Michigan Science In Action: Michigan's Blooming Industry*, included an article and drawing that outlined a vision for the industry's future. That article is titled "Bedding Plant Factories – Research For The Future" and subtitled "Automation And Assembly Line Production Of Bedding Plants May Result In A More Efficient Operation."

### Making The Vision Reality

The next step after the vision was the mission – and a number of people took up that mission. Ken Diller, Fred Blackmore, Leo Merzweiler, and others worked on plastic flats and made a significant change in our industry, leading to more standardization. Ray Sheldrake, Jim Boodley, and others worked on soil mixes, and their zeal lead to peat-lite mixes and uniform growing media. Among those first involved in plug technology were George Todd with his Speedling cells and Skip Blackmore with his waffle sheets for plugs.

Mechanical seeders were developed by many companies, including Blackmore Co. and the Hamilton group in England. More recently, various individuals and groups, including Tom Van Wingerden and Jack Van de Wetering, have worked to automate the transplanting process.

Thanks to hundreds of individuals, today there are bedding plant factories, and the vision from 25 years ago is a reality. (Please forgive me if I have omitted a name.)

### Looking Ahead

Let's look at some newer visions for our industry. Who will have the forethought to see what the industry will look like in 25 years?

Remember, 25 years ago, cut flowers were the biggest part of the U.S. floriculture industry. Today, these crops are the smallest part. Conversely, bedding plants were the smallest part of the industry 25 years ago, but today they are the largest.

What new technology will become available and how will this influence each segment of our domestic industry? Who will have the vision and who will make it happen?

Over the last 25 years, the vision and new knowledge came from industry groups made up of universities, companies, and individuals. In the early stage, people didn't worry over who got credit or who patented the process of cultivar. But today the world has changed. The free exchange of information has tightened. This leads to the question for the next 25 years: Who will develop and control the new knowledge?

There are those who think all future research will be done by private companies and that public research institutions won't exist. This is the route plant breeding has taken. There are fewer breeding programs, especially the breeding of new cultivars, at land-grant institutions.

Remember, new knowledge is power and the potential for great profits.

### My Vision For The Future

Where is our industry going? What will it be like in the year 2000? That depends on the vision we have now.

Here are several visions I have heard over the past year or so. I believe they can happen if we all work toward them.

• **The industry will be highly automated; computer-controlled plant factories will reduce labor costs by 50%.** As we all know, labor is the most expensive production cost, in most cases accounting for 20% to 25% of these costs. While large companies will be first to adopt this technology, it will also be cost-effective for medium-sized growers. This vision could be a reality by the year 2000.

• **International distribution systems will provide a greater variety of plant material than ever before.** Plant breeders introduce hundreds of new cultivars each year within a relatively few species. With international cooperation, many new plant species could be introduced to the gardening public.

• **The industry will increase in size with fewer growers.** Although 80% of product will be produced by 20% of growers, specialty growers will survive and in some cases flourish. If the distribution networks and cooperatives work, growers can become more specialized and, therefore, more productive. However, a good selection of cultivars must continue to be developed to fill out the product mix.

• **There will be four to six floriculture research centers in the United States.** These will be developed as regional centers or as centers of excellence in specific areas. The cost of physical facilities to conduct floricultural research work is expensive. Future scientists will need to be well trained and will need a large support staff. The cost to operate each center will be $5 to $10 million a year. The cost to build and equip each center will be $30 to $50 million. Floriculture and horticulture departments are being merged or eliminated. It is uneconomical to teach, do research, and provide extension programs at each of these universities. It will only make sense to have a few strong programs rather than many one-scientist operations.

• **Special interest groups will develop to serve as centers of creative thinking on specific crops and topics – thus providing vision.** These groups will provide the vision for each crop/topic, and many within the group will work to make certain the mission is achieved.

*– September 1994*

# Fooling Mother Nature May Be Profitable

## Research has helped growers give their customers the products they want, when they want them – and make money along the way.

The U.S. floriculture industry has developed into more than a $2 billion industry because it understands what makes plants flower. Researchers have been involved in this process for more than 200 years. When greenhouses were first built, they were used to overwinter plants that would normally die in cold climates. Thus, growers tried to control or moderate temperature.

Historically, you can find pictures of greenhouses on the East Coast that were used to protect and save tropical and citrus plants that would not have normally survived in that climate. But it wasn't until the early 1900s that researchers looked at factors other than temperature.

### Mum Mania

In the 1920s, W.W. Garner and H.A. Allard studied the effect of photoperiod on plants. They wrote an article in a USDA handbook on flowering and fruiting plants controlled by the length of day. This was probably the most significant finding that helped the floriculture industry. While their work at that time was not directly related to floriculture crops, it took only 10 years when Drs. Ken Post, Alex Laurie, and Gus Poesch studied the photoperiod effects on the chrysanthemum.

From that beginning and with the help of other researchers, notably Dr. Marc Cathey at the USDA, the year-round flowering of chrysanthemums became a reality. So from starting at no value in 1920, the greenhouse-potted chrysanthemum provided the floriculture industry $85,531,000 in 1996.

### Turning On Bulbs

Another plant, the Easter lily (Lilium longiflorum), can be traced back to Japan from articles dating to 1681. It grew in the wild on coral rocks and in limestone areas. It was also found in Bermuda, where it loved the calcareous soils and maritime climate.

Easter lilies were introduced to the United States in the 1880s. Most came from Japan. In 1936, more than one million bulbs were imported. Then, when the war started, growers had to rely on U.S. production. There were several areas that produced bulbs, but Pacific Northwest growers became the major suppliers.

Drs. Alfred Roberts and Lawrence Blaney, along with Dr. Neil Stewart from the USDA, developed a system to force *Lilium longiflorum* to flower. They provided the information to growers on the proper cooling requirements to reliably force the bulbs in time for Easter. This was difficult because Easter can vary by as much as a month in any given year. However, their research information provided the necessary tools to force the flower at the desired time. It wasn't natural. It did make money. Last year, Easter lilies accounted for more than $40 million to the floriculture industry.

Let me give you a third example. More than 30 years ago, Dr. A.A. DeHertogh started a Holland bulb forcing program at Michigan State University. He had the skill to manipulate the cold and photoperiodic requirements and developed the most comprehensive book on bulb forcing in the world: *The Bulb Forcers Guide*.

It wasn't natural to force bulbs, but it made the floriculture industry money. While we do not have the USDA statistics on these crops, I will venture to say that DeHertogh's work and the Dutch growers support have added hundreds of thousands of dollars to the U.S. industry this year.

### Manipulating For Money

These are only three of many examples of how researchers have provided the basic information to allow growers to produce or force a crop to provide consumers a product they want, when they want it. We also make money along the way.

Therefore, floriculture has always fooled Mother Nature. We have manipulated the temperature, photoperiod, and the cold requirements to produce a crop when the customer wants it. The floriculture industry is looking for any plant that can be manipulated to flower at any time we would like it to flower.

We also must remember that what is one person's annual plant is another person's perennial plant. What we consider an annual in the North, may be a perennial in the South.

I gave these examples so that one can see floriculture is based on flowering and forcing plants at a time they do not normally flower. I've said that we will "bedding plant-ify" the perennial. We have done that.

There are those who have said that forcing just isn't natural, therefore, it isn't right. My argument is that the floriculture industry has been using unnatural means to provide the best quality and most desirable product to consumers for more than 100 years. Perennials will be the next plants to be produced in this manner. They may be a little more difficult, but they will become a part of the greenhouse industry.

### What's On Tap

A year ago, we introduced 10 perennial plants using this forcing technique. This year, eight more will be added. We have the opportunity to raise this list to 50 by the year 2000. The reason it will happen is because it is what the consumer wants. Market studies show the consumer today wants a plant in flower. They want convenience, and they want it *now*. That is why you will see more perennials in flower at the retail level and most of them will not be "natural."

However, a most important point should be stressed: While we have forced them to flower early in the first year, they return to their natural cycle for the remaining life of the plant. There is no indication of ill effects on the plants we have tested.

The bottom line is flower forcing will increase the number of consumers who buy perennials, it will increase sales, and it will have people grow more plants more often. In fact, this last year more than $10 million worth of perennial plants were sold this way. It won't be long before it will be more than $100 million. Believe it because it is true. It may not be nice to fool Mother Nature, but it may be profitable.

*— September 1997*

# How To Survive In The 21st Century

*While we cannot predict how the industry will look 100 years from now – planning, organizing, influencing, and controlling our operations can help us prepare.*

When I thought about this topic, I wondered what a person in 1897 would have predicted about the 20th Century. I wondered if anyone at that time could have predicted two World Wars, hundreds of other smaller wars, a major depression, and all the technological achievements, such as going from a horse to a rocket, a typewriter to a computer, or a dirt road to a super highway.

I have taken the time to reflect on some of the written material of the late 1890s and early 1900s. I believe no one knew the tremendous changes that would occur. I know that of the top 10 businesses in Michigan prior to 1900, none are still in operation.

In fact, I believe that if we look over the whole world only one business in 10,000 will last at least 100 years. Actually, 80% of all businesses that are started fail within the first five years, 90% fail within the first 10 years, and less than 5% last more than 25 years.

Floriculture was basically an art in the late 1800s. It was at a time when people could enjoy the finer things in life, like flowers! I am sure the entire U.S. floriculture industry in 1900 was less than $5 million and most of that was for the private production of flowers for affluent people.

The industry grew very slowly until the 1920s, then a major discovery happened. H.A. Allard and W.W. Garner, working at USDA, determined that some plants were photoperiodic. While the plants they worked with were not floriculture plants, their concepts could be applied to our plants.

### A Look To The Future

When we look at history, we can see no one can predict what will happen. The reason our industry survived and developed was because people saw an opportunity and capitalized on it. Therefore, I don't believe it is possible for anyone to tell what will happen in the next 100 years.

But I do believe there is a great deal of information to help someone prepare for the next 100 years. The first thing we must realize is no one who reads this article will be alive in the 22nd Century. Just think, in the year 2000 Christianity will be 2,000 years old, a tree in the center of the MSU Children's Garden will be 300 years old, MSU will be 145 years old, and the average person in the United States will live 75 years.

So this puts our task in perspective. How will you survive as growers in the next century? Perhaps the same way someone in 1897 survived. The basics are simple to follow: "Inch by inch any thing's a cinch" and "Row by row we will make a garden grow."

The survivors know planning is the key to their success. Our group at MSU is working on a plan (or vision) for the year 2005. That will be the 150th anniversary of MSU. We are working to be one of the major plant science institutions in the United States. We hope to build facilities and have the ability to conduct research, perform extension work and teaching, and show professionals, as well as lay people, the value of plants in their lives.

Ask yourself: When I plan, do I plan for one day? One week? One month? One year? Five years? Ten years? One hundred years? I think we would all agree in floriculture we must plan for at least one year, and there are a few who will plan for two to five years. Most of us would not think further than that. But if you want to survive in the 21st Century, you might have to think beyond the five-year time frame.

To be successful in our business it is fairly simple. You must plan, organize, influence, and control your operation. This was true in the 20th Century and it will be true in the 21st Century. There will be no magical change that occurs in the last second of the 20th Century. January 1, 2, or 3 of the year 2000 will not change the basics of the 20th Century, but we can say that the 20th Century has certainly developed the floriculture industry.

### From Different Standpoints

From a technological standpoint, we have gone from an art to a science. Most of the problems that were destroying our crops in the 1900s have been solved and cured. Our structures have been greatly improved and we can produce crops in much less time and effort than in the early 1900s.

From a human resources standpoint, it takes much more talent to produce a plant today than 100 years ago. People have a greater level of skill and knowledge and are able to use tools, mechanisms, and computers to reduce their physical work.

From a creative standpoint, floriculture is on the verge of thousands of new crops that will flower out of season for whomever wants them, and at any time of the year they want them.

If our industry can accomplish as much in the next century as we did in this one, it will be unbelievable. I wish you all the best for the next century. I hope to see you there.

*— December 1997*

# Will Floriculture Continue To Grow?

*To survive in this industry, you must find the stars, milk the cows, look carefully at the question markets, dump the dogs, and keep squintin'.*

I recently was interviewed by one of my colleagues who was preparing a talk on horticulture's future in Michigan. He had collected government statistics, noting while floriculture continues to grow, other segments of horticulture have started to face a more difficult situation with increased competition, lower prices, and a grim economic position.

I told him floriculture has potential to increase market size and share for several reasons. One is because our industry sells more plant products than any other horticulture segment. The average greenhouse may grow between 75 and 100 different species. In fact, even within a given species there may be 400 to 500 different cultivars, giving the average greenhouse grower tens of thousands of specific plants from which to choose.

This broad product mix can provide something different to grow and sell. It helps niche markets and allows growers to easily change their product ranges. Also, this diversity enables growers to adjust to market demand more quickly.

Secondly, floriculture has developed a system to efficiently and effectively produce crops. Many of our large operations are truly plant factories. Any profitable plant, whether ornamental, fruit, or vegetable, can be grown in this system. All we need to know are the physiological requirements to produce it for the requested selling date.

Finally, our industry has built a sophisticated distribution system to all the major retail players. For the most part, this system is owned and operated by large independent growers or grower cooperatives. Some wholesale distributors also seem to work well within the system and have both the growers' and retailers' interests at heart.

### Survival Of The Fittest

While we can take great satisfaction in these reasons for floriculture's success, we have to constantly remind ourselves of the following strategic points to survive within our industry.

**1. The industry constantly changes.** In the 1960s, cut flowers were the largest part of floriculture and bedding plants were the smallest. Over time, the two segments have traded places. Major crops in 1960 were roses, chrysanthemums, carnations, azaleas, potted chrysanthemums, and poinsettias. In 2000, impatiens, petunias, geraniums, New Guinea impatiens, hanging baskets, and perennials are major items.

Crops change constantly. Someone who left our industry 10 years ago probably couldn't name one cultivar that still exists in a given species – 80% of the products we sell today were not available 10 years ago. Look at greenhouse structures in the 1950s – more than 95% were made of glass. Today, plastic accounts for about two-thirds of production space.

Twenty years ago no one thought greenhouses would ever use computers. They didn't fit our businesses then, but today we can't operate without them.

We may not know what changes will occur next, but we do know there will be many and they'll happen quickly.

**2. Riding the product life cycle.** Each product has a life cycle – the introduction phase, the growth phrase, the maturation phase, and the product's demise. We have to realize where each product is in the cycle and know what to do with them in each phase.

When it is introduced, a product might be considered a question market. Will it be great or a dud? In the growth phase, it may be a star making growers money. When it matures, a product enters the cash cow stage. Here, the market doesn't grow but the product makes us money. We then move to the demise phase, where a product is a dog and no one wants it anymore.

The solution is to find the stars, milk the cows, look carefully at the question markets, and dump the dogs.

**3. Develop new products constantly.** Growers who are the first to market something new can reap the greatest rewards, but they also take the greatest risks.

Consider the 'Winter Rose' poinsettia which was introduced two years ago. With consumer appeal and no competition, everything has been right for big profits for this new variety. But as more people grow 'Winter Rose' over time, it will become more familiar to consumers and its novelty will wear off, and thus there will be less profit.

Fortunately, our industry is blessed because there are about 100 new cultivars introduced each year and thousands more waiting in the wings. This diversity is the lifeblood of floriculture and why we are successful while the fruit and vegetable markets have offered consistently less new material.

**4. Fail quickly.** Not every new product and marketing scheme growers attempt will be successful. Failures are often more common than successes. It's important to realize that failing quickly cuts your losses, allowing you to move on to another idea and potential success.

One of my marketing failures was introducing spring flowering poinsettias in the early 1970s. I placed 100 six-inch white, pink, and bi-color cultivars in a local supermarket the Wednesday before Mother's Day. I had great hope for success, but on the Monday after the holiday, there were 99 plants left in the store. People complimented the store manager on the display, but said poinsettias are Christmas plants – they just aren't for Mother's Day. It was a good idea that had bad execution and no market demand.

**5. Develop your plant factory.** You must develop your production systems to produce and market your plants. If you have sent your salespeople to prebook sales, the retailers expect the product to be delivered without excuses. You can't afford production, packaging, or delivery mistakes.

Because many of our operations, ship 80% to 90% of their product in a six- to eight-week window, planning and organization are essential. Production action plans must be made, with all the details thought out before the season begins. Remember, the plant factory needs a viable step-by-step system to run smoothly.

**6. Use new technology.** It's hard to believe, but in the last 30 years, there has been more new technology developed in floriculture than in the previous 970. From automatic seeders, transplanters, and subirrigation systems to plastic coverings and containers to computer-controlled systems, greenhouses have evolved into plant factories. New technology continues at a rapid pace and each new development can make changes to the whole system. It is extremely important to keep abreast of new products and implement them as soon as they are economically valid.

**7. Revisit products and procedures.** In the 1920s, many of the plants grown to flower in greenhouses were perennials and forced-flowering shrubs. Once growers started producing year-round flowering potted plants, many of these earlier forced plants were forgotten. Then, in the 1990s, these crops were revisited with new technology that had developed, resulting in the plants' reintroduction into commercial greenhouse operations.

Likewise, production techniques need to be revisited. The Ohio State University developed the first use of subirrigation in the 1890s but, because of disease problems, this technique did not last long in commercial plant production. With the introduction of soilless media mixes and new chemical and biological controls, subirrigation has made a major comeback and is used in many large commercial ranges.

**8. Remember your roots.** The greenhouse is only a tool and tools must be changed or redesigned to accommodate changing products. You must get rid of plants, structures, benches, and equipment that are no longer profitable to grow or use. I've seen concrete benches built in the 1950s and '60s for cut flowers that were demolished in the 1980s and '90s. They were replaced by movable benches or subirrigation floors for bedding or potted plants.

Old greenhouses are like old tools – they make great conversation pieces but they usually aren't profitable to use. Don't get so wrapped up in the greenhouse structure that you forget it's there to help you produce plants profitably, If it doesn't, it's not useful.

**9. Exploit new products in their early growth phase.** The most profitable growers are innovators who are the first, or nearly the first, to introduce new plant material or technology. Some growers get so carried away with a new plant or growing technique, that they forget their objective is to make money by exploiting it rather than perfecting it.

If you ride the top of the wave or are on the cutting edge, the returns can be great. If you fall off, the risk can be tremendous.

**10. Feed the market.** Remember, fads are short-lived and trends continue for a longer period of time. For example, it looks like bedding plant flat sales have leveled off while hanging basket and other container sales are increasing.

People like our flower products but they don't want the work of planting 30, 50, or 100 little plants. In response to this trend, one might develop products in containers or flats that can be placed directly in the ground without transplanting. People who can provide these products will reap the rewards.

### Floriculture Will Flourish

Yes, floriculture will continue to grow. New plants, technology, and consumer trends will develop with your help. All you need to do is be the first to react to them and know what to do with them.

When his students couldn't answer a question he asked about plants, W.J. Beal, a botany professor at Michigan State University in 1870, said, "keep squintin'." He meant look closely at the plants and technology until you know what they are and how to use them.

*– March 2000*

# How Big Is The Floriculture Industry?

*Statistics from the 1998 Census of Horticulture Specialties and the 1999 Floriculture Crops Summary bring perspective to this frequently asked question.*

I recently joined a group of industry leaders to discuss the results of the 1998 Census of Horticultural Specialties and 1999 Floriculture Crops Summary with members of USDA's National Agricultural Statistics Service (NASS) in Washington, DC.

Our main goal was to improve future statistical reports by providing valuable input to NASS members regarding the floriculture industry. This in turn will help NASS capture the total value of floriculture in the United States more accurately. More importantly, the survey data is used by the government when it considers research grants and investments in the Agricultural Research Service and land grant universities.

### Breaking Down Floriculture

Here are some statistics we discussed at the NASS meeting:

Floriculture's value worldwide is estimated at $22 billion annually, led by the United States at $4.9 billion. I was surprised to learn that Japan was the second largest flower-producing country at $3.65 billion per year.

Europe is the largest flower-producing continent with more than $10 billion in sales. Europe is led by The Netherlands ($3.14 billion), Italy ($2.2 billion), Germany ($1.36 billion), and France ($1.01 billion). North and South America combined produce flowers at $6.25 billion annually. Other continents include Asia ($4.37 billion), Australia ($434 million), and Africa ($243 million).

California ($829 million) and Florida ($617 million) are the top flower-producing states in the United States. Potted flowering plants account for $868 million in total U.S. floriculture sales. The poinsettia has widened its lead in this category. The top five plants are: poinsettia ($259 million), orchid ($92 million), chrysanthemum ($76 million), azalea ($43 million), and Easter lily ($41 million).

Orchids have grown significantly in the potted plant category in the past 10 years. While the number of potted orchids is much lower than poinsettias (90 million pots vs. 260 million), their price per pot is much higher. Potted roses also have increased their market share since the last census.

The rose is still the largest cut flower at more than $114 million in annual sales. It is followed by cut lilies ($56 million), gladiolas ($35 million), and chrysanthemums ($31 million). All other cut flower sales total less than $25 million.

There have been significant changes in this category, too. Many cut flower growers have diversified their crops to develop a profitable mix for their market. One grower in our group said he grew more than 100 different cut flowers, indicating small quantities of a large number of flowers may be a key to success for small cut flower growers.

Annuals (73%) and perennials (27%) account for $2.4 billion in bedding plant floriculture sales. The top-selling annuals and perennials produced in the United States are: vegetative annuals, impatiens, petunias, chrysanthemums (hardy/green), pansy/viola, New Guinea impatiens, begonias, vegetables (other than tomato and cole crops), seed geraniums, marigolds, vinca, herbs, tomatoes, hosta, ornamental grasses, daylilies, and other flowering annuals and herbaceous perennials.

The "other" category of annuals and perennials represents more than $660 million or about 29% of total sales. This includes new introductions of minor bedding plant and perennial items, which is a great strength to this part of the floriculture industry.

### A Successful Meeting

I've had many meetings with the USDA in the past, but I felt this was one of the most productive industry-government gatherings I've ever attended. NASS members were receptive to our input for future reports.

We hope the USDA and federal government will realize that our industry (Horticultural Crop Specialties) represents more than 10% of total agriculture and is probably the most profitable segment today. We also hope the government will invest taxpayers' money accordingly and offer the support needed to provide accurate statistical data to help the industry continue to grow and prosper.

*– September 2000*

# LEGENDS OF FLORICULTURE

The columns that follow are some of the most difficult I have had to write – and some of the most meaningful.

As you will see when you read through this book, I have a firm belief that people make our industry great.

Those whose lives are celebrated in the following pages have made tremendous contributions to our industry and to me personally. While most of them are no longer with us physically, their spirits live on in our industry and in the many people whose lives they touched and influenced. Dick Meister, who has been part of Meister Publishing Co. for more than 50 years, continues to bless my life with his wit and wisdom.

One of my favorite books is Robert Fulghum's *All I Really Need to Know I Learned In Kindergarten*. Among the things Fulghum learned are to "live a balanced life – learn some and think some and draw and paint and sing and dance and play and work every day some," and "when you go out into the world, watch out for traffic, hold hands and stick together."

These are lessons that the individuals celebrated in these columns learned and lived. I feel privileged to have known and worked with them over the years.

# People Make Our Industry Great

## John Carew – master teacher, diplomat, coach, poet, and friend.

Over 13 years ago, I had the opportunity to come to Michigan State University (MSU) and interview for an extension position. That was the first time I had the opportunity to meet John Carew. I'd wanted to take a job in Pennsylvania, but after meeting Dr. Carew and seeing the opportunity in Michigan, I accepted the position.

John Carew was a master teacher and a diplomat of the highest order. Every time I got into a bind or corner in my early extension days, I was off to his office for the next set of instructions. I always asked him what he did when he was in a similar situation. He always passed on a few pointers from his experience and sort of coached me on my way. He viewed his staff as if they were all-star players and he was the eager coach.

Dr. Carew loved to plan and dream with his staff. On one particular day with John, when, with his advice and counsel, he started us dreaming about an extension program for bedding plant growers, he told me to plan the best national bedding plant meeting I could. I spent the next few days calling friends, growers, colleagues, and everyone who knew the name of someone who knew something about bedding plants. I discussed the program with John and he said, "It looks great! Go ahead and put it on." I was delighted and said, "Fine. Where is the money?" John smiled and said, "That's your problem!" Well, the meeting was held (the First International Bedding Plant Conference), attended by 150 people and it paid for itself.

Over the years, John continued to supply thoughts and ideas for the conferences along with suggestions for the formation of Bedding Plants, Inc. He felt strongly that the growers should be organized and in a position to express themselves to other groups.

Words of wisdom seemed to come from John whenever a staff member was depressed or felt like they lost a battle. His favorite expression to me was "Be happy, but not content." He always preached that actions were better than words, and he spent most of his time working to provide support, leadership, and aid for his staff and the Horticulture Department at MSU. Being able to talk about any facet of horticulture was John's delight, and he loved nothing more than to visit growers and speak at industry meetings.

A leader in horticulture education, John was eager to tell of its virtues to students in all areas of horticulture. In fact, John has been called the teacher of Department Chairmen, since many of his former staff members and students are now chairmen of departments across the country.

Even after his surgery, when most people would have given up, John stayed right in there, coming to work every day, enjoying the opportunity to meet and discuss horticulture with students, faculty, and industry people.

At a mutual friend's funeral last January, I had the opportunity to discuss death with John. He said he believed death to be just a change of address. His view impressed me and I've thought about it many times. When John died on November 1, his view of death came back to me.

John was a poet, rhyming his thoughts on many subjects. I remember one poem by R.L. Sharp that certainly fits John's life:

*Isn't it strange, that princes and kings, and clowns that caper, in sawdust rings,*
*And common people like you and me are builders for eternity.*
*To each is given a bag of tools, a shapeless mass, a book of rules,*
*And each must build, ere life is flown, a stumbling block or a stepping stone.*

It's people like John Carew, Carl Dietz, Loyd Viet, Walter Good, and many, many others who have made contributions to improve the bedding plant industry during their lifetime that have left stepping stones and examples for us to follow. The opportunity of knowing and working with an individual like John Carew has been a rewarding and meaningful experience. While physically he is gone, spiritually he just moved to another address.

*– December 1977*

# A Tribute To Leonard Bettinger

## The third president of Bedding Plants Inc. had an abiding enthusiasm, a drive to get things done – and a heck of a time finding Detroit Metro Airport!

It was with great sadness that I learned of Leonard Bettinger's death this past January. Only the week before, I had joked with Leonard about the bedding plant business.

The large crowd at the funeral attested to the scope of this man's influence. My wife, Barbara, and I joined more than 250 other friends and relatives on this occasion to express our grief. It was a difficult time for his wife, Marie, who was his right hand, working with him in business and also in raising their fine family.

I first met Leonard about 20 years ago. He was one of the first members of Bedding Plants Inc. (BPI) and its third president. He attended the early conferences and was instrumental in the early development of the association. During his presidency our membership doubled.

He worked with second BPI president, Jim Perry, to move the organization's annual conference to different parts of the country for better access to all our members. During Leonard's presidency, the conferences were held in Raleigh, NC, in 1974, and Newport Beach, CA, in 1975.

Leonard was always willing to help people. I've heard reports of how he helped farmers and neighbors in time of need. Leonard had an abiding enthusiasm and a drive to get things done – and in spite of all odds, he generally did just that.

I remember one instance where Leonard's intentions turned out to be better than his results. In retrospect, it turned out to be a great source of amusement – and I offer the story as a representation of the great times we had at the early BPI meetings.

At the end of one of our first conferences, Leonard offered to drive Henry Levy of Tennessee and Ernie Cuzzocreo of Connecticut to Detroit Metropolitan Airport. This 90-mile drive usually takes about 1½ hours from Lansing. I knew they were in trouble as soon as Leonard got into the car and couldn't find his way out of the parking lot. However, the five to six minutes of parking lot confusion turned out to be nothing compared to what followed.

The next day, Ernie called me to relay their misguided journey to the airport. It seems Leonard began talking and took the wrong exit from the expressway. Just as he realized his mistake and admitted he was lost, Ernie spotted an airplane in the skies ahead.

"Follow that plane!" Ernie cried. Leonard followed, and a half hour later they arrived at an airport, the Widow Run Airport, a cargo airport about 10 miles away from Detroit Metro!

This 1½ hour trip wound up taking three hours; both Henry and Ernie missed their planes. Henry had to stay overnight in Detroit and Ernie caught the last plane to New York. When Ernie finally arrived home in the wee hours of the morning, he snuck into his house, trying not to disturb his family. Unfortunately, he tripped the burglar alarm; his own dog almost bit him!

From that time on, Ernie and Henry refused to travel with Leonard and always teased him about following that plane. Leonard had a great sense of humor and retold this story frequently with great relish and he always laughed when anyone said, "Follow that plane!" He would say, "I hope I don't have as much trouble getting to heaven as I did getting to Detroit Metro Airport!"

Though Leonard may have been lost on the way to the airport, he was certainly on the right track in his business and community affairs. His helpful accomplishments are well known in horticultural and agricultural associations, as he assumed many roles as an officer and committee member.

Leonard directed his time and money toward helping others. He and his wife were active in their church as well as in community activities. Leonard had a genuine concern for other people and his pleasant, sincere manner of working with people was his trademark.

Leonard will be truly missed by his family and friends, but we can be glad that his work here is over and he's done a fine job.

I'm sure Leonard won't have as much trouble getting to heaven as he did to Detroit Metro Airport, because the exit ramp to heaven is well lit with his good works and unselfish deeds.

*– April 1987*

# Let Me Tell You About My Friend, Ernie

*Ernie Cuzzocreo – the "George Washington"*
*of the bedding plant industry.*

It was quite a blow when I learned of Ernie Cuzzocreo's death this past April. It's difficult to believe my longtime friend and colleague in the bedding plant industry is no longer with us.

I first met Ernie 20 years ago when he spoke at the first International Bedding Plant Conference at Michigan State University. John Carew, my boss at that time, knew Ernie when John was extension vegetable specialist at Cornell University.

Ernie grew vegetables, bedding plants, and ground covers in Orange, CT. He was a friendly, low-key farmer. He seemed nervous, since he wasn't used to speaking before large groups, but he got up in front of the 150 people attending that first conference and did a great job.

He liked that conference so much he helped organize the second one – and was instrumental in developing BPI itself. He was one of "The Original 13" who laid the groundwork for the association – and served as our first president from 1969-1972.

I have always considered Ernie the "George Washington" of the bedding plant industry. He had the vision to see the need for an association like Bedding Plants Inc. (BPI). There were florist groups, vegetable groups, and nursery groups but none represented bedding plants. Truck farmers fell between the cracks of the other groups. He knew that all these people would benefit from getting together and discussing bedding plant issues.

In the 20 years since Ernie helped form BPI, it has grown. Then it was a small group of 13 with $500 and a good idea; now it's the definitive growers' association, representing 3,700 members of the greenhouse industry across the United States and Canada, plus nearly 100 members in other countries throughout the world.

Ernie not only helped our association get started, he was instrumental in getting many growers involved in the business as well. In Connecticut, New York, and the entire Northeast region, growers will tell you it was Ernie Cuzzocreo who helped them get started and encouraged them to stick with it. He was a proud, loyal, hard-working person who really loved to help other people. If you were Ernie's friend, he would literally give you the shirt off his back.

Ernie was also a well-known and respected member of his community. He was one of the first volunteer policemen and he served on the town council. Everyone there called him "Uncle Ernie."

One of the first lessons I learned from Ernie was to keep my information simple. He'd always say to me, "Will, we're a bunch of poor farmers; we didn't go to college. You've got to talk to us so we can understand you. It doesn't do any good to bring us in from all over the country and then talk over our heads."

But Ernie was no "poor farmer." He could have bought and sold all of the educators in the group, but he kept his humble attitude. Whenever we got together for a BPI conference, he always made it a point to talk to the growers, not above them.

### Food For Thought

Let me tell you about some of the good times we had together:

Ernie was a connoisseur of Italian food, and so is my wife, Barbara. They made a point of searching out the best Italian restaurant in any town where we met to have our annual meeting. With Ernie as our guide, we have eaten in the finest Italian restaurants from coast to coast. Every meal was an experience.

First, Ernie would locate the maitre d', converse with him in Italian, and sometimes even make his way into the kitchen to "help" the cook. We generally consumed enough food on these outings to feed five times the number of people who were there.

On one of these occasions, we were with a group of about 18 BPI members at an Italian restaurant outside Denver, CO. During this excellent meal, George Oki kidded Ernie into ordering a better wine. As a group, we responded by consuming a generous quantity of it. I'll never forget the look on Ernie's face when he got the bill and realized how much "better" the better wine was – $35 a bottle!

Ernie never let George forget that incident. Not long afterward when we were all together again at a Japanese restaurant, Ernie made certain that George was in charge of the wine.

The funniest story I remember about Ernie was an incident with our friends, Leonard and Marie Bettinger. Ernie and his wife, Sylvia, went with Leonard and Marie to tour the area for one of our conferences.

Because Leonard was driving, it was not surprising that they got lost. After they had wandered for some time, Ernie's wife had to use the restroom, so they stopped at a service station along the way. While they were there, they filled up the car with gas, asked directions, got a soft drink, paid the attendant, got in the car, and left Ernie's wife in the restroom!

Eight or 10 miles down the road they remembered Sylvia, turned around and drove back to pick her up. Needless to say, she could have been happier. They all arrived about an hour late to the BPI banquet. Ernie made his way sheepishly to the head table to find his seat, muttering, "You'll never believe what happened to me."

At Ernie's funeral, the priest who gave the eulogy did an excellent job of extolling Ernie's fine traits. One line in particular struck me: "I'm sure from now on, there'll be pachysandra planted around the pearly gates of heaven," he said. "And myrtle will probably be planted within a week," added Ernie's son, Ernest Jr. and his wife, Michelle, as I talked to them afterward.

Ernie may have played the role of the humble farmer who was not too smart. But those who really knew him realized he was one of the smartest, most astute business people in our industry.

If you knew Ernie, you'll agree he was a modest man – so if he were here right now, he'd probably say, "That's enough; time to get back to work!"

I can't express in words what a personal loss both my wife, Barbara, and I feel at Ernie's death — but we'd better get back to work if for no other reason than to make Ernie proud of us.

*– July 1987*

## Jim Perry: The Gentleman Of The Bedding Plant Industry

*His broad smile, friendly gestures, and homespun, common-sense wisdom were well known and an inspiration to the industry.*

James C. Perry, second president of Bedding Plants Inc. (BPI), died June 18, 1988, in Camarillo, CA, following a stroke he suffered on June 5. Jim had been confined to a wheelchair for the last eight years – but though his body was hindered, his mind remained alert as always.

More than 200 attended the funeral at Rose Hills Memorial Park overlooking the Los Angeles area. Represented were the leaders of the California growing industry as well as Jim's family, friends, and present and past employees of Perry's Plants.

Carl Zanger, his lifelong friend and former business partner at Perry's, offered the following eulogy:

"In all of our lives, certain individuals stand out as major influences, with a direct effect upon our personal lives. Jim Perry was such a man to me. His broad smile, friendly gestures, and homespun, common-sense wisdom were well-known to all who came into contact with him.

"Jim loved the nursery business. It was his major interest – second only to his family. Jim started in the nursery industry during the Depression years of the 1930s, working in a retail nursery in West Los Angeles, where he gained broad knowledge of the horticultural trade. During the years of World War II, he worked for a large bedding plant nursery where he developed his interest in this phase of the industry.

"Following the war, he purchased a very small bedding plant nursery in Montebello which he named Perry's Plants. Through years of hard work, he developed Perry's Plants into one of the largest nurseries of its type anywhere. It has been visited by growers from all over the world. Today, the business remains as a testimonial to Jim, continuing its role of leadership that he established.

"Jim was without peer in his unselfish giving of himself to the causes he espoused. He gave unstintingly of his time to further the cause of the nursery and horticultural industry, serving in many ways:

• "He was among the founders of the Bedding Plant Marketing Order, established in the early 1950s. Although it was subsequently disbanded, its principles remained to stabilize the industry.

• "He was very active in the California Association of Nurserymen, served on innumerable committees, and was president in the early 1960s.

• "He was among the charter members of the Nursery Growers Association of California and served as its president.

• "He served as chairman of the Los Angeles International Flower Show, the largest show of its kind in Southern California.

• "He was active in the Los Angeles Chamber of Commerce and the 'Los Angeles Beautiful' committee.

• "He was a member of the *Sunset Magazine* Southern California Garden Panel for more than 20 years.

• "He was a charter member of BPI, served on many committee assignments, and was president from 1972 to 1974.

• "He was interested in the education of young people and in developing their interest in the horticultural industry, serving in advisory positions with various boards and school districts to develop meaningful and practical programs.

"These are just the highlights of an outstanding man, a leader in the industry he loved and upon which he left his mark. Those of us who were privileged to work with him will remember him with the highest respect and regard. Personally, I have fond memories of Jim as a close friend and associate. He will always remain in my heart. We entrust him to God, knowing he will be at peace."

Another eulogy was presented by Willis Stribling, who knew Jim well. He told a story about Jim walking on the rocks at the sea coast, when he noticed a big, old sea lion lying on the rocks, near death. Jim approached the beast, kneeled next to it for a moment, then returned to Willis with the comment, "It ain't over till it's over."

Jim was a faithful husband, taking care of his wife for more than eight years after she had a stroke. He was a faithful father and grandfather to his three children, Dennis, Landon, and Janice, and five grandchildren. The youngest, James Dean Perry, was born just one month prior to Jim's death.

Jim was also faithful to the ornamental plant industry. He attended every BPI annual conference – the last eight in a wheelchair with his nurse, Florence, at his side. When introduced at the Grand Banquet, he would summon all his effort to stand and be recognized. What determination!

James C. Perry was a faithful, honest, friendly man. We who knew him will miss him, but we know that his spirit – a double portion of it, we hope – will inspire us all to continue to be faithful as he was, to our families and to our industry.

*– August 1988*

# A Tribute To Two Industry Legends

*Fred Gloeckner – the "banker" for horticulture, helping growers solve short-term problems while taking the long-term view for the industry.*

*John Holden – consistently positive, persistent, and always a gentleman, known for his knowledge of bedding plant cultivars.*

The industry lost two of its legends in the last few months. It was with great sadness that we learned of the deaths of Fred Gloeckner and John Holden. Each of these individuals had a great impact on the floriculture industry.

### Fred Gloeckner

In my first floriculture course at Penn State University, I was given a Gloeckner catalog and told that it was the best in the industry because it contained all the technical information required to grow chrysanthemums. That was only the beginning. Since that time, hardly a day has gone by in my horticultural career that someone hasn't mentioned Fred Gloeckner, or the Gloeckner Co., or the Gloeckner Foundation.

Fred took great care to make sure his salespeople were knowledgeable – for example, sending them to Yoder Brothers to learn about chrysanthemums. One of the highlights of my career was spending a six-month sabbatical at Yoder Brothers. It was a real challenge to discuss chrysanthemums with the Gloeckner salespeople. Yoder sales training was more thorough and extensive in chrysanthemum production than the curriculum taught in most four-year universities. Fred's company provided this production information to growers. The informal method of teaching through his sales staff helped many growers succeed.

Fred was also the "banker" for many horticultural businesses. I've heard stories of how he would carry accounts for many months to help a small business succeed. If it weren't for Fred, there would be far fewer successful horticultural businesses today.

Besides helping growers solve short-term problems, Fred had a long-term view of the industry. He saw the need for research and started the Gloeckner Foundation, which has spent more than $2 million on research at public institutions across the United States. I received several grants from the foundation and I have several students who would not have been able to complete their education if not for Fred.

There aren't many people in our industry who can say they started their own business and saw it thrive for more than 50 years, or that they were responsible for providing more than $2 million to floricultural research, or that they provided guidance, financial help, and reliable products to growers – making the difference between success and failure for many. Fred Gloeckner has a unique claim to these accomplishments.

Fred's values contributed both to his success and to the success of those whose lives he touched. He believed in hard work and long hours. He encouraged many to think positively and take aggressive steps toward bettering their futures. It is not surprising that Fred was considered a member of the family by many to whom he was not directly related.

I remember getting phone calls at all hours of the day or night from Fred – excited about some new information, curious about some question, asking for information on some project, or announcing he planned to stop by for a brief visit. I'm sure there are many besides myself who hear the phone ring and still half believe it will be Fred on the line. Fred's ideals, work ethic, and compassion are examples for us all to attempt to follow.

### John Holden

John Holden is another individual who contributed much to our industry. John was a warm, outgoing, dedicated person. He traveled extensively. I don't think there is a growers' meeting in the United States where John didn't speak. He also was greatly respected by plant breeders and traveled to all the seed trials. John knew as much about bedding plant varieties as anyone.

As with Fred, my first contact with John was when I was at Penn State. He attended the seed trials and a conference or two while I was there. When I came to Michigan State University (MSU) and started experiments on bedding plants, John was there to provide seed for the experiments. He bent over backwards to be accommodating. He made sure the order was delivered on time and filled correctly. If anything was wrong, you could be sure John would take care of it.

When we began talking about forming Bedding Plants Inc. (BPI), John was involved. He was one of the 100 attending the very first BPI conference in 1968 and he spoke on our conference program many times. He served on our board of directors and was our membership chairman for several years. He received the association's Meritorious Service Award in 1982 and a special Outstanding Committee Chairman award in 1985.

John served as a judge, and later as president of All-America Selections. He was president of the National Garden Bureau and chaired committees of the American Seed Trade Association. In all his dealings, he was consistently positive, persistent, and always a gentleman.

Like Fred, John had a forward-looking attitude about the industry and was supportive of research. He served as president of the Bedding Plants Foundation, Inc. (BPFI) in 1986-87. In 1988, as a tribute to John, the Geo. J. Ball Co. created the John Holden Research Fund administered by BPFI.

Only three weeks before his death, John was at the MSU flower trials discussing cultivars with many of the seedsmen in attendance. Both he and his wife, Nancy, toured that day and then stopped by the Professional Plant Growers Association (PPGA) office to discuss an ambassador program in which John was planning to speak at various grower meetings across the country as a representative of PPGA. John had no thoughts of retiring – only of how he could continue to be of service to the industry.

Outside the industry, John was active in his church, singing in the choir for many years. I remember John being the one designated to offer the invocation at many PPGA banquets, breakfasts, and luncheons. Because of John's example, many of us looked to him not only as an industry leader, but as a spiritual leader as well.

I can truly say that I have known no kinder, nicer person in the floriculture industry than John Holden. His warmth, personality, and breadth of knowledge in bedding plant cultivars are qualities to be emulated.

John was made an honorary member of PPGA in 1986, as was Fred in 1988. I have portraits of all the PPGA honorary members on my office wall, John Carew among them. I'll never forget what John Carew told me at a funeral of one of our close friends. He said, "I believe death is just a change of address."

It's true that Fred Gloeckner and John Holden have had a change of address, but I believe they still play an important role in our industry. I hope you will join me in remembering each of them fondly and drawing strength from the memories of the good times we had together.

*— November 1990*

# A Legend Is Gone

*No one needs to give a sermon about Aart Van Wingerden. They just need to follow his example – have faith, believe in your family, help people, and work hard.*

Webster says a legend is "an unauthenticated story from early times, preserved by tradition and popularly thought to be historical."

I will add to my Webster's definition. In 1948, Aart Van Wingerden came to the United States from Holland with $6 in his pocket. In 75 years after his birth, including 38 years in the United States, he has become a legend.

In my life, I have had several role models – my father, Dr. John Carew at Michigan State University, Ernie Cuzzocreo from Connecticut, George Todd from Florida, Egon Molbak from Washington, Lou Brand from Michigan, and Richard Meister from Ohio to name a few. High on my list is also Aart Van Wingerden.

### Our First Meeting

I first met Aart in the late 1960s. I was a young assistant professor and was told by industry people that Aart was one of the sharpest growers in the country. I knew he worked with Dr. Ray Sheldrake of Cornell University on soilless mixes and with Dr. Bill Roberts of Rutgers on double-layered polyethylene greenhouses.

My first meeting with Aart was awesome. I had never met a man with as much self confidence, self control, and vision of what needed to be done, yet he treated me as an equal. We talked about the bedding plant industry. He told me what needed to be done and that we must work to make these improvements happen. By spending one hour with Aart, I had at least two years of research work to do when I left.

I always enjoyed my visits with Aart and Cora Van Wingerden. They were always on the move. He had more ideas than any 10 people. His mind was always working so I knew the business side of his life early on. It took me a few years, though, to really understand the total Aart Van Wingerden.

He and his wife raised 16 children of which 15 are still in the bedding plant industry. Cora is certainly the saint of the bedding plant industry. I hold her in the highest regard. The family has developed greenhouse operations in New Jersey, California, Ohio, Illinois, North Carolina, and also in Honduras, Indonesia, and Haiti.

### A Free Man

One of the most moving times in my life was when his son, Leonard, gave an acceptance speech for his father at the Professional Plant Growers Association conference in 1994 when Aart became an honorary member. Leonard said, "Our father is a free man in three areas of his life. He is free economically, he is free ethically, and he is free eternally. Free in body, soul, and spirit."

Aart can be given credit for many improvements to the industry: packs, plastic flats, double poly greenhouses, cart transportation, plugs, heating systems, watering systems, etc. He was always thinking.

The last time I visited with Aart was about one year ago. Bedding Plants Foundation, Inc. sent me to present a plaque to him and Cora for their research contribution to the foundation. I had heard he was sick so I expected to see him in a bed at his home. No way. When I arrived, I was told that he had been at the hospital for a blood transfusion but would be back in 15 minutes.

He showed up ready to go and gave me a two-hour tour of his operation. Along with that tour came a list of things that the university people should be doing. Like, let's get rid of thrips. Have you looked at ultrasound? Have you looked at UV light? We need to do something besides pesticides. His mind was in high gear. When I left, I felt he still knew exactly where we were going.

### Following The Golden Rule

Aart was also a humanitarian. He believed in the Golden Rule: He always tried to treat people as he wished to be treated. He worked with people from all parts of the world. He worked closely with his church, and because of his great mind and business skills, he helped people in many other countries. "Love your neighbor as yourself" was a cornerstone of his lifestyle.

I was recently on vacation in Missouri and drove past a church where the bulletin board said, "A good example is the best sermon." I can think of no better example in the bedding plant industry than Aart Van Wingerden. His son also said that Aart was free eternally. He realized business was part of his life and his family was part of his life. He believed life on earth is only part of the total journey.

### Cornerstones Of Living

Since Aart's death in August, I have reflected on his accomplishments. I have seen how important his wife and family have been, and I have tried to distill the tenets he and his family have used to be successful in their business, family, and spiritual lives. I also must say my mother, who passed away February 2, had many of the same strong-willed attributes of Aart Van Wingerden. She also had very similar ethics. Upon reflection, I believe with their European backgrounds they developed very similar goals. I have obtained these five cornerstones from both of them:

**1. Have faith.** People have a choice of having faith that things will happen for the best or fearing things will happen for the worst. Faith will provide a less stressful and happier route through life.

**2. Believe in your family.** Aart had a large, close family. My mother had four children, and all were very close. We took great joy in the good times in each life, and we protected and supported each other in the bad times. A strong family is a cornerstone, the rock of life on earth, a strength that helps in good and bad times.

**3. Help people as much as you can.** Aart helped thousands of people in many different countries. He knew the importance of helping people, as did my mother. She knitted afghans for hundreds of people just to be helpful.

**4. Work hard.** Aart worked all the time. In fact, I bet he could not tell the difference between work and time off. His mind was always working. The best job to have is one that you cannot tell whether it is work or play. Make your hobby your work. Aart did this. He had fun doing his work.

**5. You can have anything you want.** What Aart Van Wingerden showed everyone is that you can come to this country in 1948 with $6 in your pocket, raise 16 children, build more than 200 acres of greenhouses, impact thousands of people, contribute to a profession and take it from the smallest segment of floriculture to more than $3 billion, and have the most significant input in that industry of any one individual in the world.

I would say to Aart and my mother, Marie, "Well done thy true and faithful servants." I would also say that perhaps today there are other people with $6 in their pockets who will have the same aspirations, goals, and values of Aart (and my mother), and 30 years from now will be the leaders of the bedding plant industry.

*— October 1996*

# Hail To The Editor-In-Chief

### Reflections on Dick Meister's 50th anniversary celebration with Meister Publishing Co.

On December 12, 1996, I had the good fortune to attend Richard T. Meister's 50th anniversary celebration with Meister Publishing Co.

In addition to his years of service to the company, Dick has a bachelor of science degree from Cornell University's College of Agriculture and an MBA from Harvard Business School. He also served as a supply officer in World War II.

### Lessons Learned

When I first started writing a column for Meister Publishing, I would visit yearly and play a round of golf with Dick and his brother, Ed. And each year I would score in the 120s for 18 holes. Dick felt sorry for me and each year would tell me how to improve.

First, he said I needed golf shoes. I spent $150 for a pair, and at the end of the year my score was 120-plus again. Next, he said I needed a new golf outfit, so $250 and one year of practice later my score was 120-plus. Then, he said I needed new clubs – $1,200 and another year of golf later, my score was 120 plus. He then said I needed to golf at better courses. One round at Pebble Beach resulted in 17 lost golf balls, a 130 score, and $500 for the round.

With all of his tutelage over the past 30 years, my score remains the same. This past year, he said he found my problem – "poor hand-eye coordination." I'm afraid he is going to send me to a medical sports facility. It could cost me thousands. I told him I think a 120-plus score is fine.

### A Champion In Life

Dick is an excellent golfer who has won many championships and loves the sport. He takes all challenges in life with the same passion that he plays golf. Most people in our industry don't realize that Dick is chairman of Meister Publishing and editor-in-chief. Meister publishes 17 magazines and yearly manuals.

Here is the list: *American Fruit Grower, Western Fruit Grower,*

*American Vegetable Grower, Greenhouse Grower, Cotton Grower, Cotton International, Cotton Grower Mid-Months, Farm Chemicals* (now *CropLife*), *Farm Chemicals International, Farm Chemicals Handbook* (now *Crop Protection Handbook*), *Ag Consultant, Insect Control Guide, Weed Control Manual, Florida Grower and Rancher, Ornamental Outlook, Productores de Hortalizas,* and the *Plant Health Guide.*

Dick is involved with all the magazines and projects. He visits with the editors on a regular basis and is never at a loss for new ideas or innovations.

When Meister acquired *Cotton International* in the mid-1960s, Dick and his daughter, Cathy, set out on an around-the-world trip to sell advertising for the magazine.

Talk about innocents abroad. They were threatened by soldiers with rifles in Syria, detained at the airport in Cairo, got sick in Khartoum, almost inadvertently smoked hashish in Damascus, and barely escaped being crushed in a crowded commuter train in Osaka. But they made every appointment and brought back many new advertisers, articles, and photos.

### Working Together

Dick has developed a very capable team at Meister Publishing called Team Meister. With more than 100 employees, it is a group that works together very effectively. His sons-in-law, Gary Fitzgerald and Bill Miller, are major players in the corporation.

Dick has also been extremely helpful to the floriculture industry. He has served on the board of directors and as president of Bedding Plants Foundation, Inc. He and his company have established the Meister Graduate Assistantship with the foundation. And Dick and Bill Miller were chairpersons of the Seeley Conference at Cornell University in 1993 on the topic "Has Success Spoiled Floriculture?"

The Richard T. Meister Internship has also been established at Cornell University in Dick's honor. The ag communications internship will allow a Cornell student to spend two months each year at Meister Publishing learning the basics of publishing monthly magazines in our industry.

Dick has always been an advocate for agriculture, horticulture, and specifically floriculture. He has helped many universities in promoting the education programs and publishing their research and extension information to help growers, allied trades, and students.

It can truly be said that more people in the world have read an agricultural publication from Meister Publishing than any other agriculture magazine publisher in the world.

### A Lasting Success

Dick and his wife, Brick, are an example to follow. They have been married 53 years, have three lovely children, and love horticulture. So I salute the chief and his wife on 50 years of working in the business and 53 years of marriage. Not many folks can do that. I've observed what makes them LAST, and I'd like to share these four tips with you.

**L – Learning.** Both Dick and Brick continue to learn, are great readers and great conversationalists, have a wide variety of interests, and are knowledgeable on many, varied subjects.

Dick plans to work more out of his homes in Ohio and Florida but learned all the new computer equipment so that his presence will still be a daily occurrence at Meister Publishing.

**A – Attitude.** Be always positive. One of the quotes in the Team Meister newsletter in December covered it nicely. "Only you can keep you down! You and only you have complete control of your mind. This is a basic truth of life. It follows, therefore, that you are the only one who can set limitations for yourself."

As a point of interest, at Dick's 50-year celebration in December he asked that the program be finished by 3 p.m. because he had a tennis match at 3:30. The can-do attitude and the competitive nature make work fun and make for an environment where people can be successful.

**S – Staying Power.** Another quote from the Meister newsletter reads. "All too often people quit when the going gets tough – often when just one more step would have carried them triumphantly to victory." Meister Publishing and its employees have staying power. I've seen them do jobs in two days that would normally take a week to finish.

**T – Truth.** Dick has spent 50 years providing information to agriculture; 50 years of reporting and observing trends; and 50 years of trying to provide truthful, reliable, and trustworthy information. I believe he, his management, and his employees are extremely truthful.

I consider Dick Meister to be the "Walter Cronkite" of agriculture publishers worldwide and most importantly my friend. I am proud to be associated with this elite group.

*– February 1997*

# The Scribe Of Floriculture

## G. Victor Ball – author, journalist, and interpreter of the floriculture industry.

G. Victor Ball helped develop the production of the U.S. floriculture industry throughout the 20th Century. In the process, he traveled more miles, saw more growers, took more pictures, and wrote more about the industry than any other individual.

Vic was truly a scribe. He wrote for the floriculture industry for 60 years. He was an author, a journalist, and an interpreter of what the floriculture industry was doing.

He started this task in 1937 with *GrowerTalks* magazine when he had his first bylined article. He was also the editor of the *Ball Red Book*, and was instrumental in editing seven updated editions. He completed the 16th edition within the last four months. While these are the written, long-lasting legacies of Vic, other contributions are just as great.

### Beyond The Written Word

First, his family. Vic's wife, Margaret, was the backbone of all of his efforts. His three daughters – Katharine, Esther, and Margaret – and six grandchildren – Chris and Katie Soper; Benjamin Victor, Flora and Mary Hewitt; and Eliza Stace – were the major joys of his life.

I had an opportunity to visit all of them at the funeral home following Vic's death in August. I spent 10 to 15 minutes telling tales of the great contribution he made to our industry – that was the highlight of my trip to Chicago. What a great group of grandchildren Margaret and Vic have.

Vic was not always a writer. He was born in 1914 in Glen Ellyn, IL. He graduated from the University of Illinois in 1936. He joined his father's company that year and worked until 1941 when he entered the military. He served as a Lt. Colonel from 1941 to 1946, spending 15 months in Italy. Then, in 1947, he became a member of the Board of Directors of Geo. J. Ball, serving as vice president of production.

Vic was very interested in students. I first met him when I was a student at Penn State University in 1963. He came to see what new research work was going on. My first impression was that he was very intense, and interested in everything. He had a piece of 8½ by 11-inch paper, folded in the middle, and a pencil to capture every word I said. He would reread it to me to make certain that he had all of the information correct. He then gave me a copy of *GrowerTalks*. It fit in my pocket. From that day until the present, I have most of the issues printed. Vic, at the time, was president of Geo J. Ball Co. In fact, he was president from 1960 to 1970.

### Investing In Floriculture's Future

One of Ball's significant accomplishments was the establishment of the DuPage Horticultural School in 1963. Vic's strong concern that students in this country have practical experience led to this venture. For more than 20 years, he and Geo. J. Ball Co. underwrote efforts to train students and give them practical experience so they could enter the floriculture industry prepared.

In the last few years at DuPage, I had the privilege of being on their board of directors. From that experience, I know firsthand how much money Vic and the company had to spend each year to keep the school in operation.

When the school closed, Vic and Margaret continued to invest their monies in floriculture education. In 1992, they provided a sizeable grant to the American Floral Endowment to fund internships for students enrolled in four-year colleges across the United States. Students can take three to six months off from school to gain practical work experience, while receiving a scholarship from the fund to help defray their expenses. This is a great contribution to our industry and is an outstanding legacy to Vic and Margaret. They helped train floriculture production people, not only in their lifetime, but for years to come.

Vic was also interested in continuing education for people who worked in the industry. Ten years ago, he started Grower Expo – a four-day conference and trade show – so growers from across the country could come together to share ideas with industry members.

Vic was also instrumental in starting Bedding Plants Inc. (BPI). In 1968, he and Geo. J. Ball Co. hosted a summer meeting of 13 people from within the bedding plant industry. That was the start of BPI. Vic and his brother, Carl, provided major support to start the organization. BPI was incorporated in 1969. Vic and Geo J. Ball Co. actually published the first three editions of *BPI News*.

Vic, along with John Holden, then membership chairperson, set the record of new members in one year. They got 250 new members. A big incentive was that everyone who became a member got a free subscription to *GrowerTalks*.

### A Lifetime Of Serving An Industry

Vic was heavily involved in the industry. Someone said he belonged to every grower organization in the United States. He helped many of them when they needed it. Vic has also received all of the major honors of the industry, among them induction into the Society of American Florists' Hall of Fame.

I would venture to say that Vic and Margaret Ball have made some of the most significant contributions to the floriculture industry in the 20th Century. He has been a business person at the head of a major company. He started a significant trade school and provided monies to help students learn through experience. He started a continuing education program for the industry and has been the main recorder of the floriculture industry in the 20th Century.

When I left the funeral home, I talked with Marvin Miller, Vic's aide the last few years. I gave Marvin an old BPI pin and told him to ask Margaret if Vic could take it with him. I told Marvin I know John Carew, Ernie Cuzzocreo, Leonard Bettinger, and Eiichi Yoshida will be there when he arrives and I know that he will be fined at least $5 if he doesn't have that pin. All of these folks built the bedding plant industry in the United States. It's only fitting that the scribe of the floriculture industry is there to continue the journey.

To Vic, I say well done thy true and faithful servant. To Margaret and his family, thank you for making Vic available for all his work and good deeds to help floriculture in the 20th Century.

*— October 1997*

# Claude Hope: Maestro Of Horticulture

*A composer and master of the art of horticulture who used his plant breeding and genetic skills to develop hundreds of flower varieties.*

On December 5, 1997, Claude Hope received an honorary doctorate degree in agriculture from Michigan State University (MSU). To my knowledge, this is the first honorary degree given to a floriculture person by MSU in 143 years.

It is only fitting that with all of his accomplishments and 50 years in the seed business Dr. Hope should be recognized in the 90th year of his life. Here is a brief history of what he has accomplished.

Claude Hope was born on May 10, 1907 in Sweetwater, TX. He was valedictorian of his high school class and earned his bachelor of science degree from Texas Tech University in 1929. Upon graduation, he assumed the position of horticulturist in the Department of Agriculture's Field Station at Sacaton, AZ.

In 1935, he entered graduate school at MSU. Within two years, he finished his course work and accepted a position at the U.S. Plant Introduction Station at Glenn Dale, MD.

During World War II, he moved through Officers Candidate School and attained the rank of captain. In 1943, he was put in charge of a cinchona nursery for the establishment of a quinine plantation in Costa Rica. In 1948, following World War II, Hope helped organize PanAmerican Seed Co. In the same year, he started Linda Vista, a seed production nursery in Turrialba, Costa Rica. He served as president of the company until 1989 when he retired.

### Breeder And Seedsman

Hope merged his plant breeding and genetic skills with numerous horticultural talents in the development of methodology for producing high quality flower seed. Nearly single handedly, he developed the production, seed harvesting, and handling procedures for dozens of flower species.

Hope co-developed the petunia 'Comanche Red,' the first red hybrid ever and an All-America Selections winner in 1953. This event is considered by many to have been the prime mover that started the bedding plant industry on a path toward a value of $971 million in 1990. This value puts the industry as number one in all categories of the floriculture industry at wholesale.

Hope is also the breeder of the first multiflora yellow petunia variety. He is widely recognized for his improvement of impatiens as a bedding plant and the development of the Elfin and Super Elfin series of hybrid impatiens. Impatiens have now become the number one bedding plant in sales and value in the United States.

In 1981, Linda Vista produced 90% of the seed for hybrid impatiens used by the U.S. market, 15% of the seed geraniums, and 8% of the snapdragon seed. His research and contributions to science have been recognized by the American Association of Scientists, MSU, and Texas Tech.

### Master Teacher

Under Hope's guidance, Linda Vista enjoyed a reputation as an outstanding flower seedhouse that specialized in quality products. At the peak of production, the company encompassed more than 230 acres with 50 acres under cover and employed more than 1,000 people.

At the commemoration of his 80th birthday, members of the Linda Vista family, many of whom Hope had nurtured in the company for more than 30 years, honored him with an engraved plaque. The inscription on the plaque read: "Maestro Claude Hope." This was a fitting description. As a composer and master of the art of horticulture, he brought credit not only to himself but to the many dedicated workers who had spent their lives at Linda Vista.

Hope's story would not be complete without a discussion of his commitment to the education, training, and personal welfare of the native Costa Ricans he employed. For more than 45 years, while political, social, and economic exploitation were occurring in neighboring countries, Hope developed and fostered a unique social structure that emphasized personal development and improvement. Many employees benefited from Hope's financial support for their secondary schooling.

Another source of training instituted at Linda Vista was the instruction provided to workers to enhance their job capabilities. Employees were divided into teams with separate responsibilities for production, breeding, and disease control. This way, the employees became knowledgeable about the "why" as well as the "how" of their responsibilities.

### Taking Care Of People

In addition to his concern for the day-to-day needs of the workers, Hope's legacy included monetary benefits from long-term investments that provide employees financial incentives. Through direct bonuses, supplemental pay, and an extended health care system, Hope provided employees with benefits in excess of those required through employer-employee contributions to the national health care system. He also established a trust fund that allowed employees to receive long-term home loans.

Dr. Hope is truly one of the major reasons the bedding plant industry has grown in the past 50 years from the smallest to the largest part of floriculture. To paraphrase an old adage: "Mighty oaks from little acorns grow."

A mighty impatiens industry has grown from the small seeds produced by Claude Hope in Costa Rica. Everyone in the bedding plant industry owes him their thanks and respect. The Captain, the Maestro, and the Doctor are all fitting titles for this great person.

*– January 1998*

# Selling Out Too Soon

*Lyle Cox – the catalyst who was willing to struggle for a good cause and kept Bedding Plants Inc. on its feet in difficult times.*

I first met Lyle Cox in the late 1960s when he worked in Ball Seed's seed department. He was sharp, and he provided integrity and great service to growers who counted on his good work and deeds.

Lyle became an active member in Bedding Plants Inc. (BPI) during this time and helped round up the largest membership in the group's history. Ball Seed Co. had more than 200 BPI members in just one year.

When BPI started, bedding plants were the smallest part of the floriculture industry. Many people in the business thought of these growers as poor, dumb vegetable producers with cheap plastic structures who didn't know how to grow any traditional plants. But now that's changed.

I knew Lyle was the key figure in saving BPI from comments I had heard and correspondence I had read. My wife, Barbara, and I were shocked to learn of his untimely death April 22.

Just a month earlier, we invited Lyle, who sat on BPI's board of directors and was chair of the 1998 Denver conference committee, to our home with Dick Goodson, BPI's new executive director. Together we shared good food, fun, and frank talk about BPI.

Losing Lyle is a great blow to many, but especially to his wife, Judy; his children, Stacey and Shelley; and to their family business, Central Iowa Floral Co. It is also a loss to the Society of Iowa Florists, the Iowa State Horticulture Society's Legislature Committee, the Commercial Horticulture Advisory Board, and the Des Moines Area Community College Horticulture Advisory Board. This loss especially hurts BPI, where Lyle was serving as director, treasurer, and chairperson of the 1998 annual convention.

### Staking A Claim In History

Here's a little piece of history. In 1976, Lyle and Judy started their bedding plant business, Central Iowa Floral Co., in Des Moines. As a small grower, Lyle supported BPI. In the beginning, he ran for office once or twice and lost, but he always remained a member and supported BPI's efforts. Fortunately, Lyle's continued support for BPI and its goals made him run for director, and he won the election just when BPI needed him most.

When I think about Lyle, I am reminded of an article I read called "Selling Out Too Soon," by Bishop Ernest A. Fitzgerald. Fitzgerald recounts a story about Russell H. Conwell, who founded Temple University in Philadelphia, PA. Conwell became famous for his lecture, "Acres of Diamonds," which caught America's attention.

Fitzgerald insisted that, if only we would use our imaginations, we would have a tool to make life meaningful. Then he told a story about a man who discovered gold in Western Nevada. He worked the claim for a while, but he thought it was running out, so he sold it for a mere $11,000.

History proved the gold mine was not at its end. Investors who bought it found the Comstock Lode – the richest gold and silver deposit ever discovered. Thirty years later, these investors had earned $300 million on their $11,000 investment. Conwell says this story was about "the man who sold out too soon."

Lyle was the catalyst BPI needed to continue working the claim. He was the one who kept BPI on its feet, and he was the one who realized that a lot of gold had been taken from the claim.

One of the deadliest enemies to human accomplishment is the temptation to become too easily discouraged. It happens to all of us.

In our own business or lives, we struggle to work for a good cause and to succeed. Yet, we find ourselves working on problems that need to be solved. It gets tougher. The load gets heavier. It becomes difficult. Only, with a little more effort and another push, the gold mine could be ours.

When BPI held its first meeting at Michigan State University in 1967, 150 people attended. It was the first time most of these people met each other and began discussing mutual problems. They needed each other.

I know people who attended that meeting with little or no money, and 30 years later, they are millionaires. Bedding plant production is now worth more than $2 billion in the United States. It was worth less than $80 million when BPI was founded.

### Fulfilling His Dream

BPI is truly the bedding plant industry's Comstock Lode. Lyle Cox must be praised for his efforts. He struggled for a good cause without throwing in the towel and selling out.

Perhaps with just a little more effort and a tiny push, floriculture's gold mine can be even bigger for the next generation of bedding plant growers.

It's up to BPI's present leaders to determine what path the association will take. I believe it will be the motivated bedding plant growers – the future Lyle Coxes of BPI – who won't be easily discouraged, who will struggle for a good cause, handle the heavy loads, and continue to find the Comstock Lode.

*– November 1998*

# The Champion Of Geraniums
## J. Robert (Bob) Oglevee – "Mr. Geranium."

After World War II, geranium cuttings came mostly from open field production in Southern California. Growers had a choice of keeping and overwintering their own stock or bringing cuttings in from California in winter or early spring. Because the plants were grown in open fields, they often contained pests like geranium rust and plume moth, as well as dreadful diseases such as geranium bacterial blight (*Xanthomonas pelargorai*). This bacterial disease reached epidemic proportions in California during the spring and summer of 1952. The whole geranium industry was on the verge of extinction. Researchers and growers held a meeting to develop a system that would greatly reduce or eliminate this bacterial disease. They were searching for a hero.

The right person at the right place at the right time with the right information was J. Robert (Bob) Oglevee.

### Getting Started

Bob attended Cornell University in the late 1940s. He became interested in the commercial application of culture indexing to remove systemic diseases and grow clean stock plants.

When Bob returned to the family business in Connellsville, PA, he worked with James Tammen of Penn State University to create the procedure for growing culture-indexed geraniums. They developed the process to identify and eliminate infected cuttings, keeping only the healthy ones to propagate and release to the industry.

It wasn't an easy sell because the price of culture-indexed cuttings was much higher than the field-grown ones. But once growers lost 25%, 50%, or 100% of their crop, cost became less of an obstacle.

Bob's effort to introduce this procedure was the first major step at reviving the cutting geranium business. But he was the type of person who was never satisfied. He was always looking for a better product and thinking of how to solve the next major problem.

Bob was truly the driving force behind the cutting geranium crop from the late 1940s until his death in March. I've often said Oglevee Co. did for the geranium what Yoder Brothers did for the chrysanthemum.

### Cleaning Up Geraniums

In the late 1970s, Penn State pathologist, Samuel H. Smith, and Bob's daughter, Wendy Oglevee O'Donovan, developed culture virus indexing (CVI). CVI eliminated bacteria and viral pathogens. While this process may take up to four years to clean up a propagation source, once it has been completed, the variety can be used as a commercial product.

Bob never compromised the integrity of the CVI process. Throughout the years, he became the spokesman for the cutting geranium, preaching the virtues of CVI and developing production systems to show growers how to make a profit on this crop.

He worked with researchers at Penn State to develop the "fast crop" geranium, producing a saleable plant from a cutting in five to six weeks. He also made contact with other industry people who worked with him to increase the production of CVI geraniums. Lou Shanke of Canada was one of his close friends and partners in this effort.

One of Bob's strongest skills was finding good people to work for or with him. He had his own plant breeding program and worked with other plant breeding companies to introduce promising new varieties. His company now offers 38 zonal geranium varieties, 25 ivy geranium varieties, 25 Regal geranium varieties, and six Stardom floribunda geranium varieties. Oglevee also offers streptocarpus, Bright Point poinsettias, kalanchoe, New Guinea impatiens, double begonias and impatiens, and Spectrum hiemalis begonias.

I first met Bob when I was a student at Penn State. He would often visit Tammen in the plant pathology department and Darrell Walker and Dick Craig in horticulture. As with most horticulture students at the time, I was taught the importance of culture indexing geraniums. I had the honor of knowing Bob for more than 30 years and was often involved with the same grower programs he was.

I first realized what a significant contribution Bob made to the industry when I became the floriculture extension specialist at Michigan State University. One day I was called to a geranium grower's range in Detroit. On one of the first sunny spring days, a number of his plants showed signs of wilting even when they were well-watered. I took samples, had them analyzed, and found the dreaded bacterial blight. More than 100,000 plants were lost in less than three weeks. The grower had infected his own stock with cheap, field-grown cuttings purchased from California. He spread the disease by splashing water from plant to plant.

### Geraniums Galore

Bob has taken the industry to new heights. In 1997, more than 50 million cutting geraniums valued at nearly $93 million were produced in the 26 states surveyed by USDA. Oglevee and its primary propagators supplied more than 30 million of these cuttings. Millions more Oglevee geranium varieties reach consumers each spring through secondary propagators.

It's safe to say that Bob Oglevee's CVI process has touched almost every geranium cutting grown in the United States and Canada today. Bob was a leader the last 50 years, and his influence will be felt for many years to come.

Bob Oglevee was fair, intense, determined, and eager to learn. He was willing to share information and experiences, and always able to get knowledgeable people to work with him. His analytical mind was focused and goal-oriented. He loved research, fresh ideas, and new knowledge. Using his abundant talents, he easily commercialized new plants and knowledge.

He truly was the champion of the cutting geranium. No other person has ever made a bigger contribution in taking a plant from the verge of extinction to the height of popularity.

Everyone in floriculture will miss Bob's presence and significant contributions. I want to thank Bob's wife, Jane, and his family for sharing his talents and good work with our industry. I'm sure those who are involved in the Oglevee family business will continue to make significant contributions to the industry. They may have big shoes to fill. But they are headed in the right direction.

Bob Oglevee is a great example of how one small family businessman in a rural community can have an impact on millions of people worldwide. Bob saw the beauty of today and helped grow beauty for tomorrow. He will forever be remembered as "Mr. Geranium."

*– May 1999*

# A Tribute To George Todd

### The "Henry Ford" of the horticulture industry – an inventor, innovator, and pioneer of plug technology.

Before I met George Todd, Sr., I thought a plug was a tired, old horse. My father would tell me that the horse was just "plugging along." My conception of what a plug was changed forever when I first met George during the second International Bedding Plant Conference at Michigan State University in 1968. He came to the conference to see if his new "plug" concept could be used to produce bedding plants. He unveiled a polystyrene flat that had 120 individual cells, which he was using to grow vegetable transplants. He coined the word "speedling" for this procedure of producing individual plants in individual cells. This event was the start of plug production in the bedding plant industry worldwide.

In their textbook, *Plug And Transplant Production*, Roger Styer and David Koranski identified George as one of four individuals who figured prominently in the development of plug technology. There is no doubt he was the first to use this concept for vegetable transplants, and he, Bill Swanekamp, Ed Pinter, Sr., and Fred Blackmore were the pioneers in this technology in the flower bedding plant industry.

When George attended that bedding plant conference in 1968, he asked me what flower I thought would be best suited for his plug concept. I suggested geraniums. From that moment on, George became obsessed in developing a procedure to produce speedlings in Florida and selling them to growers across North America.

Every time George ran into a problem, he would aggressively work toward the solution. He would call others for advice, read textbooks and research articles, or do anything necessary to find the solution. In our early work with the plug, George funded three graduate students to solve the problems facing geranium production using this system.

In addition, I remember how we would develop our own experiments, collect the data, and present the results. George would have the information immediately transferred to commercial production. For example, he funded our research to prevent ethylene damage to plug geraniums shipped from Florida to the North. We solved this problem in one year.

### Cultivating An Industry

George was an inventor and innovator, developing many patents throughout the years. He also was able to take new knowledge and apply it to a commercial system. This knowledge has been used by all his friends and colleagues within the bedding plant industry.

George also had the knack for making lemonade out of lemons. For instance, once he was involved in a lawsuit where a group of growers in the Southeast sued his company because the tomato plants they bought from him developed bacterial leaf spot.

After a legal battle, which he lost, he told me, "Will, this will never happen again. I lost the suit because I couldn't prove that I didn't water the plants on their foliage. Therefore, the bacteria, the plant, and the environment were present at my business. If the disease occurred there or in the growers' field, it would still be very difficult to prove scientifically."

But George didn't take this lawsuit as a negative. He turned it into a positive. He invented the plug float system, which waters the plant from below the container. It essentially ensured there would never again be water on the foliage of any plant grown at his facility in Florida. This production concept helped increase production and efficiency at Speedling and is still used today.

### Rooted In Horticulture

George had strong roots in horticulture, growing up on a cauliflower farm in New York. He worked with his father on the concept of producing two cauliflower crops a year, one in New York and one in Florida.

During these early years, George valued the cooperative extension service. For advice, he often called John Carew, an extension specialist at Cornell University, who later became my boss at Michigan State University.

George also became actively involved in Bedding Plants Inc. (BPI), becoming the association's fourth president. He has held every office for BPI and probably been on every committee. Also, when others took their money and ran from BPI, George continued to be involved and worked with it to the end. The association's America In Bloom program will survive and exist because George didn't run from a difficult situation. Instead, he helped make lemonade.

### Tennis, Anyone?

After selling one of his businesses, George decided to use his free time to learn everything there was to know about subirrigation. He would call me on nights and weekends to ask: "Who are the experts? What research is going on? Where can I learn about this? Who should I see in Europe? Where can I go to understand this concept?" I thought George was starting another greenhouse business and couldn't wait to see it launched.

To my great surprise, George, along with his son, George, Jr., got into the business of building clay tennis courts. With my simple mind, I had no idea what George was up to. He and his son invented a system to water clay tennis courts by subirrigation. Within five years, they were one of the largest tennis court builders and maintainers in the United States.

### Lasting Legacy

Another definition for plug in Webster's Dictionary is "anything used to stop a hole." Before George Todd entered the horticultural industry, there was a hole in which each seedling had to be transplanted from a seed flat and placed in the hole of a transplant flat. Because of George's invention, more than 95% of all plants are directly seeded in plug flats and, in many cases, automatically transplanted to finished flats or the field.

To give you some idea of the impact of his efforts, in 1965, there were no plants produced in plugs. In 1997, there were more than 25 billion plants a year produced in the world by plug production, and in 2001, I would estimate at least 40 billion plants will be grown by this method. I would also estimate more than one trillion plants will have been produced by the plug system by 2010.

I, therefore, consider George Todd, Sr., the Henry Ford of the horticulture industry. He helped develop the mass production of seedlings. This will forever be a legacy remembered by everyone who enjoys growing plants.

*– August 2001*

# He Lived His Dream

*Paul Ecke, Jr. – "Mr. Poinsettia" – a visionary who gave so much of himself to floriculture, his business, his community, his family, and his friends.*

The many friends and colleagues of Paul Ecke, Jr. were deeply saddened by his death on May 13, 2002. While I was unable to attend Paul's funeral, I did take the time to stop and reflect on all the times he and I interacted with mutual interests in the floriculture industry. I'd like to share some of these memories with you.

### Looking Back

Someone once said, "Memories are bits of history that you record in your heart and soul."

The first time I met Paul was on one of his visits to Penn State. I was a graduate student and he and one of my professors, John Mastalerz, were in the greenhouses when I was on my rounds checking temperatures. I knew Paul only by reputation and was honored to have a chance to shake his hand and talk with him. He took the time to ask me questions and seemed interested in my work and what I'd found from my research. My first impression was that he was a "down-to-earth" person who truly seemed interested in people.

With his background and his worldly experiences, Paul seemed to have a vision and knew what he was doing. Paul was also enthusiastic about promoting the poinsettia – his job was to know more about the poinsettia than anyone else in the world.

When I came to Michigan State University (MSU) in 1966, Paul would visit once or twice a year. When Dr. Tolbert in biochemistry and Dr. Richard Lindstrom in horticulture used Cycocel to control stem elongation in poinsettias, Paul was eager to use the results and commercialize them. It wasn't long before almost every grower in the United States used this material to control plant height.

Paul gave me my first research grant for poinsettias and Dr. Ken Sink and I developed a method to produce a specific number of shoots per plant. We called it precision pinching of poinsettias. This production method also became widely used nationally.

### Advocating Floriculture Education

In the 1970s, I found that Paul was keenly interested in training students in floriculture. He and my boss, Dr. John Carew, worked with John Henry Dudley and the American Floral Endowment (AFE) to start the Mosmiller Fellowships. These were awarded to students who then would train with a selected commercial floriculture company for three to six months. At the time, it was the only program of its kind in floriculture.

Paul also developed an extensive internship program at the Paul Ecke Ranch. He usually hosted eight to 12 students at a time, who were not only from the United States but also countries across Europe. He provided housing, transportation, and wages to expose these interns to poinsettia production practices used at The Ranch. Several of these interns became employees of The Ranch and the others became excellent customers or allied tradespeople. Paul was truly interested in students and worked with universities, colleges, trade associations, and the industry to promote floriculture education.

### Being Mr. Poinsettia

From the continuing education point-of-view, Paul had few equals. He talked to every local, state, and national floriculture group. I'd wager he has talked to industry members in every state, most Canadian provinces, and countries all over the world. As the spokesperson for the poinsettia, he made it the largest selling potted plant in North America. He also promoted the poinsettia to consumers through his contacts with the American Horticulture Society and became well-known to the gardening public. Paul often provided his poinsettia varieties to the national news networks during the holiday season.

Another one of my memories is when we tried to make the poinsettia a spring-flowering plant. Dr. Sink and I talked with Paul about the idea. He indicated that red probably wouldn't work well but other colors might. Providing them was no problem but when we tried to sell 200 plants of nonred poinsettias in a local supermarket the week before Mother's Day, only five plants were bought. The plants were beautiful and the store owner said he thought they looked great except for one problem: All his customers thought the plant was only for Christmas. We all had a good laugh over our experiment.

### Being Mr. Floriculture

Paul spoke several times at the former Bedding Plants International (BPI) conventions and was supportive of the organization's efforts to mobilize growers to work and learn together. He provided product, exhibited at BPI trade shows, helped build its office buildings, and provided a great deal of personal support for the association's efforts.

Whenever a yellow envelope with a red poinsettia logo arrived, I knew Paul had something to share with me. Just to make certain I wouldn't miss the main point, he would always highlight what he wanted me to remember or do with a pink highlighter pen. In fact, I have two of his most recent letters in front of me with one of his requests still to accomplish.

Paul's strongest industry support was with the Ohio Florists' Association. Few people have given as much as Paul Ecke has to the organization. He graduated from The Ohio State University and the institution has no stronger supporter of its work and research. I have often said to my colleagues that if only Paul had attended MSU, we would have the largest floriculture short course and trade show in Michigan – not Ohio.

Paul's work and collaboration with the Society of American Florists (SAF) and AFE also have resulted in groundbreaking and tremendous accomplishments. His involvement and efforts in governmental affairs, education, and research have been of great value to our industry. Paul often identified major problems and opportunities, and then set to work quietly to further industry goals. There are truly few people who have donated as much time, money, and effort for the betterment of floriculture than Paul Ecke, Jr.

### Being Mr. Generosity

Paul made significant contributions to many other organizations inside and outside the floriculture industry – from the YMCA, to local botanical gardens, to other causes he was interested in. Back in 1990, I contacted Paul and told him we were going to develop a Horticulture Demonstration Garden. I told him it would only cost $2.5 million and that more than a quarter of a million people would see it every year.

Together, we developed a set of plans for a feature we thought would be appropriate to honor his father. Soon after, he stopped by for a visit, looked over the project, and a short time later the check arrived to build MSU's Conservatory Plaza.

In the January 1993 issue of *Greenhouse Grower* on page 16, Paul's and my pictures appeared on the same page. It was quite an honor to be considered with Paul as one of the growers and researchers who have enlightened production and marketing techniques. His father's picture appeared in the same issue as a captain of the industry. Both Paul and his father, Paul Sr., truly were and continue to be the masters of poinsettias – and of floriculture. Their good works and deeds will long be remembered.

I consider Paul Ecke, Jr. a visionary. Every industry, business, and cause needs to have people with vision or, as it says in the Bible's Book of Proverbs, "Where there is no vision, people perish." My first boss, John Carew, also was a visionary. I'm still trying to fulfill his vision to create new knowledge and distribute it. Both Carew and Ecke are great examples to follow.

Paul Ecke, Jr. lived his life to the fullest and, in the process, he has given so much of himself to all of us – to floriculture, to his business, to his family, and to his colleagues and friends. In passing, as well as in life, I'm sure Paul will continue to be an influence on all of us who have memories of our contacts with him.

*– July 2002*

# TAKING THE LEAD

If you want to have a winning operation, you have to develop a team that will work together to get all the tasks done. Family members may be key players on the team. So will others who are part of your operation. You have to coach them to help them become star players. You have to let them know what the plan is and what you expect of them. In other words, you need to be a leader.

The major difference between successful businesses and ones that go bankrupt is that the successful ones have people who can make things happen. No matter how bad the weather, no matter how bad the conditions, they can get the product to the customer and make the sale.

It isn't hard to get into a negative rut. Many people think we are fools to be in this business. Often, after a long, hard winter, we wonder if anyone will ever buy our product. Negative talk, negative reactions, and loss of profit go together. A positive outlook can go a long way toward developing a winning team and a winning operation.

In his book, *Maybe, Maybe Not,* Robert Fulghum illustrates how important we are to each other, using the children's game of musical chairs. You know the game. You place one less chair than the number of players, start the music and walk around until the music stops, at which point everyone grabs a chair. The player who doesn't get a chair is out of the game. Fulghum suggests a new variation. When the music stops, those without chairs must sit on someone else's lap. When the last chair is removed, everyone is sitting on someone else's lap, supporting each other in an interlocking chairless circle – everyone's a winner.

A good leader can help create these win-win situations. Following are some columns that have ideas on how to become that kind of a leader in your business.

## *It Takes A Leader*

*The best bedding plant operation in the country is best because someone within the operation is a leader. Apply Charles "Tremendous" Jones' seven laws of leadership to your operation.*

It takes a leader in any group, whether it's in government, industry, education, or other aspects of life, to get a job done. This doesn't mean that they do all the work themselves, but that they are able to get the job done.

Getting a job done just doesn't happen by mistake, it usually happens because a leader exercises the seven laws of leadership. These laws have always been at hand, but it took Charles "Tremendous" Jones to develop them in his book *Life Is Tremendous*. I'd like to review these seven laws and interpret them as bedding plant growers might use them.

**Law 1: Get Excited About Your Work.** Most bedding plant growers are really interested in their profession. In fact, they usually eat, drink, and sleep their work. If this atmosphere can be passed on to your employees, they will catch your excitement and the usual result is that they will do a better job for you. Some owners never tell their employees anything. They treat them in a very cold, uninformed manner. This can only cause conflict between the employer and employees. Getting excited and getting other people excited about the same thing – our bedding plant business – usually is the first step toward everyone working together for a successful business.

**Law 2: Use Or Lose.** Everyone has talents they usually obtain by working and gaining experience. If you use these talents, you will increase your ability. If you don't use these talents, you will usually lose them or at least decrease your effectiveness. The object then, if you wish to remain proficient in something, is to continue to use and practice it. If you do not continue to practice, you will lose the talents you once had.

**Law 3: Production To Perfection**. Everyone tries to produce a perfect crop. That should be the goal for all of us. However, we all know this is very difficult. The one prayer I always say is "O Lord, let me do one thing perfect in my lifetime, but in the meantime, help me do something." While we are always trying to grow perfect crops, we must continue to grow every crop as best we can. Some are better than others, some have insect and disease problems, and some have other problems that we hadn't thought we would encounter. We all have problems to overcome. Our biggest problems usually occur when we build greenhouses or get involved in other jobs at the same time we're attempting to grow the crops. It's difficult to do two or more things at one time, but no matter what the obstacles, a crop must be produced.

**Law 4: Give To Get.** This law doesn't mean trying to give something to someone so that you will expect to get something back in return. That's only trading. What it means is that you're learning to give, to keep giving of yourself, or your time, your talents, or money to others that need it. And, you will be surprised what you get back in return. Usually you get respect, admiration, and your own peace of mind. What you get in return is not a gift, but a greater capacity to go beyond where you are now. You'll usually find that you get much more out of life than you ever give in return.

**Law 5: Exposure To Experience.** Each exposure that you receive is like a key you place on a chain to be used in the future. When you run into a situation in your own greenhouse, you usually draw from past experiences to solve your problem. If you never go anywhere, if you never attend any educational meetings, if you never visit with fellow growers, you have no keys on your chain from which to draw and so, therefore, you must learn by your own mistakes. However, if you have been exposed to a wide set of circumstances, you'll find that the problems you face probably will be solved from the experiences you've had in the past.

**Law 6: Flexible Planning.** This is the year of the planner and of the organizer, but we all know that unexpected things always develop. The good leader knows how to be flexible. One grower told me "I always write down 10 things to do each day in the order I want to do them. But many times at the end of the day so many unexpected things have developed that I still have those 10 things to do plus another 10 jobs that also need to be done." The point is be flexible. Be able to adjust to things that you cannot foresee and be able to solve these problems as they come along. Remember, those people who cannot adjust usually aren't leaders.

**Law 7: Motivated To Motivating.** Once you are motivated and are practicing the other six laws you will eventually become successful at motivating other people and be happy doing it. There are many professional motivators who are successful and motivate everybody but themselves. They lose their own sense of purpose and, therefore, they have forgotten to learn how to motivate themselves. Remember, you've got to not only motivate other people, but keep yourself motivated also.

Leadership makes decisions. Once the decision is made, leadership requires persuasion, and a supervisor must be able to convince his employees of the advantages of a change.

Leadership achieves results. The effectiveness of leadership can be measured in the amount of influence one person has over the behavior or job performance of others. Also, leadership is willing to be different. Being different means being able to implement change and to overcome all of those 30 objections I've listed plus thousands of others.

Lastly, remember a leader renders service. No leadership is exercised when employees are serving supervisors. Leadership begins to function when the supervisor begins to serve the employees. That is the most important characteristic of leadership. The best bedding plant operation in the country, no matter how big or small, is best because someone within the operation is a leader. Work at this skill and you'll be well on your way to being the best operation of your size and type in the country.

*– December 1977*

## Plants Aren't The Problem – People Are

*Perfect plants are the result of people doing things right. Go-Go growers have their whole act together.*

One of the interesting aspects of my job as extension specialist is that of troubleshooting plant problems – evaluating why plants aren't growing properly. It often is like playing detective, trying to determine what happened. In all cases, the conclusion is that plants aren't the problem – people are. Usually, it boils down to someone not doing something or doing it improperly, causing the plant to perform abnormally. While plants don't talk, they sure can show exactly what's been done to them. Anyone who has worked with plants closely and seen how they react to different conditions can identify a similar looking plant in another greenhouse. Plants will always respond to the way they are treated. That's one good thing about our business; you can tell us how good a grower you are, but you also have to produce the plants to prove it. Perfect plants are the result of people doing things right.

Winning starts with beginning. Every successful grower has a plan, develops proper scheduling, and mentally grows the plant before seeds or cuttings are planted. Without a plan or schedule, it is impossible to grow the plants properly.

There is no gain without pain. It takes time and dedication to produce a good crop. You can tell if a grower is spending time and attention on his crop or if he is just giving it the once over. Many problems occur because the grower becomes a carpenter, electrician, or adds on to the greenhouse at the same time he is supposed to be growing a crop.

The hardest part is getting started…developing a plan, gathering all the materials, putting it together. If you've done your planning properly, you're over half way to a perfect crop. Then it is just a question of implementing your plan. To be a good grower, you've got to be observant; you have to anticipate problems. For example, if you're growing a petunia crop, what can go wrong? What diseases and insects could damage the crop? What do the symptoms look like? Constantly check your crop to make certain that problems don't occur.

It is also important to analyze your problems properly. If a disease like Botrytis develops, while a chemical will stop the disease, you must search to discover the cause of the problem. Perhaps overwatering has occurred or the mist cycle is too frequent and this has resulted in a high moisture condition. The problem then was caused by a person who must be told to adjust his watering practices to reduce or eliminate this disease.

It is important to organize your operation. Divide responsibilities so the people involved will receive all the credit or blame for the condition of the crop. It is important to give people responsibility and authority. This system of organizing to divide and conquer your problems is important and, thus, makes the big job of growing many crops in many situations a more manageable condition which usually results in better crops.

I've seen four types of growers during my experience in working with greenhouse people. They can be classified as follows:

**1. No-No Growers.** You've seen the type. It can't be done. We don't have the time. It costs to much. We don't need it. And nine million other negative statements to rationalize away improvements and stay content with a rundown, old greenhouse that is losing money.

**2. Yo-Yo Growers.** One time they produce a fine crop, the next time it all dies. They aren't consistent. They can't do the same thing twice. Their mind wanders, sometime doing things well, implementing new technology, and other times forgetting the basics. The up and down cycle of this type of individual always has you wondering what he will do next.

**3. Blow-Blow Growers.** All talk and no product. He is the type of individual who can talk a good crop but can't produce it. He usually makes a great impression, handles himself well in public, but when it comes time to deliver what he has to say, there becomes a great credibility gap. It usually doesn't take anyone very long to identify this type of individual.

**4. Go-Go Growers.** These are the people who have their whole act together. They know what they are doing and can produce a good crop consistently. They are well organized, have the plan thought out, and are able to put all the factors together with the proper end result. Everyone should try to be this type of grower; for in the end, these will be the only types that will survive as our business becomes more competitive and more competition develops.

More and more our industry will need its share of leaders. Those people who will not only be concerned about their business, but with the industry as a whole. We have been fortunate in the bedding plant business as we have had individuals of this type who have helped develop the industry within the last 10 years.

Remember, there are five traits that a leader must have:

**1. He Grows.** He constantly is learning, developing, and working at improving himself. This is a continual process and one can never stop. Reading, attending meetings, and searching for new information is essential in becoming or remaining a leader.

**2. He Knows.** He takes the information he has and draws from it. He knows what to do and when to do it. His mind is his built-in computer, with the right answers at his finger tips.

**3. He Shows.** He acts like a leader. He handles himself well. He has the respect of his employees, his peers, and with all those he comes in contact.

**4. He Goes.** He travels and is exposed to many different experiences. He understands the entire picture and is able to use this worldliness toward being a leader.

**5. He Bestows.** He builds up others. He helps develop the most valuable resource he has – people. A leader doesn't demand respect, he commands respect because others believe he can lead them to a better, fuller life.

I hope that everyone who reads this column is a go-go grower who is a leader. The year 1979 will be a challenging one, and, hopefully, the best bedding plant year ever. It will be for the people who do it right!

*– February 1979*

# BPI: 10 Years And Growing

*Having E-N-E-R-G-Y can unlock the secrets to success.*

In November 1969, Bedding Plants Inc. was incorporated as a non-trade association in the state of Michigan. This incorporation resulted from two previous conferences that were held at Michigan State University (MSU). The first was held in September 1968, with an attendance of slightly more than 100 people. From this first conference, the need for continued information and dialog was apparent. The next year more than 150 people attended the conference.

Ernie Cuzzocreo, of Orange, CT, was elected first president of BPI, with Jim Perry, vice president, and Bob Soos, treasurer. The first board meetings were knock-down, drag-out affairs with many meetings running 12 to 15 hours. BPI started with 50 members and less than $500. We had to borrow a typewriter to get started. Our first major purchase was a secondhand mimeograph machine. I'll never forget at our organizational meeting, I was elected executive secretary because, as one grower said, "Will, you're the only one in the room without an honest job, therefore you're elected."

It was a challenging time getting 25 people, officers, and the board to agree on how to develop and run the association. We learned by doing. The board told Bob Soos and I to get BPI incorporated in the state of Michigan. It took us three to four months and about $100 to do the job. Years later, when we became more sophisticated, we incorporated the research association with a lawyer. It took him six months and more than $1,000. This proves we can make up for money with a lot of our own time and effort.

Cuzzocreo's phone bill during his two years in office was probably enough to purchase a round trip ticket for him and his wife to Europe. His early morning phone calls were a regular event. If the phone rang before 6 a.m. it was always answered, "Good morning, Ernie." Ernie guided BPI from MSU to St. Paul, MN, to Rochester, NY, increasing membership to 523 as the meeting moved to these locations.

In 1972, Jim Perry became president, Leonard Bettinger was elected vice president, and Bob Soos was again treasurer. Jim helped greatly to develop BPI and place it on sound footing. Under his presiding, meetings were held in Columbus, OH, in 1973 and Raleigh, NC, in 1974. Membership during Jim's tenure as president doubled, so by the end of 1979 there were 1,205 active members.

Leonard Bettinger became president in 1974. Our seventh and ninth year conferences were celebrated in Hershey, PA, and BPI had grown to 1,731 members by that time. It should be noted that Bob Soos spent seven years as treasurer and was very instrumental in BPI's early growth. In 1976, George Todd, of Sun City, FL, became president, Harlan Hamernik, of Clarkson, NE, vice president, and Bob Schmidt of Lubbock, TX, treasurer. Under this leadership, two conferences were held at Denver, CO, in 1977 and Toronto, ON, in 1978. Membership rose to 2,557 at this time.

In 1978, Harlan Hamernik became president, with Bob Schmidt, vice president, and Egon Molbak, of Woodinville, WA, treasurer. The membership in this past year rose to 2,948. It should be noted the increase in growth can be attributed, not only to the president and officers, but to the board of directors, committees, and many individuals who gave of their time, talent, and money on BPI's behalf.

Many industry people have been impressed with the growth rate of BPI, almost 3,000 members in 10 years. They ask, "How can it be done?" The answer is simple – energy. Whether a business or trade association, energy is needed. Not only fuel, like coal, gas, or oil, but, more important, human energy. Look at the letters of the word "energy." They can be used to unlock the secrets of success:

• **Enthusiasm.** If you can't get excited about your business, and if you can't motivate other people to get excited about it, it is doomed to failure. Enthusiasm is the key ingredient to developing a successful venture, and the key to the energy you need.

• **Navigation.** There has to be a plan. Someone has to develop the map indicating where you're going and how you're going to get there. Goals have to be set, objectives defined, and strategies and tactics worked out. People have to be responsible to get the job done.

• **Enlightened.** It is important to remain current on the crops being grown, new procedures and techniques, and information related to greenhouses. This new information on new plant material must be utilized or

your business is doomed. How many of the same varieties are you growing that were grown 10 years ago? How different are the cultural practices
of 10 years ago? Your answer is probably more than 90% for each.

• **Refinement.** Constantly make improvements, make your operation more efficient. Use better scheduling and hire better employees. Try
to improve working conditions. Closely monitor all factors and refine
your operation to make it the most profitable.

• **Growing.** A business or trade association must continue to grow
and not be static. It can't stay at the same level. Every business has an
introductory phase, a growth phase, a maturation phase, and a declining phase. These phases happen with people, products, business, and
trade associations. The object is to keep the growth phase existing for as
long as possible.

• **You.** Nothing will be successful without you. If you are working,
active, and planning for your business success – if you are willing to
make a commitment and follow through, then you are on the way to success, but it takes energy.

Remember, everyone is concerned with all types of fuel energy. Do
all you can to conserve. The most important energy is your energy.
Use it wisely.

*– November 1979*

# Managing Your Business Growth

*Half of all businesses fail in the first two years. Most fail due to a lack of management and leadership skills. What kind of a leader are you?*

Whether or not you have labor problems depends on your ability to lead people. Consider the following example:

A group got together to learn about leadership styles. A facilitator broke the group into three sections and had each select a leader. The facilitator then took the leaders aside, telling each how to lead.

The first was a dictator. "Don't let the group do anything without your approval. If anyone does, reprimand that person in front of the group. You must make every decision."

The second leader was democratic. "Ask the advice of the group. Vote on each point, allowing the majority to determine what to do. Let the members have a good time while they're working."

The third leader was laissez-faire. "Let the group do what it wants. Don't give any direction or make any decisions."

### Three Leaders – Three Responses

The facilitator then gave each group a box of tinker toys and instructed them to build the tallest free-standing tower possible within half an hour. Upon completion, the groups had built very different structures and had varying responses to the three unique leadership styles.

The dictator's group built a strong but short tower. It was sturdy and well-designed, but the workers weren't happy. Many reported they resented their leader for not allowing them to express their creativity, and for forcing them to do everything in a certain way.

The democratic group built a tall tower that was unsteady and looked as if it would fall at any moment. However, they were a happy group, enjoyed working together, and thought their leader was great.

The laissez-faire group didn't get very far. They had a difficult time getting started and felt frustrated with their leader, complaining he didn't know what to do. Several tried to elect another leader, with the group spending more time trying to get someone to lead than building the tower.

### Choose A Style That Works

This example illustrates that what gets done and how it gets done relate directly to the leadership style or styles of a manager. In business, you might use all of these styles at different times to accomplish different tasks.

Most managers in horticulture have one style and only one style – and the employees know it.

The dictator runs a tight ship, making sure everything is done and in its place, but may have many unhappy employees. The democratic leader may not be as well organized, but employees usually enjoy their jobs and like the boss. The laissez-faire leader not only has a business out of control but also has several employees who would like to get rid of the boss and manage things themselves.

What type of leader are you? What's your style and how is your business organized?

Evaluate yourself to see if you are ready to grow not only plants but also your business, organization, and relationships with people. This is an important step toward success in any kind of business.

*– June 1992*

# Partnering: A New Word For Cooperation

*Working with someone who has strengths where you have weaknesses can result in a win-win situation for both partners.*

"Partnering" has been a recurrent theme at recent industry meetings. Perhaps using the word "partnering" instead of the more familiar term cooperation is just a way to focus new attention on an old concept that can still be helpful today. Either term can be defined as: Working together for mutual benefit.

### Find A Partner

When developing a business plan, completing the strategic-planning step in which you list your weaknesses can be a humbling experience. When you've recognized your weaknesses, you have two choices – either learn the information you need to eliminate your weakness, or partner with someone who is strong in your weak areas.

Let me give you an example: I know a grower who produces the finest spring plants around. His life revolves around the greenhouse and how to fine-tune production practices for the ultimate in plant quality. Certainly no grower can succeed without strength in this area! This particular grower's weakness is in sales and cost accounting. He has neither the time nor the talent to market his plants properly, he just hopes people will come along and buy them. He has no idea what it costs him to grow his plants; he just hopes he'll have more money in the bank this year than last. This grower needs to partner (cooperate) with someone who has the sales and cost accounting strengths he lacks – and that person may know virtually nothing about how to grow plants!

To shore up their individual marketing weaknesses, groups of growers have successfully banded together to form marketing cooperatives. For example, the Kalamazoo Valley Plant Growers Cooperative is made up of 54 growers who have banded together to hire professional sales and marketing people. This cooperative started with 17 growers 25 years ago and today markets more than four million flats throughout the United States – a great job of partnering (cooperation).

One large grower, Russell Weiss, produces most of the azaleas for growers in the eastern United States. He even applies the growers' labels and includes their marketing materials – another example of growers working together to market a product.

In many parts of the country, growers trade flats or plants back and forth to keep their customers supplied with a full line of material. This is probably the most basic partnering within the floriculture business. Many suppliers and allied trades people are major partners in this industry, going out of their way to help growers. Beyond their basic function of delivering their products to growers in a timely fashion, they also provide technical help – and in some cases act as banks by extending credit to help growers with cash-flow problems.

In time of natural disasters or other unexpected problems, it is not uncommon for suppliers to go out of their way to support growers and help them get back into production. This has been a long-standing tradition within our industry. More than one grower has told me how the Fred Gloeckners, the George Balls, and other suppliers have helped pull them through the rough times. That is certainly an example of partnering.

Another partnership is the one between the grower and retailer. Some of the most successful marketing efforts are a result of this partnership. For example, in Canada, the Woolco chain works with growers six to 12 months in advance so they can provide special material to help make their famous "$1.44 Days" a great success.

### It's A Global Community

As we start looking at global marketing of flowers, partnering takes an international dimension. One of the most interesting examples of global partnering is the VisaFlor Group. A French rose hybridizer and a Mexican entrepreneur had worked together for 10 years when an American grower stepped in and helped improve their system. Then in 1990, two U.S. wholesale florists and a Japanese floriculturist got involved in the marketing end of the group's activities. Today, VisaFlor has 300 acres of production, 70% roses. This group is also becoming one of the largest sources of Asiatic lilies in the world. Products are shipped to both Mexico and the United States.

I believe global partnering of this type will continue to develop over the next few years. As the United States, Canada, and Mexico become one trading block, we will see growers of all three countries developing production and destination systems that will allow them to be competitive.

Dr. Edward W. McLaughlin, professor of Agricultural Economics at Cornell University, presented a lecture at the Seeley Conference called "Competitive Options In A Global Environment." In the summation of his lecture, he made the following observations about competing for trade in discretionary purchases:

• **Any discretionary purchase must compete with many other alternatives (often commodities), and flowers are no exception.** Consumers have a choice of many other products to satisfy their desires. How will we as an industry work together to make sure flowers are the product of choice?

• **Products must be differentiated.** McLaughlin pointed out the tremendous explosion of new products. In 1970, 1,000 new products were introduced; in 1992 there were 16,000. No wonder the consumer is confused.

• **Products must be uniquely identified.** Growers try to differentiate product by means of size, number of plants per container, and the like – but these may offer only a temporary advantage. Some growers have started using trade names – some with success, some without. The important element is quality. Once consistent quality has been established, then brand identification will differentiate the crop by color, size, fragrance – and, perhaps, shelflife.

• **McLaughlin's proposition.** A differentiated product of high quality will more than pay for the costs of differentiation. It is important that our flower crops aren't handled like commodities. We must differentiate them so that they are different (special). This then will allow a value-added price so we can profitably produce our product.

• **Recognize limitations and develop strategic alliances.** With this point, McLaughlin recognizes the need for partnering. He recommends finding people you can work with and developing a system that will benefit all the partners.

At the International Floriculture Industry Short Course, Russell Weiss held a meeting to discuss bar coding and the use of a universal cart. The first problem was well-identified: the clash of a universal bar code for floriculture with the different systems required by different retailers. The large growers, however can't agree on a united front. Similarly, the cart issue is difficult to address because growers design and develop carts of varying shapes and sizes to fit their individual needs.

There is still a great need for partnering (cooperation) among growers in the United States. It would be worthwhile to address these issues and work toward developing a win-win situation in which all growers and retailers would benefit. If we do not, we may see vertically integrated production and marketing companies emerge which are made up of many partners developing their own systems. These companies could then become the major players in U.S. floriculture.

As the old saying goes, "You'll always get more by cooperating than by going it alone." To use our "relevant new term," today we'll have to say, "You'll always get more by partnering than by going it alone."

*— September 1993*

# Maximize Opportunities, Minimize Threats

*Look at your strengths, weaknesses, opportunities, and threats. Companies that are proactive in analyzing their products and services can usually survive. Those that only react are often eliminated.*

At the end of the bedding plant season, growers I visit invariably ask "What is going to happen next year?" or "Will this type of business be here in 10 years?"

While no one really knows, every business must plan ahead, partly through external analysis – looking at the situation outside the company. What effect will government have on the industry in the next 10 years? Will your competition be greater or less? Which businesses will survive?

Will you actively try to influence external factors, or will you just wait until things happen and then complain they are driving you out of business?

Remember, that 25 years ago, cut flowers, potted plants, and foliage were all larger commodities than bedding plants. But of the businesses leading the industry at that time, many no longer exist. The cut flower business has moved largely to Colombia and Central America. Even the rose now has more stems produced offshore than in the United States.

Did those businesses see the changes coming and plan to take action to survive? Apparently not. Yet, while this part of the industry declined, the bedding plant industry grew by 10% to 15% per year.

History suggests this: Companies that do external analysis and adjust products and services accordingly usually survive. Those that only react after the fact are often eliminated.

A useful planning tool is SWOT analysis – looking at your business' Strengths, Weaknesses, Opportunities, and Threats.

Let me share what some Michigan growers perceive as their top 10 opportunities and threats.

### Opportunities

1. **Increased demand.** The market for bedding plants has

increased 10% to 15% per year for the past 20 years. We must capitalize on this growth.

**2. New cultivars.** As many as 100 new cultivars may be introduced
every year, each with potential to increase sales. These are the lifeblood
of our industry.

**3. Better production technology.** Plants that took 150 days to bloom
in 1966 now can be flowered in 50 days. Plugs allow quicker turnaround for
finished product. The loss rate in production has been drastically reduced.

**4. Improved mechanization.** Automatic transplanters are making
their entrance into commercial production. Once fully operational, they
will reduce labor needed.

**5. Computerization.** Greenhouse control computers that can perform all necessary environmental tasks are here and on line. The next
step is to interface such a computer with a plant model computer: A
grower will just input desired flowering date and desired plant height,
and the environmental control computer will provide proper temperature, water, nutrients, etc. to produce the plant on the day needed. On
certain crops, this system will be on line within two to five years.

**6. Bar coding.** Initially required by the retailer to track sales and
speed check-outs, it has become a method of inventory control for growers, allowing a more accurate plant count. Bar coding is also used to
track the time employees spend on each crop.

**7. Developing plant factories.** We can now develop a greenhouse
that can produce plants with a minimum of labor. Automatic seeders,
automatic transplanters, movable tables, automatic watering devices – all
are available. Growers who spend the money to build the factories will
have a competitive advantage in the future.

**8. New flats and containers.** We could replace the amount of wast-
ed plastic thrown into landfills through recycling. Use of peat pots or
other nonplastic-type materials may see a comeback.

**9. Supplying mega chains.** There is tremendous demand for bedding plants by large chain outlets wanting large quantities, excellent
service, and low prices. Just be careful that they don't tie up all your production and then dictate price. Growers not large enough to handle the
mega chains may sell product to larger growers who in turn supply the
chains. Look for more cooperatives formed by medium-sized growers to
get the chain business.

**10. Smarter consumers.** They're looking for varieties that perform well, and they're buying perennials as well as annuals. Bedding plant growers can capitalize on the interest in perennials produced in plugs, grown in greenhouses, and flowered when consumers want them.

*Threats*

**1. Competition.** More growers and larger growers making more product are vying for the same market, often reducing price to gain entrance to the new market.

**2. Buyers' increasing demands.** Large chain buyers dictate what they want, when they want it, and what they will pay for it. Some growers have an almost adversarial relationship with them.

**3. Government intervention.** Growers are extremely upset about all the government regulations. While regulations on U.S. growers increase, product flows into the United States from growers offshore who need to follow few, if any, of these regulations.

**4. Labor.** Growers think the quality of available labor has decreased. Availability is poor because of so many regulations and because much of our labor is seasonal.

**5. Understanding the market.** There is little or no market information directly available to growers; there is an oversupply of seasonal markets; and there is little or no education of the consumer and retailer. It is very difficult to anticipate future customer demands.

**6. Shrinking profit margins.** Many growers are poor managers, have poor buying abilities, and sometimes produce poor quality.

**7. Poor communication between buyer and grower.** Growers must be concerned not just with starting a product, but with making the sales happen by planned promotion.

**8. Bar coding.** Too many numbers are needed for all of our products. Grower to grower sales have wrong grower numbers. Suppliers can't buy from any grower but their own. If these problems can't be solved, many growers will be left out of the chain business.

**9. Standardization.** What size flat or pack will plants be grown in? Will they all be the same? How can you grow in five different sizes for five different chains? Not all retailers want standardization.

**10. Distribution.** If you're not involved in a distribution network, you may be left out of major sales just like the U.S. cut flower growers. U.S.

wholesalers buy and resell offshore product before they even think of buying U.S. cuts. This could happen to small bedding plant growers also.

Look over these opportunities and threats. Ask yourself how your business would respond to each. You might want to initiate action plans – step-by-step outlines of how to take advantage of the opportunities and minimize the threats.

Remember, if you don't plan your business, someone else will – and their plans just might help your business to fail.

Take advantage of the opportunities, manage the threats, and stay in business for the next 10 to 20 years. Good luck.

*– August 1994*

# Who Took The Fun Out Of Floriculture?

*Life is like a milking stool – it must have three legs or it will be unstable. Balancing work with time for family and friends will keep floriculture one of the most dynamic, fun-filled areas of agriculture.*

For the last four years, I have taught a course in Horticulture Management at Michigan State University. In preparing to teach the course, I discussed what text book I should use with Dr. Tim Rhodus of The Ohio State University. We had a great discussion about horticulture management. From this visit, I chose *Modern Management* by Dr. Samuel C. Certo. It covers all the basics of management and it's amazing how the basics are universal to all industries.

In his first chapter, Certo discusses the various stages of a career and of life. He defines four basic stages.

**1. Exploration Stage.** This stage usually occurs from age 15 to 25. It is characterized by self analysis and looking at different types of jobs.

**2. Establishment Stage.** This stage occurs from age 25 to 45. During this phase, individuals become more productive and settle into their jobs.

**3. Maintenance Stage.** The third stage is from age 45 to 65. Usually one of three things happens in this stage. The individual becomes more productive, stabilizes, or becomes less productive.

**4. Decline Stage.** The fourth stage occurs near retirement, with the individual declining in productivity.

These stages can be applied to people, products, or a business.

### The Circle Of Life

On one of our Professional Plant Growers Association tours, we visited Oslo, Norway, where we saw Oslo's Vigeland Sculpture Park. This is a spectacular display of the works of Gustav Vigeland that depicts the various stages of life from birth to death. It contains 121 struggling figures around a 60-foot granite monolith.

These works have great meaning and to me they show what life is all about. People struggle at each stage of life and feel that the next phase will be easier and have fewer problems.

For most people, however, one set of problems or opportunities is exchanged for another. In the beginning of life, you are usually healthy but have no money. Toward the end of life, you may have the money but not the health.

At first, you worry about how to make money to live. In the end, you worry about how to pass on your money to the next generation.

Vigeland has captured the stages of life in his sculpture. Certo has defined the stages of working life in his management book. No one – not even people in floriculture – can ignore these basics of the life cycle.

### Compounding The Stress Factor

However, no one can say we haven't increased the stress of life given all of the new high-tech information and equipment we have today.

I remember trying to talk growers into using computers in their greenhouses. They said, "It would never work." Now, there are computers for the office, production, environmental control, inventory control, and personnel management.

We continue to bring in new technology. Plants that took 150 days to flower now flower in 50 days. Bedding plant flats that took eight to 10 weeks to flower now are turned in 17 days.

We must realize, however, that 80% of the floriculture businesses owners do less than $100,000 a year in business and they do only 20% of the business. The other 20% of the floriculture owners do more than 80% of the business.

Both groups may be stressed to keep up with all the information that is available and they are all working to implement it and profit from it when possible.

### Don't Lose Your Touch

While we in floriculture have become high-tech junkies, what have we done to the area of high touch? While we are keeping up with the latest in high tech, there has become little time left for the high-touch area like spending time with our spouses and family, our community, our church, and in volunteering to help others.

At each stage in an individual career, problems occur. I have students in stage one – the exploration stage – who come to me and say, "Where will I get a job?" "What will I do in life?"

In stage two – the establishment stage – they say, "Where will I get the money to pay the bills, to expand the business, to keep the help?"

In stage three – the maintenance stage – they say, "If only I had some free time." "I cannot get away from the business." "I need to spend more time with my family." "I need a vacation."

In stage four – the decline – they worry about their security. "Do I have enough money to last?" "How do I pass this business on to my children?" "How do I get out of this business?" (Getting out of business is as difficult as getting into it.)

There is an old Danish proverb Laina Molbak told to me when I was high-teched out. It says that life is like a milking stool. It must have three legs of equal length or else it will be unstable and you cannot do your job.

Those three legs are body, mind, and spirit. You must take care of your body. You must use your mind for work and creative thoughts. You must nurture your spirit by spending time with your family, your community, your church, and to mentally know who you are and why you are here.

### Balance Your Life

I have seen too many cases of people who have spent so much time on their business that they have neglected their family and spouse. They may be considered a success in business, but were failures in their personal and family lives.

I have 45 students who are going to enter the horticulture industry this year. They are planning to invest their lives in this field. I have been part of the group of professors to train them and encourage them to become involved in this field.

I have told them that they can make a living, have a great way of life, have fun, and be happy while in our area. I hope that the old folks in stage four of their lives will not discourage them too much.

Certo and Vigeland are not wrong, and floriculture will continue to be one of the most dynamic, fun-filled areas of agriculture that can provide a great way of life.

*– May 1996*

# Dreaming And Scheming To Success

*Dream, glean, beam, scheme, and team your way to success.*

Every week someone calls and wants to explore the possibility of introducing a new idea, new product, or new plant material into floriculture. Just last week, a person had an idea for a unique cemetery planter. The ideas were all over the board, and it was obvious he had only been in the dreaming stage of this project.

Years ago, a minister had a neat set of words he used to express how an idea can be accomplished. The words of Rev. Robert Schuller were Dream, Gleam, Beam, Scheme, and Team. If you use these words in that order, you can take a new idea and logically follow it through until you have enough information to make a decision as to its merits within our industry.

### First, All You Have To Do Is...

**Dream.** This is the stage of getting the idea. Sometimes it may come to you when you're sleeping or driving in an automobile or riding in a plane. It can come from visiting a trade show, seeing another product, or having a discussion with other people. Sometimes it comes to you in the form of what if we could do this or had this item. That would really cut production costs, etc. Once you identify what you think is a good idea, you move to the next step.

**Glean.** I've changed Rev. Schuller's gleam to glean because this is the stage where you need to start collecting information about similar products. You may even ask other people questions about the need for such a new product. How can it be made? Who would buy it? How big would the market be for it? Would it be a fad or a trend? Would it be worth all the time and effort to pursue it?

Once you have explored all of the angles, you then develop a prototype or produce enough of the plant material to test market the product. From a legal standpoint, you would talk to your lawyer and patent or trademark the item or process. Once this initial testing is done, you would then consider marketing the product, but you have to be ready for the next step.

### Beware Of The Soothsayers

**Beam.** Be ready for the negative reactions. Any new product or variety will receive some negative response. You know the soothsayers and their usually negative responses as well as I do: "We tried this before," "It can't be done," "Nobody will want it," "It will cost too much," and at least 50 other objections.

Many great ideas have never passed this stage because the inventor agreed with the negative soothsayers or gave into them. Remember it is easy to be a critic, but it is 20 times harder to be a constructive contributor to a project.

However, it is good to go through this stage because, if the idea has no merit or the variety really is just another red petunia, it is best to determine that early in the process rather than spend thousands of dollars to find that out when the product or variety is marketed. If your project or variety can withstand this stage of development, then the real work begins.

### Have A Plan

**Scheme.** This step requires the most thought and effort. It is relatively easy to think of an idea, get excited about it, and even withstand the criticism about it. But when you have to determine all the details of how to develop, produce, and market it, it takes a great deal of time, effort, and skill, and also the financial resources to accomplish the task. Many projects never see the light of day because the inventor can not obtain the financial resources.

Most people forget the operating cash needed. From the financial reports of businesses I've seen, it usually takes three to five years for a new business to run in the black. Once people understand these facts, many do not proceed.

But the scheme part is much more than just the financial part. It requires a business or strategic plan. My definition of these two terms is this: A business plan is a one-year plan that includes a budget and the action plans of how to produce each item and sell each item in the plan. A strategic plan is not only a business plan, but also a plan in either general or specific terms of what will be accomplished in the next three to five years.

If you are going to seek money from financial institutions or outside investors, they will insist on seeing your scheme (business or strategic plan), and they will try to evaluate if the risk is reasonable for their investment. You must work on this phase to be successful in obtaining financial help.

### Dreams Do Come True

Let me give you an example. I had a student who wanted to grow field vegetables in Michigan. I told him it would be difficult or impossible to make any money on this effort. He said he had a different way of producing the crops. Yields could be three to four times greater and be in fruit two to three weeks earlier than the regular market. I worked with him to develop the plan, and he needed $300,000 in capital to start the project. His total assets were less than one-sixth of this loan request. I said, "The bank will never loan you the money."

He was not discouraged. His strategic plan was one of the best I've seen. He called me the day he was going to meet with the bank. I wished him good luck. I thought he had no chance at all, but it would be a good experience for him. To my surprise, he called the next day and said the bank was very impressed. The loan office said he was only one in 100 farmers who had a plan and a scheme written on how to accomplish their goal. The officer at the bank helped this young man apply for a federal guaranteed loan.

The result was because of his highly developed scheme the bank with federal backing gave him more than $300,000 for his project. Usually, the bank will loan only 70% of your assets. I thought this former student would get a loan of $30,000 to $40,000, but because of his scheme, he got 10 times that amount. Today, 80 acres are planted, and harvesting has begun. He will make it happen, because he has the scheme. I can't tell you how proud I am of him and his efforts. Most people would have quit at the beam stage.

### Work Together

**Team.** All the ideas, the excitement, the resistance to negativity, and the scheme will be of no value unless you have the right group of people to make it happen. How many people will it take to make the project successful and do you have them? Do they have the skills necessary? On small projects, the team may be just you or you and your spouse. Larger projects may require more people. The key to the right team is enthusiasm. If they know what the project is, its significance, and their part, they will be enthusiastic.

The key to remember in enthusiasm is the last four letters IASM, which stand for I AM SOLD MYSELF. The right team is a joy to watch – whether it is the U.S. Women's Olympic Gymnastics Team of 1996 or the employees of Wonderful Greenhouse Co. When people work together to accomplish a goal, all things are possible.

*– September 1996*

# Lead, Follow, Or Get Out Of The Way

*Responsibility, authority, and delegation – the keys to organizing a successful business.*

It has become obvious to me over my 15 years of working on planning projects that there are definite management styles within our horticultural industry. These styles can stop a business from growing. I've identified three specific management styles.

### King – Slaves

The king usually started the business himself and lets everyone know that without him the business is doomed. He handles all the decisions and money, and dictates what every employee will do and when they will do it. This system is the predominant style in horticulture for businesses that are just starting up to those that do about $500,000 in sales a year.

### King – Assistant King – Slaves

Once the business gets above $500,000 in sales a year, the king usually worries about dying and what will happen to his business and family. He begins to look for an assistant.

However, because of his entrepreneurial background, he only wants someone to carry out orders and does not want to lose his authority. He tells the assistant king what he wants, but spends his time making sure the assistant carries out the assignments. There is still no delegation of authority.

This type of management can probably hold a business to about $1 million before it starts to "shake." It will be impossible to "grow the business," which leads us to the third system.

### Chief Organizational Officer – Product Manager-Sales Manager – Maintenance Manager

This system occurs when businesses reach about $1 million. Everyone realizes that one person cannot do everything. If the original owner is still the leader, he or she usually has received enough on-the-job training to realize it takes a team to build the business beyond this point.

Usually three or four people then work together to manage the company. Many times this is a difficult, if not impossible, step for the owner of the enterprise to take, and thus the business never gets any larger. I'd estimate more than 70% of horticultural businesses have sales of less than $1 million, and the limiting factor is the owner and the management style.

To build a business beyond this first $1 million, the owner and management must understand and know how to use three important words. These words – responsibility, authority, and delegation – are the keys to organizing a business and are the cornerstones for any business' success.

**1. Responsibility.** Webster states responsibility is "the state of being responsible or answerable or that for which one is available; a duty or trust." Most small business owners only trust themselves. They probably can tell stories of how other people have let them down.

This reminds me of the old story my father told me about a clothing store. The owner always told his son – "Never trust anyone." He would say that to his son every day.

One day the son was on a ladder placing clothes on the top shelf when the ladder began to fall backward. His father said, "Jump, son. I'll catch you." The son jumped, and the father stood by and watched him fall to the ground. The son said, "Why didn't you catch me?" The father said, "I told you never to trust anyone."

While this is a trivial anecdote, many older people feel they have learned the hard way they can't trust other people to do their business like they would. However, it's surprising to find in most cases other people can and will do the business better than the original owner. However, it is hard for owners or managers to give responsibility to others.

Most owners or managers make one or two mistakes in giving responsibility. One mistake is overlapping responsibility. They want to make certain a job is done so they make more than one person responsible for it. The result is the job will probably not be done because everyone thought someone else was responsible. The moral: Never have more than one person directly responsible for a task.

The second mistake is a responsibility gap. Owners or managers forget to make anyone responsible for a job, usually due to poor or no planning.

**2. Authority.** Many owners or managers give responsibility to workers, but they give them no authority. The definition of authority is the right to perform the job. In many small businesses, owners will tell employees they have a responsibility to do the job, but they better check with them before they do anything. Or they can buy anything they need, but owners will have to sign the check. Never take the responsibility without the authority. If you do, you and your employer will have a difficult situation to solve.

**3. Delegation.** This is the process of assigning job activities and related authority to specific individuals in the organization. First, assign employees a specific job. Second, give them the authority to do the job. And third, create an obligation for employees to do the job.

Owners or managers who know how to delegate get more work accomplished, usually because employees have more freedom to do the job the way they want. Owners or managers show they trust their employees by giving them authority.

It is also important that owners match the right person with the right job. Employees must possess the proper skills and training to be successful at the job. In small companies, not much delegation of duties occurs. However, as companies become larger it is essential that many tasks get delegated. And the more products they handle, the more delegation is used to accomplish these tasks.

### Believe In Your People

Good managers believe delegation is a frame of mind, which states "I believe in other people. They can do the job as well as or better than I can, and we must all work together to get the entire job done."

In the spring, when 60% to 80% of our product is sold – usually in a very short period of time (four to six weeks) – it is essential that an overall plan be developed and management organizes the tasks to be performed. Owners and managers who know how to delegate and build a team of people who can assume the responsibility and authority will have a much easier time of surviving the spring season.

Those owners or managers who act like kings and refuse to delegate the responsibility and authority will have a long spring season and a stressful life. The choice is yours. Remember – responsibility, authority, and delegation are the keys to organization of a business. Use them wisely.

*– April 1997*

## *Getting What You Want*

### *Seven steps to successful negotiation – joint problem solving can result in a win-win situation.*

Today, selling is more than a take-it-or-leave-it process. It is a give-and-take procedure. Often, it involves trying to do your best while being cooperative with customers. A good sale is a win-win situation. In other words, growers can feel good about a transaction without their customers feeling like they have been beaten to the ground.

But be prepared. Go into negotiations with a plan. Know how much you want for the product, how much you can give on a product, and what the break-even point is.

Often you will find that buyers will have several people sitting in on a meeting. In fact, for high-level bargaining, five people are usually present: the spokesperson, chief, observer, analyst, and specialist.

What chance does one grower or grower salesperson have against such a team? You better know what you want and how to get it.

#### *The Extremes Of Negotiation*

**A Win-Lose Situation.** There are two extremes when it comes to negotiators. At one extreme are the wily, old vegetable growers with the farmer market mentality who only believe in pure bargaining. In this situation, one person wins and one person loses.

The belief at this end of the negotiating spectrum is "I'm going to make more money than the other person will and I'm going to make the other person lose." There are conflicting interests that arise here. Each person is very competitive and each one has a goal of showing the other person that they have more power and strength than their adversary. Also, the old vegetable growers have a great deal of emotion. They work hard, the world is against them, and they need the money to survive.

I always enjoy going to the farmer market to see how pure bargaining works. There you will find that the old vegetable growers thrive on distorted communication. They love to tell everyone how bad their situation is and how there is no product available.

One grower used to call me every Sunday morning for 10 years just to let me know how bad the market was. He had his own network of 10 to 20 people he would call to find out what was happening so he could set his price, and then he would tell everyone how bad the market was. His distorted communication made him money, but caused problems with his friends.

**A Win-Win Situation.** Over the years, we have tried to move from pure bargaining to joint problem solving which is a win-win proposition.

Growers and buyers work on common interests. Everyone involved realizes that to have a lasting relationship everyone has to survive. If they work together, they can make more money over the long run than if they attempted to beat each other out of what money they perceive is there. It takes cooperation and trust to make this happen.

*Seven Steps To Negotiation*

**1. Know Yourself.** What kind of communicator are you? What is your confidence level and what kind of personality do you have?

**2. Develop Power.** What titles do you have? What rewards can you give? Do you have charisma, expertise, or information that you can use to help the situation?

**3. Understand Your Opponent.** Know what your opponents are after and know how badly they need it.

**4. Learn About Your Opponent.** Ask questions about your opponents; make them feel important. Know everyone around them.

**5. Get Ready.** Before you start, know what you want to accomplish and have a plan on how you are going to get there.

**6. Be Straight Forward.** Build trust and be honest. Speak in a simple language and remember to restate your position at regular intervals so that no one loses track of what the goal is.

**7. Close Effectively.** Don't hurry when ending the negotiation. Make certain that everyone feels good about what was said and is to be done. If there is a problem, make sure it is solved before the deal is made.

*— June 1997*

# Change: A Necessary Process

*While there is sadness in letting go of the past, every time we introduce something new, changes occur and growers need to adjust.*

Any floriculture grower knows that change occurs every day. We have to take a seed, cutting, or plug and provide the proper environment and materials to produce a flower or mature plant in a given period of time. Our job is to make it a beautiful, salable product that people want to enjoy in their homes and gardens.

We all know plants change every day, and as growers we have to be very observant to make certain they are growing at the proper rate and they don't encounter any poor conditions that will affect the beauty of the finished product. To accomplish this task, we must all realize our job is an art and a science.

Recently, researchers have spent a great deal of time and effort in developing normal growth curves for plants so we can make certain they will be at the proper height when they flower. Once we have produced a great crop, we would like to reproduce it each year. Unfortunately, every year is different (i.e., a new variety, a different soil mix, a new fertilizer, a new structure). Every time we introduce a new factor, changes occur and growers need to adjust.

### A Natural Progression

Over the holidays, I read an interesting book titled, *You Can Make It Happen*, by Stedman Graham. He lists a nine-step plan for success. It is well worth reading for everyone in floriculture. He makes the statement that mastering change is accepting that "change is not an event, but a natural process." And each change occurs in a predictable sequence of events that will get you to the next level.

My favorite floriculture example is the seed geranium. In the 1960s, we took the varieties 'Nittany Lion Red,' 'Morton Hybrids,' and 'Carefree' and tried to grow them to flower as quickly as possible. It took somewhere between 120 and 160 days, depending upon which of these vari-

eties was used. Over the next 30 years, 400 new varieties were introduced, cultural techniques were improved, and we learned to use growth
regulatory chemicals to reduce the time to flower. The result: The timing
can be less than 70 days from seed and less than four weeks from plugs.

We need to realize that more than 80% of the varieties we grow
today were not on the market 10 years ago. I've often said that if a grower left our business five years ago, he or she would have great difficulty
in getting back into it today.

It can be difficult letting go of an old variety, an old cultural program, or an old environmental control system. You may have to learn a
whole new set of skills. There's no more "one hand on the vent and one
hand on the hose." Now it's "one hand on the computer and one hand
on the manual to read the instructions."

There is a sadness in letting go of the past. At Michigan State University,
we are closing the old teaching greenhouses built in 1929. Thousands of
students have used them for classes, yet they are old and beyond repair. The
students loved that environment, but safety was a problem.

We built new greenhouses to save the plant material and are in the
process of designing a new complex that will be a plant science visitors'
center and botanical collection greenhouse – a $10 million project! Yet,
there was a major uproar by the students who did not want change. They
will be sad to see the old greenhouses go.

### Seasons Of Change

In the greenhouse business, we make changes like following the sea-
sons. This is also one of the theories Graham suggests in his book. He says:
fall is the season of change; winter the season of reflection; spring the season of doing; and summer the season for evaluation and affirmation.

I believe the average bedding plant grower follows these steps exactly. In the summer, we evaluate what happened the past spring: What
went right? What varieties will we keep? Was the media good? The fertilizer schedules right? And the insect and disease program adequate?

In the fall, we usually start making changes: order the materials we
need, improve the structures, hire additional personnel if needed, begin
training them, and, in some cases, obtain additional training ourselves.
We usually attend national meetings in the summer and fall to see our
peers and to get a feel for what is happening out in the real world. Then,

we develop our action plans: What will we grow? How much will we grow? And when all the scheduling is done, we can make certain we have thought of all the details necessary to make it happen.

When winter comes, we usually get together with family and friends – perhaps hibernate for awhile – and build up an energy level to face the task ahead in the spring season.

Anyone in our business knows that spring is the time to make it happen. Long hours, hard work, high energy, and great anticipation are all necessary in getting the money to pay our bills. There is no time for getting sick, taking vacations, getting married, or personal matters. In fact, I believe there is an unwritten rule among bedding plant growers that makes sure they don't have personnel problems in the spring. One old grower who worked until the day he died told me, "Will, I can't die in the spring because they won't have time to bury me."

### Changing For Growth

As the business gets bigger, it gets more complicated to run and manage. It can be run by the owner with a dictatorial management style until it reaches about $750,000 to $1 million in sales. Then there will be a need for change in management style or the business will cease to grow. If changes are not made in personnel and organized properly, problems will occur in production and/or sales. These will not be because of a lack of knowledge, but because of a lack of a team to carry out what needs to be done.

Therefore, you have to build your dream team – the fab five, the green machine – some group that will make the plan happen. All parts of the business change continually: production, sales, maintenance, and management. A change in one area will affect all the other areas. Remember the familiar psalm from Ecclesiastes, "To every thing is a season and a time to every purpose under the heaven."

I hope this will be your time to grow, change, and provide the beauty of our product to all those who love and want it. Have a great spring season.

*– March 1998*

# F-O-C-U-S On Floriculture

## Our industry needs F-O-C-U-S. Make it your key to success.

Readers are leaders. Charles "Tremendous" Jones, a motivator and book store owner in Harrisburg, PA, stressed this point in the late 1950s and early 1960s. To help motivate his customers, Charles sold "power pack" books, a package of five to 10 paperback books on various subjects. He also wrote a book, *Life Is Tremendous*, which was his personal formula for success.

I've taken Charlie's advice and I read books on management, business, and leadership. One of these books could apply to everyone in floriculture, *The Power of Focus – How To Hit Your Business, Personal, And Financial Targets With Absolute Certainty*, by Jack Canfield, Mark Hansen, and Les Hewitt.

A chapter in this recent No. 1 bestseller is entitled, "It Is Not The Hocus-Pocus, It's All About Focus." In meetings I've attended over the last month, most of the folks talked about generalities instead of focusing on what needs to be accomplished. This inspired me to define "focus" in my own terms, as I relate it to floriculture.

### F Is For Future

At the Bedding Plants International (BPI) convention in Vancouver, BC, in September, a speaker provided population demographics for the next 25 years. What a gold mine this information is for floriculture business owners.

For example, by 2025, the U.S. population is expected to increase by 30%. Correspondingly, floriculture product sales will increase by 30% to 40%.

People between the ages of 45 and 64 contribute most of the revenue spent on gardening products and services. These people spend more on services, such as lawn care and landscaping, than any other group. They love our plant material but don't want to do the work. Furthermore, this age group is willing to spend money on products, but want them in a package that doesn't require time and effort to get a beautiful end result.

This is just one example of how to focus on your business by look-ing to the future. If you can recognize trends, you can focus the future of your business accordingly.

### O Is For Opportunity

Once you digest information about the future, you must constantly relate it to your business. How can you provide products that will satis-fy the market? If you know customers want a product but not the work associated with it, how can you provide a finished product that doesn't require any consumer effort? If you don't believe this trend is true, then why have planter and hanging basket sales greatly increased while flat sales have remained flat?

We should also exploit all the plant material available to us. While we are seeing more brand names, trademarks, and other ways to control the product and marketing of a particular plant, it will be extremely dif-ficult to control all of the plant material that's available to adapt and pro-duce commercially. Choosing your signature plant and exploiting it could make you millions. For example, I picked purple fountain grass and learned how to grow, flower, and exploit it. Five years ago, fewer than 5,000 purple fountain grass plants were sold in Michigan. This next year more than 500,000 plants will be produced in the state. Look for opportunities to exploit, based on what you think or know will happen in the future.

### C Is For Customer

Customers are regarded as problems by most businesses, but they are your operation's lifeblood. If consumers enjoy your products, they can be your best salespeople.

One of the great joys of my job is being the faculty coordinator for the Michigan Master Gardener program. In the last 20 years, we've trained more than 20,000 people. I've found that the more people know about plants, the more money they spend on plants. If you provide infor-mation to a chain store buyer or a customer who visits your garden cen-ter, you will most likely sell your product to these audiences.

In the next 10 years, the 45- to 64-age group will increase, and, therefore, many more people will be looking for plant information, serv-ices, and products. What is your plan to attract these customers and satisfy their needs? Remember, your business is only justifiable, tolerated, and permitted to exist in people's minds if your business learns how to give more. More product, more service, more information – how will you put this all together? Only by focusing on what needs to be done.

### U Is For Utilize

This is the key word in FOCUS. Many businesses write business plans and talk about strategy, but fail to achieve their goals because they can't pull it together. They can't focus because something always comes up – another idea or a chance to do something outside the plan. They don't utilize the resources they have. Instead of focusing on their natural talents, they spend their time trying to learn other areas. A great grower who tries to learn how to be an average salesperson can lose a business, and a great salesperson who starts a production business may be doomed to failure.

The secret to a successful business is to identify your weaknesses, then find someone who has those talents and use their strengths to help you accomplish your goals. The old adages, "I can't afford someone with a college education," or "I don't want to hire someone smarter than I am," are insecure phrases that indicate you will never utilize your total potential.

Successful growers have learned how to draw from all their resources. They develop and use their physical facilities, human talents, and financial and management resources. If you can't utilize what you have, you'll never achieve your goals.

### S Is For Science

Knowledge is power. With information and facts needed to accomplish a task, all that's necessary is execution. In the last 10 years, more new information has been developed in floriculture than in the previous 100. Ninety percent of all varieties on the market today weren't available 20 years ago. Today, they represent almost $100 million in sales. Forcing garden perennials into flower in greenhouses wasn't even considered 10 years ago. It now represents 10% to 20% of total production. Twenty years ago no one believed a computer was capable of controlling greenhouse environments. Today, computers can control everything from bar coding to production.

It's hard to imagine how our industry will change in the next five or even 20 years. Those who can keep abreast of new developments in production and sales and then implement them quickly will profit most.

### Change Is Constant

Once you think you have found the answer to make your business successful, remember that every answer in a successful business is only a temporary solution reached on the never-ending path of the search for more. That's the major reason every floriculture business should invest in research and development. We are a $4 billion industry and we should be investing $400 million a year into research and development. But the entire industry's investment in private and public research totals less than $100 million.

Focus is the key word for our industry. Make it your key to success.

*— November 2000*

# Find Your Cheese In Floriculture

*Not everyone's "cheese" is the same. Learn the important points of change, how to recognize it, and what to do to keep your "cheese."*

In the book, *Success Is No Accident*, author Lair Ribeiro says, "If you go on doing what you've always done, you'll go on getting what you've always gotten." This statement may not always be true – sometimes you might get less and end up with nothing.

We have many examples in the floriculture business in which growers who once were extraordinarily profitable filed for bankruptcy. There are retailers, and even allied trades people, who have experienced the same fate.

After several people at September's Bedding Plants International (BPI) conference raved about *Who Moved My Cheese?* by Spencer Johnson, I attended a Michigan State University training session that discussed the popular book. It's less than 100 pages and takes about an hour to read, but it's worth every minute. The book is a parable that reveals the profound truths about change.

When you read the book, you'll find cheese represents what you most want in life. The first thing I learned is that not everyone's cheese is the same. For one person, cheese signified money. Another said it represented health, another personal relationships, and another said trust. Out of a group of 25 people, there were 20 different answers to what cheese represents.

### Floriculture's Fondue

The same is true in floriculture. Not everyone agrees on what they want in life. The book's four featured characters go through a maze that represents life. Inside that maze you have to find your own cheese. I know people in floriculture who have run their own small greenhouses of fewer than 10,000 feet, raised their yearly crops, had a family, were active in their community and church and never made more than $30,000 a year; yet they will tell you they really enjoyed their cheese.

Also, within the same maze there are people who have 50 or more acres of greenhouses, 100 or more employees, and sales of over $20 million a year; and they are still looking for their cheese.

Whenever I build a strategic plan for a floriculture company, I start by asking the client, "What is your vision?" This equates to, "What do you want your company to be?" or "What kind of cheese are you seeking?"

Some companies take several hours to determine what kind of cheese suits them. While many groups visualize money, some actually think about and spend a great deal of time on customer satisfaction, employee development, community involvement, and quality of life issues. But once their vision (or cheese) is realized, they can proceed through the maze to achieve their goals.

In Johnson's parable, there are four main characters – two small people and two mice. The little people are Hem and Haw and the mice are Sniff and Scurry. It is amazing how much alike these four characters are to people we all know and work with. They all react differently to change and each has his or her own way to survive and cope with it.

Sniff, the mouse, always looks around skeptically, and once he makes his mind up, he just goes for it. Scurry is the opposite, always running into walls and acting without thinking. The little person, Hem, always resists changes and wants old times to return. He is always deeply vested in the present no matter what. The other, Haw, changes but with resistance. When he does change, he does it happily, leaving signs along the way to make it easier for others to follow. Obviously there is a little of each character in all of us, but one of these traits probably dominates us as individuals.

As long as you get what you want in life (your cheese), you can survive as any of these character types, but once the cheese starts to run out, you must find a new cheese source.

### Beware Of Today's Mouse Traps

This parable illustrates exactly what is happening to floriculture. In the old days, the industry was strong in cut flowers and potted plants, with very little bedding plant production. Those growers who have stayed in cut flowers have decreased greatly in numbers, had a difficult time surviving, and may have lost their cheese. Potted plants have not grown in size greatly. It has become a commodity market and the share of the cheese is probably shrinking for each business.

Many growers are searching for new cheese in the form of new crops to grow. Even within the bedding plant industry, the cheese is moving. In the old days, the flat was king and our biggest problems were deciding the flat, the number of plants to put in a flat, and what material the flat should contain. Those were the days when we had plenty of time to think about how we would react next year. Cheese was plentiful and life was good, but now the cheese is moving much faster. The flat is no longer the sole bedding plant product. Hanging baskets, various size patio pots, container planters, and numerous pot sizes are all in the market place. The number of plant items offered for sale has increased drastically. Before, 10 species represented 80% of sales, and, while today this percentage may be close to the same, many more varieties within each species are offered for sale. The introduction of "new" minor species is making it harder for growers to not only find the cheese but to try to figure out where it's going.

The book implores you to constantly smell your cheese to make sure it's still good. The same is true of our choice of products to grow each year. Every product has different marketing growth phases, including introduction, growth, maturation, and decline. You must constantly keep track of each product phase.

If you have grown a product for many years and sales have not increased but rather decreased, you may not have smelled the spoiling cheese in time. Or, if you start a new product and it doesn't sell, you may have arrived before the cheese was ready to move to that location.

In the book, Hem wants to keep his cheese and thinks it will remain fresh and stable forever. He reminds me of people who think branding all floriculture products will keep the cheese from moving. While there are many values to people who brand a product and develop a market for it, once that market is developed there will be people who develop a similar product without the brand and sell it at a lower price. Therefore, it is a constant process of keeping track of your cheese, making sure it doesn't get old, and knowing when to find new cheese.

In floriculture, the speed at which the cheese moves is getting faster and faster. Once you get your marketing and production systems in place to deliver a product, the demand may change, new varieties will appear, a different marketing approach may develop, and a major retailer could enter the market. The dynamics of our industry can be mind-boggling.

**Buy The Book**

To stay up with all the new developments and changes, requires you to read the handwriting on the wall. I hope you'll get a copy of the book and learn the important points of change, how to recognize it, and what to do to keep your cheese. In the process, you may enjoy the rapid and exciting changes floriculture is going through.

*– December 2000*

# GETTING STARTED IN BUSINESS

My extension colleagues and I frequently receive requests from individuals who want information related to purchasing or starting a floriculture business. Many are people who want to embark on a second career. Others are young persons who think growing plants would be a great way to make a living.

There's good news and there's bad news! The good news is that, in the column written in 1982, I believed, and I still believe more than 20 years later, that you can get started in the business. The bad news is that it isn't easy! Keep in mind that the Small Business Administration reports that 80% of small businesses fail within their first five years.

We have provided growers with the technology and skills to develop plant factories. With computerized plant modeling, bedding plantizing of perennials, thousands of new varieties of plants, high-tech greenhouses where computers control the environment inside, we have the capability to produce a tremendous amount of plant material.

You will find me saying again and again that success in business involves more than just growing plants. It involves business management and marketing.

Business management requires:

- **planning** by identifying specific goals and objectives;
- **organizing** by developing strategic tactics and action plans;
- **influencing** by getting suppliers, employees, and customers involved in making the plan happen; and
- **controlling** by knowing the costs of production and having a well-thought-out and developed business plan complete with a monthly statement of revenues and expenses.

The following columns highlight some of the lessons I have learned over the years that are helpful for businesses starting out or contemplating expansion.

# How To Get Started In Bedding Plants

## Back up a decision to start or expand a business with thorough planning.

Every year many people ask for information on how to start or expand a bedding plant business. Some of them have given it a great deal of thought and collected most of the information they need to make an intelligent decision. Others wake up one morning and think it would be a good idea to grow those lovely little plants.

Starting or expanding a business requires a great deal of thought and the decision to go ahead is not a simple one. Here is an outline I've used at arriving at a decision. I hope you will find it helpful if you're ever confronted with these questions.

### Information Required For Starting Or
### Expanding A Bedding Plant Business

This section of the outline is really a history of your past and present greenhouse operation. If you have not been in the greenhouse business before, relate your previous business experience.

I. Background
   A. Background of your present business (when started, by whom, rate of growth, history)
   B. Physical structure (size, area, number of buildings)
   C. Location (in one area or in various areas)
   D. Major activities (products you grow)
   E. Biographical sketch of management people (number of managers, their ability)
   F. Principal stockholders (who owns the company – a corporation, partnership, or single owner)
   G. Directors (if it is a corporation – who are the directors)
   H. Bank references (expansion or starting a business requires capital and good credit references)
   I. Current balance sheet and five years of financial history

II. Clearly describe the new venture you wish to undertake
   A. Specific plan
      1. Location
      2. Blueprints
      3. Size of operation
      4. Products to be grown
      5. Manpower needed
      6. Local economic factors
         a. Availability of labor
         b. Zoning laws

III. Describe the management of the project
   A. Your people involved
   B. Contractors involved
   C. Consultants involved

IV. Materials, labor, and transportation involved
   A. Environment and land
      1. Cost of land
      2. Soil (type, condition, etc.)
      3. Water (quality, costs, amount of soluble salts, restrictions)
      4. Temperature (winter lows, summer highs, mean temperature – to determine heating and cooling costs)
      5. Sunshine (daylength, total energy, etc.)

   B. Electricity (costs, restrictions, limitations)
   C. Communication (costs, restrictions, limitations)
   D. Materials for building
      1. Type of structure
      2. Sources of material
      3. Location of suppliers
      4. Quality of materials
      5. Cost of materials

   E. Labor
      1. Consider availability
      2. How many people will you need
      3. Types (skilled, unskilled, quality)
      4. Costs (wages and fringe benefits)
      5. Training involved

   F. Transportation
      1. Type of transportation needed
      2. Availability and reliability
      3. Cost
      4. Trucks
         a. Road conditions
         b. Maintenance

V. Market Description
  A. Market analysis

    1. Where is your market?        4. When can you start delivery?
    2. Number of accounts           5. List specific accounts
    3. How will they be serviced?

  B. Sales forecast for next five years
  C. Type of market you're after

VI. Expected Operational and Financial Requirements
  A. Expected revenue
  B. Costs (detail)
  C. Taxes (federal, state)
  D. Expected profits
  E. Construction and start up dates

    1. Raw material                 4. Sales and production expenses
    2. Labor                        5. Depreciation
    3. Administrative expenses       E. Taxes

  F. Cash flow statement during construction

VII. Studies you made that justify all of the above planning and
    expenditures

While this outline may seem too involved and too detailed, these topics will all be encountered and each of these hurdles will have to be overcome before your new venture will be operational. Advance planning will help you in making wise decisions. It will also show your financial sources that you've provided the thought and information necessary for a successful operation.

Finally, I never encourage or discourage anyone from going into business. The decision is yours, but back it up with thorough planning.

*— October 1973*

# Getting Started – It's Still Possible

*Getting started in the bedding plant business is more difficult than in the past, but it can still be done. Are there enough rewards and satisfaction to make it worthwhile?*

Question: What has four arms, four legs, and works for less than minimum wage? Answer: Mike and Linda Klooster. In fact, this past April and May, the young husband and wife growing team put in more than 100 hours a week between their first-year growing operation and a small lawn-maintenance business, and still brought home only $300 per week! But they made it through that tough first year and now they can truly say they've got a growing business (in more ways than one).

What prompts a young couple like this to start their own bedding plant operation? Are there enough rewards and satisfactions to make those long hours worthwhile? I interviewed Mike and Linda on their six acres in the Comstock area of Kalamazoo, MI. I wanted to find out what that first year was like for them, how they got started, and why they chose this way of life.

Mike is a third-generation grower. He says that ever since he started working with his father in the sixth grade, he has wanted to work full time in the greenhouse. Mike and Linda's own business began to take shape in August of 1981. They had practical, well thought-out plans to start a growing operation, a good deal of ambition, and she had a talent for combining outside work with raising a family (Michelle, 5, and Scott, 2½). What they didn't have, but needed, was capitalization – 100% capitalization.

In today's economic climate, 100% capitalization is not easy to get, so Mike made sure he'd done his homework before approaching his credit source. He brought with him a totally itemized list of greenhouse construction costs, along with another list detailing proposed expenditures for equipment, seed, and flats – any and every cash outlay he could anticipate. He also brought a detailed schedule of production costs; but perhaps most important, he had to prove on paper that his projected output was not only great enough to enable repayment, but was something he could reasonably expect to achieve. Even with all this documentation, Mike readily concedes that his father's name as a successful grower was a great help in obtaining final credit approval.

By September 1, financing was out of the way, and construction could begin. First, the land needed filling and leveling, then water lines had to be laid, forms laid out and built, concrete poured, posts set…all in time for the arrival of the greenhouse. Unfortunately, they had to wait almost a month before the greenhouse structure arrived. Because of this untimely delay, they needed help fast and got tremendous support from other growers in the area. With their help, the greenhouse was completed in two weeks' time.

Mike started his seedlings at his father's greenhouse in December because his own greenhouse wasn't completed until January 15. He recalls the start was rough and he was short on seedlings, but again was helped by his fellow growers who gave him flats to augment his supply. Finally, things were under way, but there were still some headaches to deal with; like the kind you get when the high-limit switch keeps tripping out your heaters. Or the one you get watching seven inexperienced transplanters and realizing you're paying an hourly rate to someone who takes an hour to do four flats!

Then there was a major headache when what appeared to be Botrytis was identified by the county extension agent as Alternaria. Two thousand flats were affected, but the treatment prescribed by the agent and a lot of extra care held the loss to 30 flats. All these headaches, added to the long hours, created a very stressful environment. Both Mike and Linda acknowledged the great pressure involved and suggested that you cope with stress by being willing to admit when it's too much and getting outside help. They are fortunate to have their family in the business as well as an extended support group of cooperative fellow growers.

Having survived both major and minor problems, Mike and Linda began to think about spring sales. Production was seven to 10 days behind in early April, so some sales were lost when crops weren't ready to go by delivery dates. But by the end of the year, 25,600 out of 26,300 flats had been raised and sold. Not bad figures for such a hectic first year. And they were close to their original projections.

What do the Kloosters think about all this? In their second year, capital expenditures will be down and production should be up. Refinancing and an addition are planned, and Mike and Linda anticipate an appreciable increase in the number of flats sent to their cooperative.

And even with all the headaches that are bound to make themselves felt, and the prospect of more long hours, this coming year is one the Kloosters look forward to.

They look forward to it because they recognize the job satisfaction you can get when you are your own boss. They know that there's a good living to be made by established growers, and they appreciate the unique satisfaction of raising seed to flower. However, the ironic part for them was to realize that they paid more money in interest payments than they received in net pay.

Getting started may be a lot more difficult today than five or 10 years ago, but it still can be done. And maybe there's just a germ of truth behind Mike's joke: "You're so greedy that you'll work twice as hard during one half of the year to have the other half off!"

*– October 1982*

# Reaching Your Goal – Facts And Foibles

*A specific financial goal helps you develop the plans necessary to work toward it.*

Over the past year, I have worked with several greenhouse operations to help them develop business plans. My first question to them was always: "What is your goal?" Surprisingly, most managers did not have specific goals.

The goals that were expressed were very general – "I want more money in the bank at the end of this year than last year" or "I want to be my own boss and have a nice home and car." These are not very helpful.

Think about specific, measurable goals; for instance, set an approximate dollar amount that you want in the bank. A specific financial goal helps you to develop the plans necessary to work toward it. Dreams can become reality, but unless you can develop a step-by-step plan to reach those dreams, they will never be achieved.

### Developing Realistic Goals

Sometimes people expect the impossible from a greenhouse business. One man quit his job at General Motors, moved his family to northern Michigan and bought a 10,000-square-foot greenhouse. He asked the extension service what he could grow in this greenhouse that would make him between $35,000 and $40,000 a year so he could maintain his former lifestyle. I do not know of a legal crop that could provide that amount of income from 10,000 square feet.

Until recently, there were no industry figures available on cost of production, return per square foot of greenhouse space, or other specific values to determine what to expect from various sized greenhouse businesses.

Last year, Bedding Plants Inc. conducted a survey of 65 greenhouse businesses in the United States and Canada to determine key performance measures. The association received figures on profitability, productivity, and financial management. The results were interesting.

Using the previous example of a 10,000-square-foot greenhouse, the owner could expect total sales of no more than $105,300 if he grew both potted and bedding plants. If he grew bedding plants only, he could expect $80,000.

He would also need two and a half employees and his total labor cost would be 21.7% or $22,850. The owner's salary and profit to net sales would be 10.2% or $10,740.

In light of these averages, it would not be realistic to set a goal of $40,000 income from a 10,000-square-foot greenhouse. Even if the entire family did all the work, the maximum return for their labor would be $33,590.

This survey shows other noteworthy comparisons: the wholesale payroll was 1.5% less than the retail payroll. Net sales per employee were $44,775 for wholesale compared to $28,800 for retail. A wholesale bedding plant operation averaged $5.88 return per square foot, while a retail operation averaged $8.29 return per square foot. A potted plant wholesale operation returned $11.35 per square foot, while a retail operation returned $10.23 per square foot.

Even though this survey is just a beginning, it can be valuable for those who want to compare their business figures with those of other greenhouse operations. Survey participants received an additional, confidential, personalized report comparing their own data with the averages.

### Don't Let Foibles Foil Your Goal

If you're not careful, even small mistakes can destroy your business. These foibles may seem minor and they may go undetected – but they can cost a lot of money and prevent you from reaching that specific financial goal. Here are some examples of careless errors that have injured or destroyed crops and profits:

• One grower painted his fishing boat in the headhouse. Unfortunately, the exhaust fan he used sent the fumes directly to the greenhouse air intakes. This pollution caused damage similar to that caused by low levels of ethylene over an extended period of time. The result – thousands of dollars in crop damage.

• Another grower painted his pipes with aluminum paint, using an automatic mixer. He used the same machine to mix nitric acid to inject into his watering system. The aluminum paint remaining on the mixer dissolved in the nitric acid and was injected into all his poinsettia plants, causing aluminum toxicity damage to the larger leaves. In this situation, my colleague discovered this problem due to differing degrees of damage in two different soil mixes used. The mix with less peat (less buffering capacity) showed more damage, earlier. The affected plants had up to 400 ppm of aluminum in the leaf tissues, compared to 25 to 40 ppm in normal plants.

• Yet another grower experienced herbicide damage because he carelessly used a hose. He filled a spray tank with herbicide for outdoor use with a hose and then used the same hose to fill another tank with fungicide. The herbicide residue from the outside of that hose was enough to contaminate the fungicide spray and result in low level damage to the entire crop.

### It's A Business

Many of us are in this business because we love plants and flowers – and that's fine. But we must not lose sight of the business concerns necessary to make growing profitable. We must get the financial facts necessary to make wise business choices – we must set realistic, measurable goals in light of these facts; and we must operate our greenhouses in a careful and businesslike manner, so that our plans can lead to an unobstructed pathway to our goals.

*– September 1987*

# Survival Tips For Small Growers

*Take note of these 10 tips on how to survive
as a small grower.*

I recently visited my brother, Vic, and his wife, Jo, who own Carlson's Greenhouses in Cold Spring, NY. They started their 1,200-square-foot operation with $5,000 and it has supported them for 30 years. The business has become a way of life for them – they are "high-touch," not "high-tech."

Here are their 10 tips on how to survive as a small grower.

**1. Know your product.** You must be knowledgeable about the plants you sell. Chain stores may be able to get away with, "I don't know," when questioned about a plant, but we cannot. Most of our customers choose us over chains because we do have the product knowledge to answer their questions.

This is a natural result of doing everything ourselves. When we buy and grow the plants as well as sell them, our expertise becomes part of our product. The customer is buying access to our plant knowledge and advice along with the plants. That makes our plants worth more.

**2. Agree upon specific goals.** All partners in a small business must agree on specific, measurable goals, which can range from determining the number of plants to be sold during a given time period, to figuring a realistic yearly budget, to creating an elaborate business plan.

Whatever you strive for, it's essential that all those involved in your business know what the goals are and agree upon a plan to achieve them. Many small businesses have been lost because goals were never defined, agreed upon, or communicated.

**3. Get good professional assistance.** The first person you need when you start a business is a good accountant, one who knows the ropes, such as what forms need to be completed, by what date, and so on. An accountant can develop cash-flow projections, a yearly budget, and monthly statements so you always know where the business stands. Don't wait three, six, or 12 months to discover a problem.

Another necessity is a good lawyer. You probably won't need a lawyer's services as frequently as an accountant's, but it's important that one be on call as needed to review all legal papers and contracts.

One other professional that should be involved is a banker because you may need to borrow money or secure an operating loan. Keep your banker informed so he or she feels like part of your business – receiving the financial aid you need will be easier.

**4. Know what customers want.** Large companies rarely have the personal touch; they may feel it's unnecessary. With small businesses, the personal touch is not only necessary, it's the secret to success.

Every time new customers walk into your business, give them personal tours. Show them what you have, what you're doing, what's new, and answer all their questions. If you can teach customers how to be successful with your product, they can't afford to lose you, and price becomes secondary.

**5. Be a part of the community**. Small businesses survive when people in the community know who runs them and what they do. Broaden your contacts by joining a service club, participating in local government, or helping on any community projects. Get to know other small-business people in your area so you can work together to achieve community goals while increasing your visibility.

**6. Start with enough money.** Most small businesses start undercapitalized. Owners may have good ideas, but they haven't planned on what it will cost to turn them into reality; they haven't considered the cash flow.

You have to be able to "tough it out" through bad financial times. If sales are lower or expenses greater than expected, you need enough money to survive. You also need to learn from that experience and adjust your business strategy to improve your financial picture. Many families have gone months without getting paid a cent in order to "balance the books" – no fancy office, no frills, just survival. This is the point at which many businesses fold, but the survivors will hang on.

To determine if your business has a good chance of surviving, calculate the money you think you'll need for your first year in business and add 50% to that number; if you have that amount, you can survive.

**7. Have a good relationship with suppliers.** A good supplier can be your most valuable resource. Look for someone who is interested in you and your business. Remember, the cheapest price is not always the best deal – having a supplier you can count on to get what you want when you want it is extremely important.

In addition, some suppliers take on the role of a banker. They will supply you with growing material, waiting for payment until your crop is sold. I've heard stories from older growers about suppliers that literally kept then in business during hard times.

**8. Be flexible.** Your business won't be the same every year; new products will come along and you'll be seeking new customers all the time. The competition changes regularly, so you'll need to pay careful attention to the market to make sure your prices are "in the ball park" with those of other businesses.

Weather is another variable that can make or break your business. You have to be flexible enough to be able to hold your product or speed it up, depending on the weather.

**9. Learn to improvise.** Most small businesses can't afford large capital expenditures, so they don't have all new equipment and facilities. Two options are to look for second-hand equipment or build your own to improve efficiency.

You must use everything you have, and that includes more than greenhouse space – some small growers produce chrysanthemums in outdoor areas and perennials in cold frames. Other growers supplement their income by making grave blankets, Christmas wreaths, or flocking Christmas trees. See what raw materials and opportunities are available to you and make them profitable.

**10. Deal with businesses your own size.** If you're too small to deal with large chains, try smaller garden centers or retailers. Over the years, you'll develop working relationships with people you know and trust.

Small-business people can only survive through strong ethics and trust. Be leery of "fly-by-night" buyers who say they'll take your whole crop because when they do, they may pay you only half. I've seen growers lose thousands of dollars on these kinds of deals.

Business isn't easy. Success requires work, planning, and long hours, but there is satisfaction in knowing that you and your family can do it.

*– October 1991*

# Developing A Business Plan

## Follow these seven steps toward developing an effective business plan.

Many growers tell me they have a business plan, but it exists only in their heads. Others feel if their seed orders are in, they have the year planned.

Nonplans may have worked in the past, but today working without a plan can mean disaster. With all the changes in the floriculture industry, it's more critical than ever that every business has a formalized business plan. I know of several growers who have gone bankrupt from making decisions on the spur of the moment rather than according to plan.

Still, some people are resistant to the idea of developing a business plan. Their excuses range from "It costs too much" to "We don't have time" to "How can I plan when I don't know what I want?"

I recently read an article in the July/August issue of the 1980 *Harvard Business Review* entitled "Strategic Management for Competitive Advantage" by Frederick Black, Stephen Kaufman, and A. Steven Walleck. The authors discuss four phases in the evolution of formal strategic management. Greenhouse growers could easily apply these phases as they take the seven steps toward developing effective business plans.

### Phase 1: Basic Financial Planning

This phase includes operational control, functional focus, and an annual budget. However, all planning should center around meeting that budget.

Unfortunately, many growers don't understand all that is involved in developing a budget. They hire accountants to take receipts and expenses and fill out tax forms. This may be enough for the Internal Revenue Service but it does not provide any information about production. What does it cost to grow a crop? Which crops make money? Which ones lose money?

### Phase 2: Forecast-Based Planning

In this phase, you attempt to predict the future, planning several years ahead. It includes capital improvements: What will your range look like in five years? It includes environmental analysis: What outside factors will affect your business? What will new governmental regulations do to your business? What's your competition doing? Use your resources to meet the budget and to make necessary improvements in your business.

Many managers will lose faith in this method because of repeated failures in forecasting caused by rapid environmental changes. That's why many companies move on to...

### Phase 3: Externally-Oriented Planning

Here you look for key factors that determine the success of your business. What does the customer want? What are your strengths and weaknesses? How does your product compare with your competitors' products? What is your market?

Avoid producing plants that don't contribute to overall profitability. Ask questions such as "What if we didn't grow poinsettias?" or "What if we grow in trays with 54 cells instead of 48?" These questions help define your market niche. You evaluate strategic alternatives based on a thorough analysis and competitive assessment.

The next step is a dynamic allocation of resources. You might need a larger cooler, another greenhouse, or a plug storage area. Such decisions are based on the products you plan to produce based on what the consumer wants. Begin thinking abstractly, then you can move on to...

### Phase 4: Timely Strategic Management

At this point, companies can actually orchestrate all resources to create a competitive advantage. What separates Phase 3 companies from Phase 4 companies is the close link between strategic planning and operational decision-making. These companies foster entrepreneurial thinking. They develop a supportive value system and organizational climate that makes planning creative and flexible.

Whichever phase your company is in, there are seven steps in the strategic management process:

**Step 1. Defining your organizational mission.** The mission is the reason for your company's existence. Ask, "What business are we in?" You can answer this statement broadly: "To provide plants for people to enjoy." Or you can answer it more narrowly: "To produce flowering annuals in the spring." Either way, the mission defines the scope of your business. The remainder of the plan must support the mission statement.

**Step 2. Formulating the organizational philosophy and policies.** An organization's philosophy defines the values and beliefs that guide the behavior of its owners and employees. The policies are guidelines that provide managers with a set of broad restraints.

**Step 3. Assessment of the company's strengths, weaknesses, opportunities, and threats.** It's important to know your company's weaknesses as well as its strengths. Action plans can be written to turn those weaknesses into strengths. Likewise, understanding threats to your business allows you to write action plans that can turn them into opportunities.

**Step 4. Determining organizational structure.** For a small greenhouse doing less than $250,000 a year, the organization chart may be as simple as: Owner–Employees. For a $250,000 to $1 million business, the chart usually looks like: Owner–Assistant–Employees. For a $1 million to $5 million business, the structure is more complex: General Manager–Office & Personnel; Production Manager; Sales Manager; Controller; Maintenance Manager.

**Step 5. Analyzing the external factors that affect your business.** These factors could be government policies; local, state, or federal rulings; consumer trends; economic problems or opportunities; and competition. You must understand the relevant external factors if you are to position your business where it can succeed.

**Step 6. Determining strategic objectives.** Each specific crop you produce and each container size you grow it in will have a plan for every time you grow it. Once you total the income and expenses you expect for each crop, you will have most of your budget established. However, there may be objectives – such as employee training – that generate expense but no income.

**Step 7. Developing action plans.** Action plans indicate what is to be done, by whom and when it will be completed – with a cost/benefit analysis of each plan. This is the most important step because it provides step-by-step instructions on how each crop is to be grown. It's a lot easier to manage when it's clear to all what is to be done. Numbering your steps makes them easier to discuss with those responsible.

*– March 1992*

## Know And Grow

*Growing plants is easy. Growing a business is a true achievement. Here are three major problems small businesses must solve to be successful.*

There is a difference between growing plants and running a business that sells plants. Many people don't realize this difference exists. This is why more than half of small businesses in floriculture fail in their first five years.

I have the joy of seeing people get excited about horticulture. They have learned how to grow plants. Perhaps they have taken master gardener courses, completed two-year degrees, or on the spur of the moment, decided to get involved in commercial horticulture.

In the beginning, it may seem easy to grow plants. But then comes the realization that it's not a hobby anymore. It's a business. When beginners reach this stage, they have many questions and are full of excitement and enthusiasm. Often, this is a difficult, soul-searching stage.

Many people believe that because they have mastered the art and science of growing plants, everyone will want to buy their product. Some mistakenly believe they will make enough money to maintain the lifestyle they had before opening the new business.

Throughout the years, many people have called me saying: "I've just started this business. Now what should I do?"

One newcomer called me, and said her husband had quit his job as an executive at GM, and they bought a small greenhouse. They wanted to meet with me to determine what to grow and where to sell it. She told me her husband had abandoned his high-paying job to help run the 10,000 square foot greenhouse. How could I help them maintain their standard of living?

In author Michael Gerber's book, *E-myth Revisited*, he gives sound advice on planning a business and explores the thought and effort that goes into it. Gerber says there are three types of people: the technicians, the managers, and the entrepreneurs. Seldom does one person possess all three talents. Few people know how to grow plants, manage a business, and understand market dynamics well enough to profit.

*Small Business Strategies*

For the last 15 years, I've helped small businesses develop strategic plans. Some have turned out to be great successes, some have just survived, and some no longer exist. I've worked with businesses that had less than $50,000 a year in sales and some that had $10 million in sales. Small businesses usually have three major problems they must solve to be successful.

**1. They don't have enough money.** The owner didn't realize how much money it takes to start a business and pay monthly bills. Oh and yes, there's the problem of waiting 30, 60, or 90 days for clients to pay for the product.

Owners soon learn what cash flow is. When no cash comes in, it is a painful lesson learned quickly. They may visit their local bank, soon to find bankers don't loan money to people who need it. Banks are not charitable institutions. They only loan money to people who have enough assets to pay back what they borrow.

Can't pay the bills? The bank can take everything a grower has, sell it, and get the money back. Growers must understand finances. In growing, soil is the dough that makes the difference. In business, money is the dough that makes the difference.

**2. They aren't managers.** Many small growers had to learn through experience. Although experience is the best teacher, the tuition is high. Growers pay a high price by learning from their mistakes.

Growing plants as a hobby, there are no deadlines, pressures, or stresses. With a business, growers must produce plants at a given time and meet specified quality standards. Growers must coordinate activities with many people – suppliers, customers, employers, and lenders. Communication with all employees is essential.

Today, many growers have been trained as managers because it can be difficult for them to handle the paper work, the details, the government forms, and rules and regulations.

I strongly suggest many of my clients take the Dale Carnegie course on how to win friends and influence people, and create win-win relationships between employers and employees. It takes as much time and effort to work with people as it does to grow the plants.

Also, a time will come for hiring help. But there may be labor shortages. The pool might not have the training you need, and each employee may have a high price tag. This is why devising a business plan is essential.

**3. Where's the plan?** Most consultants will suggest developing a business or strategic plan. In reality, most people get started with an idea, a little planning, and working nights. They do try to make it happen.

When they get a moment, tired and stressed out, they realize more than one person should know the nuances of the business. Then the idea of a plan becomes important. The plan can be very simple. It can address a variety of questions. Where are you at now? Where do you want to be? How will you get there?

This is the technique to use for expanding or improving your business. The more formal plan addresses: your mission; beliefs; strengths; weaknesses; opportunities; organizational charts; and competitors.

What are their strengths and weaknesses? What are their objectives? What are your plans to reach these objectives?

Then develop the yearly budget, the production plan, and the marketing plan, and make it happen. It sounds easy, but it takes a lot of thought, decision, and soul searching to put it on paper. But when it is done, all these who help develop the plan will know how to make it work.

The entrepreneur must get an idea that will attract customers, employers, suppliers, and lenders. Only when the product will satisfy all groups will that business be successful.

In his book *The Power Point*, Michael Gerber says the management of impressions is the management of people. Your business has to convey the impression of a being a place where plants are grown by happy, knowledgeable people. With that impression, you have given people confidence that you not only grow plants but people, customers, bankers, and your business.

Growing plants is easy. Growing a business is a true achievement. I wish you all the best in your venture.

*– March 1999*

# The ABCs Of Starting A Successful Business

## Four factors lead to the success of a new business.

I realize that 20% of growers sell 80% of the product. I realize how high tech our industry has become and that we have developed plant factories. I know that big chain stores will control the marketing and sales of our product.

But, I also understand how the bedding plant industry started. Families worked together night and day learning to grow plants. It may have taken several generations for a poor vegetable grower's family to become a mega bedding plant grower.

It is almost deja vu for me. When I became the extension specialist at Michigan State University (MSU) in 1966, I was told who the biggest and best growers in the state were. They dictated what happened to our industry. But I also noticed that because they were the best, they were not interested in learning anything new. They knew all they needed to and were making plenty of money. The status quo was maintained.

At the same time, I met a group of former vegetable growers who were looking for another way to make a living. They were eager to learn about greenhouses, bedding plants, and how they could survive.

Today, 30 years later, the six major growers in Michigan have died. Their businesses have ceased to exist or are no longer major forces. The major businesses of today are those that were learning about greenhouses and bedding plants 30 years ago.

There is a cycle in life and in business. New businesses are born. They attempt to grow and if they are successful, they develop and mature, and become the leaders of tomorrow.

### Helping The Co-op

Recently, I took an assignment to develop a business plan with a small cooperative in Massachusetts. I'm working with 10 to 12 ornamental growers to develop a plan to produce about $1 million worth of product to sell to the chains.

The co-op is comprised of a great group of people, and the manager is a saint. In the group, most have less than 20,000 square feet. The largest grower has about one acre of covered area.

We started off with a strategic plan and then a business plan, but the group needed production and marketing plans, as well. After several meetings, they were sent home to do their action plans, but they did not have the information or facilities to accomplish the task.

We needed to start at the beginning. That wasn't a problem because they were eager to learn. They could follow instructions, and they all wanted to work together. As a group, they met at least twice a month to see how the project was going. They discussed mutual interests and problems.

This was a big gamble by everyone involved. Most had never forced a perennial. We used the information published in *Greenhouse Grower* on forcing perennials to help develop production and marketing plans.

Recently, I checked on the co-op's progress. When I had a chance to see how it was doing in March, I found there were four important factors that could lead to its success.

**1. Structures.** Most beginners are undercapitalized and many structures are homemade. They have to do everything themselves as cheaply as possible. Instead of purchasing a standard structure, they buy some 2 x 4s and plastic and build a greenhouse.

This is usually the first mistake. In most areas, it will limit success. Once the structure is up, they face the next set of problems: how they will heat it; how they will bench it; and how they will install a watering system.

Typically, heating is the biggest problem. In small greenhouses, growers should contact a greenhouse supply company, buy a gas-fired or propane-fired unit heater, and have it installed with the proper air intake and venting. Then, 99% of problems would be eliminated.

But most people getting started buy old, used oil or gas furnaces and put them inside double poly greenhouses with no air intake and improper ventilation. On cold, winter nights, they discover the greenhouse is so tight that the furnace uses up all the air and does not have complete combustion. As a result, the plants are damaged by air pollutants. This has caused several new businesses to go bankrupt in their first year.

Watering systems are another concern. Most beginners think one hose that's 100 feet long will be all that is needed. Installing the proper system greatly reduces the labor required to water plants.

**2. Planning.** By developing a plan, you will know how many flats and baskets at what time and how many turns will be required to meet your financial goal. Then you can determine the size and type of greenhouse you will need.

Notice, I listed planning second. Most self-starters build the structure first and then find out they need a plan of what to do with it. Of course, the right sequence is to develop the plan first, then build the structure.

**3. Soils And Nutrition.** If growers know how to handle, control, and manipulate the nutrition and the media, then there will be no problem in production – 80% of the problems in production are soil and nutrition related.

New growers should find a greenhouse supplier and get premade media. Most are variations of the old Cornell mix developed by Ray Sheldrake and Jim Boodley in the early 1960s. I've often called this mix the dough that made the dough for the bedding plant industry.

Another major contribution to our understanding of media and nutrition has been made by MSU's John Biernbaum and his students with root zone management lectures and short courses.

Also, there are two items every grower should have – a pH meter and a soluble salts meter (EC meter). If you can test your soil weekly and keep these two factors in the proper range, you will not have a problem with soils or nutrients.

**4. Family.** The great part about small businesses is that families work together. Men and women, their children, and grandparents all help make plants grow. Many people say they are in our business not for the money, but for the way of life. Some have started a second career in floriculture because they enjoy the plants and people.

As we approach the new millennium, we should take great satisfaction in knowing that while technology changes and we become more high tech, every day there will be someone who starts into our business with only the hope for a better way of life.

*– June 1999*

# Make The Next Millennium Profitable

*In the next millennium, floriculture businesses must know their costs. Otherwise they will fade away quickly.*

Entrepreneurship is risky mainly because so few entrepreneurs know what they are doing. I've worked with four greenhouse businesses in the last six months to help them develop strategic plans. Several were in financial trouble. They had to clean up their acts or face losing their businesses.

Three of the four groups I worked with did not know how to calculate their cost of production. They didn't know which crops were profitable and which ones lost money. They also didn't know how to determine their cost per square foot per week.

They walked in with financial statements from an accountant who indicated they lost money last year. Some only used the accountant to fill out their year-end tax forms on a cash-based accounting system. They did not develop the proper accounting tools for their businesses.

My colleagues, Drs. John Biernbaum and Bridget Behe, gave a talk at the Ohio Short Course in 1998 – "Greenhouse Crop Production: Counting the Costs and Making Cents." This talk should be mandatory for anyone entering the floriculture business or for those who are veterans.

One of Biernbaum's sections is "Don't Let Mathematics and Numbers Intimidate You." He says the phrase "I am not good at math" ranks up there with "I have a black thumb" as some of the most useless words ever spoken.

What chance would you give someone who starts a floriculture business with two strikes against them – they don't know how to grow plants and they don't do math? Sounds like a formula for failure, right?

You would be surprised at the number of people starting floriculture businesses who are in this situation.

### Getting A Handle On Costs

There are two types of costs – direct and overhead. Some growers call direct costs variable costs.

Direct costs include plant material, containers, media, fertilizers, chemicals, and labels. Labor, energy, packaging, and shipping can fall into this category. But to keep it simple, most people will lump these costs with property, structures, equipment, property taxes, and insurance in the overhead cost. Overhead costs also are called fixed costs or indirect costs.

With this background, you can use a step-by-step system to find out how much it costs to grow a crop and how much you must grow to make a profit.

**1. Develop an action plan.** Create a step-by-step outline of how to grow a plant and determine when to do each step. Use this outline to figure out the amount of time it will take to produce your crop and the space you need to grow it.

**2. Develop a cost-benefit analysis.** First, list the number of plants to be sold and the price per plant – the total income. Next, list direct costs – plants, pots, soils, and labels. Then list the overhead cost per plant. This indicates the cost per plant. Multiply this by the number of plants and you will have the total expense. The difference between total income and total expense will be the profit for the item grown.

The problem is recovering all the money spent on overhead costs from the plants grown and sold from the greenhouse. The easiest way to do this is by taking the total cost of all overhead and dividing it by the square feet of bench space in the greenhouse.

For example, if your total overhead expenses were $100,000 and there are 10,000 square feet of production, you'll need to get $10 per square foot per year to pay the overhead costs. This equals 2.7¢ per square foot per day.

But few, if any, greenhouses are filled all the time. Most are filled at 50% to 60% of the total space available. If the greenhouse was filled to half its capacity, the cost per square foot would be 5.4¢ per square foot per day. Most successful greenhouses have overhead costs of 2.2¢ to 3.2¢ per square foot per day.

**3. Determine the cost to produce one plant.** Consider the number of plants that will die in production. Most production facilities allow a 2% to 3% loss – then decide on a profit goal. Once this has been determined, you can reach the selling price. Determine this price for every product you grow before you sell your plants. If you don't know the proper selling price to cover your costs and your profit, you are doomed to failure.

Remember, buyers are taught to get the best price possible for your product and to sell it for as much as possible. They will see how low you will go. There are many growers who have made big sales and lost big money.

In a business analysis I once did for a poinsettia grower, we found that each year he sold 100,000 six-inch poinsettias and lost 50¢ per plant. He was Santa Claus to the buyer, and it cost him $50,000.

Finally, consider that profitability is the result, not the cause, of business performance. Businesses that know their costs set their selling prices properly and will profit.

In the next millennium, floriculture businesses must know their costs or they will fade away quickly, just as the Vikings of the first millennium faded in a few short years of the second millennium when they met William the Conqueror.

*— November 1999*

# Competing With The Big Boys

*Formulas for success help small businesses survive in the "big box store" environment.*

My wife Barbara and I recently invited several small growers to our home to talk about how they survive. Some have been in business for more than 50 years, others for 10 to 20 years, and one was just starting. We discussed the development stages of a business and determined many seem to go through similar steps to become successful. My observations indicate there are three distinct phases.

**1. Getting Started.** Most new growers are extremely ambitious people who love plants. However, many of them know little about running a business and some just don't have the money to develop their idea without borrowing. For these people, the first dose of reality comes when they visit a bank for a loan. Bankers are wonderful people but they typically don't loan money to people who are at risk of not paying them back.

However, banks are in the business of selling money at a profit. Therefore, they will loan money to people who have the assets to cover the loan they want. Usually, banks will loan between 70% and 80% of your assets.

When someone starts a small floriculture business from scratch, the banker is the one who makes the most money from the business. It takes five to 10 years before new business owners can see the light at the end of the tunnel and the debt can be reduced to a reasonable percent of their overhead costs.

**2. Early Development.** When businesses enter the early development stage, they typically start to make money. It's also the time when most businesses will need to invest more money to make them more efficient. Improvements and facility updates are often needed, prompting many owners to consider expanding their operations to satisfy the demand of their product. Once they reach the end of this stage, a major decision must be made. Will they remain content being small growers or will getting bigger be better?

**3. Growth Phase.** When businesses reach the growth stage, the owners must decide whether to take them from family operations to true small businesses. Not only will they have to expand the physical facilities, but the owners also will have to develop personnel to operate the businesses, which may mean hiring full-time, nonfamily employees.

In addition, if the business starts to produce more product than it can sell at farm markets and retail outlets, it may choose to approach the big box stores. Unfortunately, many growers will experience buyers who only want to treat their plants as commodities. They must decide if they want to swim with the sharks or be the biggest fish in their own small ponds.

I can give you examples of people who have been successful with either choice. I can also give you examples of people who have gone bankrupt attempting to go from a great, small grower to a large one.

My brother Robert, the financial guru of our family, has always said, "Show me a company that expands at 25% per year for four years and I'll show you a company that will be bankrupt in the fifth year." He makes a valid point – many businesses at the growth phrase attempt to grow faster than they can obtain financial resources.

One large grower I know doubled his operation in three years because the buyers loved his product. He added a great financial debt to his operation and ended up selling his product at the same or a lower price in the fourth year than he did the previous three years. That year, he was on the verge of bankruptcy. Only through working with excellent accountants and his banks did he survive a financial disaster.

There are a lot of horror stories about mega growers. Many large corporations have come to the rescue, taking over the supply chain of such growers' products to the big box stores. Frequently, these takeovers fail.

Still others continue to dig the same hole. For example, one mega grower in the southwestern United States has filed for bankruptcy at least three times, only to rise from the ashes with a new financial source to continue the fight again.

### Stay Low And Keep Moving

During my discussion with my grower friends, we rehashed all the gory details of large grower horror stories. Then they explained their strategies for surviving within the big box environment. We came up with six formulas for success.

**1. Offer niche products.** You will never compete with large growers on price by offering commodity plants like petunias. Your customers will think you're overpriced, and if you're overpriced on petunias, you're likely overpriced on all items. Differentiate your product from the commodities. Offer varieties featuring cultivar name – don't just market red petunias. Use cultivars that may be more expensive but proven to perform the best.

**2. Provide specialized service to customers.** Perhaps plant knowledge is your talent. Promote yourself as the "Plant Expert" who knows more about the plants you sell than anyone else in your area.

Knowledge is critical for any business. For example, one of my friends is a pet shop owner who grew his business from a small corner store to the biggest pet shop in the area. He built his whole business on new products, product knowledge, and unique advertising. He installed fish aquariums in the post office, local restaurants, doctors' offices, and many other public facilities where people visit daily. His business cards are always near the display and now everyone knows if you need help with your pets, his shop is the place to go.

**3. Develop and promote new products.** Choose a plant you know will do well, develop it, and promote its use to your customers. The example I'm closest to is purple fountain grass. I helped take this from a plant that sold fewer than 5,000 plugs in Michigan to one that sells more than one million plugs statewide in just five years. First, I knew the product had great consumer appeal. I tested it in my yard and several people stopped and asked where they could get it. Next, I learned how to grow and flower it for May sales, and then had growers sell it to major retailers.

**4. Provide a unique buying experience that's different.** Build a new attraction and make it a family experience. If you can get children involved, they will repeatedly bring their families back. Some retailers keep a play pen available or let kids take little red wagons around the garden center. Offer plants that are easy for kids to grow and sponsor contests such as who can grow the biggest pumpkin.

**5. Once you start making money on your business, use that money to grow your business.** Therefore, you will not be borrowing more money and increasing your debt.

**6. Try to promote some new, unique aspect of gardening that can also help the environment.** Today, a lot of folks are interested in organic gardening, or sustainable home gardening. It may take more time and effort but it can save some resources and may even cost less. You must know all the approaches to sustainable gardening. Find out what your customers' goals and objectives are and have the services and products to help them succeed.

*– February 2002*

# TAKING CARE OF BUSINESS

It's hard to believe that so many greenhouse growers still don't have a business plan. They keep all their records in a shoe box, which they give to their accountant once a year to fill out tax forms. They figure if they have more money in the bank this year than last, then they've made money. If they have less, then they've lost money. While that might be true, it's also true that they don't know why – and consequently have no idea how to improve the trend for next year.

A number of years ago, I worked with a grower who was losing $100,000 a year. Within two years of drawing up a business plan – including scheduling of each crop – he had a profit of $100,000 a year. And five years later, he had a $200,000 profit from the same operation.

Growers who "don't have time to plan" lose a lot of money.

Whenever a group of growers meets there always seems to be a discussion on production costs. If one grower presents his figures, they are usually viewed with a critical eye and many times subjected to words of skepticism.

One of the biggest fallacies with these discussions is the fact all growers do not keep their records in the same form. One does not calculate his own labor in the cost, another does not calculate interest on investment, while still others do not consider depreciation factors. It boils down to comparing apples with oranges.

Another fallacy is everyone will have the same answer. There is only one right answer for your operation – that is what it costs *you* to produce your product. I know of no other business that can be as competitive as the floriculture industry.

You've heard me say, "if it is to be, it's up to me." Following are some of the ideas I've come to feel are important for you to consider implementing if your goal is to have your business survive and thrive in the 21st century.

## Ten 'Ps' For Perfection

*Predict your potential for perfection with a plan that applies the 10 "Ps."*

Every grower, whether he knows it or not, is a manager and is involved with 10 words that start with "P." They create the cornerstone for striving for perfection in the bedding plant or any other type of business. Let's briefly review the 10 "P's" to see how important each is and how they can be applied to your business to make it perfect.

**1. Planning.** Every successful business requires a plan. No one can accomplish anything if there isn't a plan developed. This usually requires discussion with key employees, family, and others involved with the operation of the business. Some businesses have a one-year plan, others have long-range plans five to 10 years ahead. The plans usually include production totals (e.g., number of flats, hanging baskets), what type of annuals to grow, physical improvements, staff additions, number of employees, their responsibilities, and marketing strategies like major accounts, amount each will take, and projected increases. All details must be thoroughly thought out before a proper plan can be developed. I'm certain your 1979 plan is already prepared. If it isn't, you'd better do it now. It should all be written down and not just some vague thoughts in your head.

**2. Preparation.** To execute the plan, every person must be ready and know what is expected of them. Raw materials must be ordered and the greenhouses ready to implement the plan. Sales-end delivery must also be organized. Contacts must be made with retailers. How did they do this year? Discuss their needs for the next season. Are they planning to increase or decrease sales? To be a good manager, you must be prepared, not only for what you expect to happen, but also for the unexpected.

**3. Production.** This is the mainstay of any business…being able to schedule the product, put all the materials together with the necessary labor and come out with the finished product. There are many decisions to be made. If proper planning and preparation are done, the manager will have smooth sailing in this phase. If there is little planning and preparation, the result will be many problems and poor quality in production.

**4. Product.** Everyone says quality sells and a good product is easy to sell. Therefore, it is important if one is to be successful or striving for perfection to produce the best possible product. The product is the end result of all the planning, preparation, and production. One can easily tell if the grower's "homework" has been done or if he or she is flying from day to day with little thought or planning. Plants can "talk." They tell any knowledgeable person exactly how they have been treated by their appearance.

**5. Performance.** What will be done with the product? How will it be delivered? Can you provide the service and the quality a customer wants? How do you perform? There are many growers who can produce a good product but can't perform. Either they feel people will beat a path to their door or they won't sell the product. Performance is important; the product alone is not enough. But a quality product and good performance will certainly lead to perfection.

**6. Promotion.** This is an essential factor in any successful business. If you're good, you've got to let people know. Promote your product, your business, and yourself every opportunity you can. There are some great examples of promoters in our bedding plant business. "The Petunia King" probably is the most well known. He lets people know about his product, his business, and that he's ready, willing, and able to do business.

**7. Provide Information.** We want people to be successful with our product. Many of them have questions and need information to be successful. Sometimes it is a simple question like, "What is the name of this plant?" By now I'm sure everyone is labeling their plant material; label not one per flat, but one label per pack or pot. Point-of-sale information, labels, display signs, and booklets all help promote the sales and increase total sales. It's good business – do it!

**8. Pride.** Everyone must have pride in what they do or it's not worth working. Bedding plant growers have a lot to be proud of. They work hard and provide a product of beauty that improves our environment and adds to the beauty of the world. At the same time we provide this product of beauty, we also help others by employing them and allowing them to participate meaningfully in society. Think about all your pluses – you've got a lot to be proud of.

**9. Price.** An important factor. What is the right price? This depends on the quantity of the product available to the market and the quality of that product as well as other factors. Determining the selling price depends on your production costs, transportation costs, quality of product, and your circumstances... not another grower's costs. Remember inflation? This year this factor may be more than 10%. Do your prices reflect this increase? Remember, don't set your price by what others do. They may have lower production costs or other advantages that can allow them to sell lower than you can. If you try to keep up with them, you will go bankrupt.

**10. Profit.** The reward for a job well done. If all the other "P's" are performed well, this will be the end result. Remember, it comes as a result of putting the total package together, managing it properly, and making the entire operation productive.

After this brief review of Perfection in business, now is the time for you to predict your potential for perfection. In other words, start today to plan your entire 1979 year. Develop your game plan, remember the 10 "P's" for Perfection and make 1979 a perfect year...Good Luck!

*– November 1978*

# Growers Give Away Millions At Christmas

*Who said there isn't a Santa Claus? Calculating the cost of producing a poinsettia crop can help you determine if you are giving away money at Christmas.*

During the last few years, I have been assisting growers with their business plans, examining the crops they produce to determine if they are profitable. I was surprised to learn that some crops are not profitable for all growers. The fact is, some growers actually lose a significant amount of money by producing nonprofitable crops. Growers continue to grow nonprofitable crops for various reasons:

- They're unaware a crop isn't profitable.
- They want to fill out their product mix.
- They have a preference for a crop.
- Their competitors are producing a particular crop.

Many growers have said, "We pay for our overhead in the fall and winter and we make our profit in the spring." These growers price their crops accordingly – the selling price is not based on making a profit, but on just paying the bills.

### Case In Point

Although many growers produce a crop of six-inch poinsettias, it may not be profitable for them to do so. But it is possible to determine if the selling price for this crop is set at a profitable level or if it's set to pay the bills.

To determine your production costs, add your variable costs to your overhead costs. Variable costs depend on your method of propagation – that is, whether you buy your cuttings or produce them from stock plants. Another factor is the quantity of cuttings purchased or produced. The price of a pot, for instance, can vary by the quantity purchased and the quality of the pot. The growing medium can also vary in price depending on the quantity purchased and its ingredients.

Overhead costs include taxes, depreciation, utilities, wages and benefits, office expenses, buildings and equipment, general products, and supplies. According to the growers with whom I have worked, these overhead costs can vary greatly depending on the amount of debt owed, as well as the depreciation that can be taken on their structures.

In the Northern states, a six-inch poinsettia crop is usually started between August 15 and September 1 and sold between December 1-10. For my example, I'll charge overhead for 16 days in August, 30 days in September, 31 days in October, 30 days in November, and 10 days in December, for a total of 117 days. Some growers feel that overhead costs should be charged until the end of December because no other crop will be produced in the greenhouses for the remainder of the month.

The lowest production cost that a grower could conceivably have would be $1.69 (34¢ variable costs + $1.35 overhead costs). But that figure does not include any marketing costs. If you apply the rule of thumb that 25% of production costs should be used to market the crop, add 45¢ to $1.69 for a total of $2.14.

But what about the crop loss factor, which is usually set at 5%? Add 9¢ for loss to bring the cost to $2.23. Finally, figure in a profit margin of at least 10%, adding another 22¢ and bringing the absolute lowest selling price for a six-inch poinsettia to $2.45.

In the case of an average grower, the breakdown of costs might be 44¢ for variable, $2.78 for overhead, 14¢ for loss, 73¢ for marketing, and 36¢ for profit, resulting in a selling price of $4.01.

However, many growers sell large quantities of six-inch poinsettias for $2.80-$2.90 each, delivered. In order to be able to do this and break even, these growers would have to produce their crops in 117 days or less, have an overhead of 2¢ per square foot per day, and have variable costs of 44¢ or less. There are very few growers in this country who can meet these financial restrictions.

### Don't Give Away Your Crop

Realistically, the six-inch poinsettia – with all the expenses attributed to it – should be priced accordingly. Overhead costs should be for 140 days because no other crop is usually produced in the greenhouses for the remainder of December. Overhead costs would then be $2.80 per pot. If you figure in the other costs – 44¢ for variable, 5% loss, 10% profit, and 25% marketing – the final cast for a six-inch pot should be $4.60 per pot.

These figures may be too low or too high for your operation, but don't disregard them entirely. Remember, the only exact costs for you come from your financial statements. Make the calculations on your own crop to see if it is profitable for you to grow.

If $4.60 is the average profitable selling price and millions of poinsettias are sold at $2.80, then growers are giving away millions of dollars each Christmas. When I calculated the exact costs for one grower, he discovered that he gave away $47,000 last Christmas with his poinsettia crop.

And who said there isn't a Santa Claus? Let me be the first to wish you a merry, and hopefully profitable, Christmas.

*— November 1988*

# 15 Ways Not To Go Bankrupt

*It is more difficult to stay in business in a competitive, fast-changing marketplace. Be better informed, more careful – and avoid these 15 common mistakes.*

The American economy has experienced an ever-increasing number of bankruptcies during the past few years: large companies such as John Mansville, Sharon Steel, and Osborne Computers; medium-sized companies such as Busy Beaver; and small, family-owned businesses.

Our horticulture industry has been a part of this trend. Well-known companies within this industry in California, Colorado, and Ohio have filed for bankruptcy within the past two years. Why is this happening? We believe the majority of reasons fall into these 15 areas.

**1. Undercapitalization.** This condition can have various causes. The company may have taken on too much debt, or in the case of a new company, it may have accounts receivable but no cash to run the business. Having few assets makes it difficult to secure bank financing, so the business becomes cash poor and unable to operate. Many people try to start a business without enough capital. They plan for the initial start-up but don't do a cash-flow projection. Some also tend to be overly optimistic in estimating sales, but expected cash does not come.

**2. Not Knowing The Business.** Take the case of a person who gets sold on a hydroponic tomato greenhouse. It sounds like a good idea, so the person buys the complete package with the greenhouse and the equipment – but how does it work? You need to know the business – or be able to afford to hire someone who does – in order to survive.

**3. Selling To Someone Who Doesn't Pay.** This is one of the biggest problems for greenhouse growers. It seems there are buyers out there who make a game of buying on credit, using the grower as their banker. They don't pay until they need to order for the following year. You're lucky if these slow-payers are only a year behind on their payments. If a grower gets tired of this game (after figuring out how much it is costing the business), the buyer just finds another sucker and keeps playing the slow-pay, no-pay game.

**4. Too Much Overhead.** A mistake some people make is starting their business on too grand a scale. They put up ultra-modern greenhouses with all the latest innovations, and leverage them to the hilt. The cost is more than 8¢ per square foot per day and not many crops can be grown profitably at that rate. Remember, the best greenhouse is profitable. All those bells and whistles have to pull their weight in profits.

**5. Poor Quality Product And Service.** Quality sells – it's trite but true. An inferior product is tough to sell, and, if you do it once, you may not get a second chance. It's amazing how buyers seem to know who produces quality and who does not, who has great service and who does not.

**6. Noncompetitiveness.** This situation can arise from a narrow-minded "We've always done it that way" approach to business. A grower may be used to producing a product that is no longer in demand, or selling it for too high a price. Sales start to decrease – but instead of studying the market and figuring out why, the grower refuses to change.

**7. Product Liability.** One only has to think of a product such as asbestos to realize the extensive problems a dangerous product can cause. Asbestos brought a large company like John Mansville to bankruptcy. There are still thousands of cases involving asbestos waiting to go to trial. When an individual comes up against a large company, juries tend to side with the individual. Screen your products for potential liability.

**8. Environmental Restrictions.** As people and governments become more environmentally concerned, more restrictions are imposed. Complying with such restrictions may be so costly that a company must cease doing business.

**9. New Technologies Making Products Obsolete.** You wouldn't want to be a typesetter in this age of desktop publishing and electronic-typesetting. Such new technology made mechanical typesetting obsolete. The advent of seed geraniums had much the same effect on cutting propagators in the North. Make sure you stay on top of new technologies and products.

**10. Fraud.** Someone in your business steals the company's money. It could be anyone who has access to company funds. This potential threat to your business requires that you institute a sound money-handling system. Such a system must have checks and balances so that even during busy times, all money is accounted for.

**11. Foreign Competition.** The Japanese auto industry is making it difficult for the domestic "Big Three" automakers. In fact, Lee Iacocca wrote the President in March asking the government to limit the number of Japanese cars entering the United States to 31% of total U.S. sales. He indicated that if Japan gets 40% of the U.S. market, Chrysler will be gone. We're seeing more foreign competition in the flower business, too. Do what you can to make your business competitive.

**12. Depressed Market Conditions.** If the size of the market decreases by one-third or one-half and you are not the industry leader, it may be difficult to survive. Many small contractors in the building industry have gone bankrupt for this reason.

If our market starts to decrease, the same fate could befall small growers and retailers. Look at the foliage industry in the 1980s; there were many bankruptcies as the size of the market declined.

**13. Being Underinsured.** What happens when a fire or flood hits your business, or when a tornado roars through? Suddenly the rationalization "I can't afford the insurance" doesn't make sense.

**14. Overexpanding.** Perhaps things are going well with your business, so you expand. You expand at the rate of 25% a year for four years; the fifth year you go bankrupt. You've expanded your way into bankruptcy.

Of course, expansion can be positive, but you must do it in a financially responsible way. Don't get too big too fast – a slow, steady growth rate is the safest course.

**15. Owners Drawing Excessive Salaries.** Sometimes an owner will take all the money they can from the business, and give spouse and kids big salaries, too. If owners drain all the money out of their businesses, they may have to declare bankruptcy. This has been done many times by people who don't care about the business or by people in business for themselves – and even large corporations.

There is no question that it is getting more difficult to get into business and to stay in business in today's competitive, fast-changing marketplace. You have to be better informed and more careful – and make sure to avoid the 15 common mistakes mentioned here so you can avoid the threat of bankruptcy.

*– May 1991*

# It's The Results That Count

*The crop tells the tale – but it means nothing if the plants don't sell. If you want to stay in business, don't get hung up on the process. Focus on the results.*

Why do we get so hung up on the process of doing something that we excuse poor results? I recently read a great article written by John R. Graham in *Flower News* titled "Don't Bother With The Process; The Results Are What Count." Graham makes a great case for results-oriented management.

You can often hear employees say, "I've worked long hours; I've been here every day; I did my job – but the crop just died." But time and effort don't count for much when the results are a dead crop.

The crop tells the tale – of jobs done well and mistakes made. People have asked me if plants can talk. I believe they can – and they never lie. An owner may tell me business is great, but if his plants look sick, I know he's wrong. When plants look healthy, odds are the business is healthy, too. Dead plants don't make money.

But healthy plants are not the whole story, either. The other ingredient of success is healthy sales. And in sales as well as production, results count. No matter how many sales meetings are held, sales objectives set, and sales calls made – they mean nothing if plants don't sell.

Graham says the current emphasis on TQM (Total Quality Management) encourages businesses to focus on the process rather than results. If businesses focus on producing the perfect product but ignore such factors as whether that product can be produced profitably or if there is a market for it, the whole system has no value.

Here, then, are the major areas, as I see them, where the floriculture industry must focus on results in the next few years.

**1. Production Isn't Enough.** We are now at the same stage Henry Ford was at the end of World War II. He could produce all the product he wanted when he wanted it, but he didn't have anyone to buy it. Mr. Ford soon figured out that he had better get his cars sold before he produced them.

Now, I wouldn't say that we in floriculture are slow, but it's taken us nearly 50 years to reach the same conclusion. It makes sense: Know where your crop is going before you grow it.

**2. Don't Forget To Get The Money.** Making the sale is easy; getting the money can be difficult. Many growers have told me tales of woe about the accounts they should not have sold. Beware, they warn, of out-of-town buyers who order large quantities on credit. When it comes time to collect the money, they're either gone or asking for more time to pay.

Check credit before the sale. For new accounts, require certified checks on delivery. No certified check, no unloading. It may sound tough, but it makes sense – maybe even dollars! Remember, the end result is not the order – it's the payment.

**3. Work Hard – But Don't Get Hurt.** Our business is seasonal; that means busy times when everyone is working at top speed. Employees work overtime, and owners and their families put in 16- to 18-hour days. During the stressful spring season when you and your employees are tired, accidents are more likely to happen.

I know a number of people who have been injured or experienced property damage due to mistakes made under spring-rush conditions. One of my friends broke his back in a fall, and I also heard about a greenhouse employee who welded a vent to an oil tank, generating enough heat to blow up the oil tank.

There is a lot of attention being paid these days to pesticide safety. That's important, of course, but we must not lose sight of physical safety hazards that cause problems like those mentioned. Many more greenhouse injuries are caused by physical accidents than by pesticide use.

Work hard – but be careful.

**4. Keep Records – For You.** Many growers have accountants who do "the books" for the federal government and for tax purposes. Owners may get a report annually, biannually, or maybe quarterly that may be dutifully filed, but is not used to help manage the business.

Most of the greenhouse financial records I've seen are designed for the government and the accountant – not for production and sales people. Remember, the government does not know how to run a business. It proves it every year by being hundreds of billions of dollars in the red. Keep your books in order to make money – not just to satisfy the government. If you're not in the black, you won't be in business for long, and you and the government will both lose.

Reports should be issued monthly and contain a balance statement and income statement. A good accountant will also provide a cash-flow statement and a report of production costs as well as income generated by each crop. This information shows a manager the results – and can help that manager make decisions about how to get even better results the next time.

**5. Bar Coding – Help Them Sell Without Losing Your Identity.** Bar coding continues to be one of the major matters of debate in our industry. The large retailers want plants bar coded so they can use their scanning equipment to speed check-out for their customers. Unfortunately, these retailers can't agree on what coding system to use.

Another problem is that many retailers want only color and species identified to the code, such as "red petunia." But when the variety name is lost to the ultimate consumer, it kills all the promotion done by seed companies and organizations like All-America Selections and FloraStar. One compromise suggested is having two labels on each plant – one bar coded for color and species and another identifying the variety name.

There is no doubt that bar coding will be used not only to help retailers, but also to help growers with inventory control. We need leadership in this area to address the issues being faced by all growers and retailers. A workable compromise could benefit the entire industry.

**6. Plan For Results.** Today, it is very important to have a business plan so you know where you're going. With increased competition and more production and governmental rules and regulations, it will be tougher to grow and market your product. Know where your crop is going, use prudent credit practices, and use your records to determine which crops are making money.

Develop your plan and then execute it – but never forget the plan is only a means to an end. Work with your employees to tie your plan to desired results, and adjust your plan until it gives you the results you want.

**7. It Is Not Okay To Fail.** Going through the motions is not enough. Many management systems will teach you their process and tell you that following it will guarantee success. But whether it's TQM or another fad or fancy title, it is not the process that will make you successful – it's the end result that will.

To be successful in the floriculture business, you have to have knowledgeable growers to execute all the little details required to produce quality plants – and then someone has to sell those plants at a price that will not only cover the cost of production but generate a profit as well. If you don't reach the bottom line in the black, producing a quality product can still add up to failure.

In the last three to four years, we have seen a number of floriculture businesses fail – and the next few years will be challenging times as the remaining growers work to overcome what these businesses could not. Those growers that succeed will evaluate their businesses from the standpoint of the desired results. If you want to still be in business by the year 2000, don't get hung up on the process. It's the results that count.

*– January 1994*

## Slow Pay, No Pay

*One of the major problems in small businesses is cash flow. Remember, you haven't made the sale until you collect the money. Follow these steps to finishing the sale.*

I recently visited a grower in Western Canada and had the opportunity to see his greenhouse operation and discuss plant production with him. The grower knew everything there was to know about growing different types of plants. He was excited about how many crops he could produce and how quickly he could turn them over.

He also told me he had dropped his affiliation with all trade associations and industry magazines because "times were tough and money was getting tighter." From what I had seen, it looked as if he was making a great deal of money, so I asked, "If you are producing all of this product and selling it, why are times so tough?" His answer was, "I produce it and I sell it, but people don't pay their bills."

He said he had more than $100,000 in accounts receivable – some more than six months – but was reluctant to ask for his money because many of his customers were friends.

I've seen this happen all over North America. I believe there are people in our business who make a profession out of not paying their bills – some growers never get paid.

It would be interesting to determine the percentage of bad debts within our industry. From the financial statements I've seen, bad debts range from 1% to 5% of total annual sales. Because bedding plants represent $2 billion in the United States, 1% to 5% could total between $20 million and $100 million a year – just in the United States!

### Know The Risk

Have you ever gone to the bank to borrow money? The bank lends money to some people at the prime rate and some people at 1%, 1½%, 2%, or 3% above prime. Why the difference? It is directly related to the bank's perceived risk for getting its money back. As your ability to pay increases, your rate decreases. Imagine a banker saying, "I'll give you the money at no interest and I'll never ask you to pay it back because I don't want to upset you." It would never happen!

In Stuart Wilde's book, *The Trick To Money Is Having Some*, he states, "You have a divine right to choose whom you will play with and under what circumstances." If only bedding plant growers would understand that.

### Know Why You're In Business

A major problem in small business is cash flow. I've seen growers take big orders and brag about the 10,000 flats they sold to one account – then wait six months for payment, or never get paid. Meanwhile, they've lost their ability to pay creditors and suppliers, and have had their reputation tarnished. Remember, the sale is not done until the money is received.

Wilde also states, "There is no other reason for being in business than to count the money." Growing, selling, and shipping are not the business – collecting and counting the money are the business.

Many growers think the business will take care of itself. You've heard the saying, "Grow a quality product and it will sell itself." That may be true, but as my longtime friend, Florida vegetable grower George Todd, has always said, "You haven't made the sale until you collect the money."

### Steps To Finishing The Sale

PPGA controller Leo LaPorte has made a list of tips he believes will ensure you collect your money.

**1. Make the deal up front.** Most growers are so thankful to get the order, they forget the business details. Ask your customers when and how you will be paid. Indicate you will add 18% interest per year if the bill is not paid in 30 days. Make your customer sign an agreement itemizing all the financial details.

**2. Ensure invoices are accurate.** Each invoice should contain:
- billing name and address;
- purchase order number, contract number, registration number;
- name of the person ordering;
- units shipped and price (double check your math accuracy);
- terms of sale (e.g., -2% 10 days, net 30 days, 18% interest per year on all bills more than 30 days); and
- Provide the name, phone, and extension number of the company person to contact for questions.

**3. Send invoices in a timely manner**. Invoices should be sent the day of shipment. Sending a copy of the invoice with the order also serves as a bill of lading.

**4. Know your client.** Get background information on each of your customers before establishing a line of credit. Learn the name of their banks and the loan officers in charge of their accounts. Do a credit check through Dun & Bradstreet. Talk to your clients' other major suppliers.

Ask your customers up front about their payable cycles and what paperwork their accounts payable departments need. This information should determine the price of your product. The longer you have to wait for money, the higher the price.

**5. Send monthly statements.** If an invoice is lost, a monthly statement will alert your customer's accounting department that an invoice was sent.

**6. Follow up quickly on unpaid invoices.** If it seems payment is "drifting," take the initiative. Contact the person who made the transaction, or ask for the head of accounts payable or the controller.

**7. Be gracious, but straightforward.** Maintain a good relationship with late-paying clients; try to troubleshoot. Don't burn down bridges.

**8. Use your phone or fax.** Don't mail follow-up invoices to your customers; fax them. Time is money.

**9. Be persistent.** If customers don't pay, let them know you are still after your money.

**10. Let your customers know you trusted them.** You provided the product and service. You helped them make money. You expect your money in the amount and timeline agreed upon.

**11. Continued business, profitable to all, can only exist if bills are paid.** Your bills must be paid to your suppliers and staff. If your customers do not live up to their agreements, they jeopardize the entire industry.

### You Could Lose A Lot

Many growers have as much as $10,000 to $50,000 out in accounts receivable. Just think of the money that could be saved if they had someone actively collecting this money. My Canadian friend could probably join every trade association and subscribe to every trade journal he wanted to – and still have money for a great vacation.

*– July 1994*

# What Is A Greenhouse Worth?

*It is as difficult to get out of the greenhouse business as it is to get in! The best deals are where the parties work together to develop a win-win situation.*

In the last two weeks, I have had three calls relating to how much a greenhouse is worth. One caller wanted to buy a greenhouse. Another was getting divorced and wanted a value on his greenhouse. And the final caller wanted to sell the business quickly.

While there are many appraisers of real estate, few know the value of a greenhouse and a greenhouse business. They can appraise the tangible values of the greenhouse, land, and equipment, but they are at a loss to place a value on the business and its potential.

### A Valuable Exercise

In my horticulture management class, I had students attempt to appraise a landscape nursery business. In the example, the nursery was doing $800,000 a year in sales and had five full-time employees and 15 seasonal workers. The business was a partnership, had all debts paid, and each partner was paid $60,000 a year for salary and profit. They had 77 acres of land, 10 of which was used for the business, and equipment and buildings for conducting the business.

I asked the nine different "sales companies" (five students per company) to bid on this operation. The bids ranged from $485,000 – just the price of the tangible assets of the land, greenhouse, and equipment – to nearly $2.5 million. Most of the groups bid $1.2 million to $1.5 million. This student exercise is a lot like putting a value on a greenhouse business.

### Tools Of The Trade

Usually the lowest bid is the one that covers the land, equipment, and structures; however, I've seen cases where the value was lower because a greenhouse had to be torn down to get the value of the land. Also, I've seen owners have to get an environmental impact statement before the land could be sold.

So, in some cases, a greenhouse will lower the value of a tangible asset. Therefore, the buyer and seller must realize a greenhouse is just a tool. It is no better or worse than the people who operate it. And if there is no one to operate the tool, it is of little value.

To determine the value of a greenhouse, the buyer must see the last five years of financial statements to see if money can be made with the tool. If no money can be made, the tool has little value. The buyer must then determine if he or she can use the tool in a more efficient way. This is the area that causes variability in market price. Once the buyer and seller agree on this area of value, the rest of the pricing is easy.

Another point for the potential seller is the larger the greenhouse, the fewer people there are who will be able to use it. A 40- or 50-acre range may be difficult to sell. The tool is big, and there are few that have the capability to manage or the capital to purchase the facility. I know of ranges of 20 or more acres that never sold. They were abandoned because no one could afford or manage such a range profitably.

The seller must also realize that the buyers must be able to handle the debt. Many buyers carry a heavy initial debt to the point the business is not profitable. Overhead costs become so high they can't compete. In other words, for them to pay off their debt, their overhead costs per plant place them at far higher wholesale prices.

For example: It is difficult to offer $25 per square foot for a greenhouse and carry that debt load while attempting to compete with greenhouses that can produce the same product in a $10 per square foot greenhouse that is paid for.

In a greenhouse sale, selling is as difficult as buying. The best deals are where both parties work together to develop a win-win situation. Also, trying to "keep it in the family" does not always mean success. When I arrived in Michigan 30 years ago, there were four major family greenhouses in operation. Today, two no longer exist and one may not exist in the next generation. If proper financial planning is not done, the greenhouses may have to be sold just to pay for the taxes upon the death of the owner.

If the buyer and seller cannot determine a fair market value, one of them will suffer. If the price is too high, the buyer will not be able to operate the business profitably. If it is too low, the seller will not obtain the monies that were rightfully his.

Remember, it is as difficult to get out of a greenhouse business as it is to get into it. It takes planning, time, effort, and a mutual goal by the buyer and seller to be successful.

### 10 Truths About Valuing A Greenhouse Business

From all my years seeing different sales of greenhouses – some successes, some failures – I would like to offer some suggestions. I call them the "10 Truths About Valuing A Greenhouse Business."

1. In most cases, the tangible value of the business is the bottom line – that is if no one can manage it or nothing can be done with the greenhouse.

2. The greenhouse is only a tool – it is only as profitable as the people who know what to do with it.

3. The most expensive greenhouse to build may not be the most valuable or profitable.

4. The bigger the greenhouse range, the fewer people who know what to do with it or can afford to buy it.

5. Bankers are poor growers – if they take over the greenhouse, you'll lose money.

6. A rapid increase in the size of your greenhouse may lead you to bankruptcy.

7. If you have to sell quickly, you'll sell cheap.

8. If there is a family feud, don't hold the greenhouse as ransom. Only the lawyers will make money.

9. Partnerships where one person puts up the money and one does the work are seldom successful. A sale of the facility usually follows shortly after problems occur.

10. A well-planned, slow transition where everyone accomplishes their goals is the best way to sell a greenhouse.

### Four Type Of Greenhouse Sales

Here are four types of transactions that occur in the greenhouse industry:

**1. The Big Business Buyouts.** These get a lot of attention from the media, but most of them have not been successful in the long run.

**2. The Friendly Takeovers.** One grower wants to increase the size of his range and purchases another grower who may or may not be financially sound. These have a fairly high level of success.

**3. The Family Buyout.** If the younger family members have horticulture and management skills, this system can work as long as the business can be separated from family.

**4. The New Entrepreneur Getting Started.** This can work if the seller will help in the transition and the buyer is willing and able to work with the seller on the change.

*— June 1996*

## Build With A Plan

*Businesses that can adapt to change will survive –
those that cannot will be eliminated. Don't build
yourself into bankruptcy.*

In the June 1999 issue of *Greenhouse Grower*, there was an excellent article on structures and coverings titled, "Building Toward Tomorrow." I might add that it was timely, too.

This has been a good year for most growers. Many have indicated they couldn't keep up with demand. In fact, one grower said he will be 100,000 square feet short of greenhouse space if he grows all the product he has booked for 2000.

I saw the pressure these growers are facing firsthand. Several growers I spoke with said, "I'm not interested in new material. I don't have enough space to produce the old stuff."

There's definitely pressure to expand production facilities or risk going out of business. A great example of this occurred recently. In 1998, 140 acres of new greenhouse construction went up in Ontario, Canada. At the same time, a Michigan cut rose operation – less than 50 miles from where 140 new acres were built – closed its doors forever in favor of a new housing development.

After some thought, I realized this is the natural cycle of the greenhouse industry. Those businesses that can adapt to change will survive and those that cannot will be eliminated.

Our industry has changed dramatically in the last 50 years. In the 1950s, cut flowers were the biggest greenhouse items, followed by potted and foliage plants. Bedding plants, perennials, and vegetables were the smallest parts of the industry.

Today, bedding plants, perennials, and vegetables are the biggest segments. Potted and foliage plants and cut flowers account for less than 40% of production. It is only logical to think that greenhouses built before 1950 are now obsolete.

While total U.S. greenhouse space has not increased much the past couple years, many newer greenhouses, offering growers more flexibility, have replaced out-of-date structures.

### Building On Profits

New construction will occur as long as the industry remains profitable. One of my friends who tracks the industry asked the question, "Are we building more and making less?" He was involved with one of the largest potted plant ranges in the Midwest in the early 1960s, only to see it closed down and sold for real estate within one year because it was no longer profitable.

There are other examples of where growers have built themselves into bankruptcy. Increasing size and sales is only good business if a profit is made in the process.

### Tool Time

While profit is important, so too is producing a quality product. One of my most vivid memories of a new greenhouse that didn't improve plant production is from my first trip to an experimental station in England in the late 1960s. This brand new greenhouse, featuring the latest in technology, was impressive. The only problem was every plant in the structure was dying from nitrogen deficiency.

A greenhouse is a tool. It can be useful if you know what you want and how to use it. Some might say a greenhouse is like a hammer. There are many different types of hammers, so you must buy the one that fits your needs. Each one will do a specific job, but there are some that will do the job better than others. While you don't need a $100 hammer to drive one nail, you shouldn't use a $1 hammer to drive thousands of nails.

The same is true of greenhouses. I have seen greenhouses built for $1 per square foot and some for $400 per square foot. They are not the same structures and don't perform the same functions. Don't buy a greenhouse until you know what you want to accomplish with it. Like a hammer, a greenhouse is no better than the person using it.

### Making The Plan Come Together

When choosing a new greenhouse, don't buy a Cadillac if you can only afford a Volkswagen. I've seen a number of greenhouse operations where the only person who made money was the banker.

A 1996 Professional Plant Growers Association financial survey showed the average greenhouse operation was 60% to 70% of its net worth in debt. That leaves little room for mistakes to occur before bankruptcy.

If you are going to expand, develop your plan thoroughly. Don't put one house up, then another, only to find they don't fit into your overall plan. Do your expansion planning well in advance of when you want it completed.

When people get started in this business, many think it's easier and cheaper to build a greenhouse themselves. Don't underestimate the value of commercial greenhouse building companies. They have much experience. Even if you plan to build a greenhouse yourself, it's a good idea to work with greenhouse manufacturers. They can offer expertise and provide the necessary materials for doing the job right.

Whatever time you anticipate the job taking, add another one to three months for unforeseen delays or problems. In addition, don't forget to get the proper permits for construction from your town, county, or state.

Finally, build during the slow season. It is tough or near impossible to build and grow crops at the same time.

### Greenhouse Of Tomorrow

Greenhouses of the future will have many changes. But no matter how simple or complicated they become, they will still require growers to oversee them.

How fast changes occur in the future will depend a lot on the profitability of the crops we grow and consumers' demand for them.

*– September 1999*

# Mechanize Or Labor-ize?

*The decision whether to hire more labor or increase mechanization depends on the economics of your business and your vision for the future.*

There's been a discussion in the bedding plant industry for some time about whether it's more profitable to mechanize greenhouse operations or substitute labor for expensive new machinery. There's no simple answer. Each case needs to be analyzed to see if the investment in equipment justifies the potential labor savings.

The answer may change as our economy changes through the years. In the late 1970s and early 1980s, when interest rates were more than 20% and unemployment was above 10%, labor was plentiful and much cheaper than borrowing money. But in the last few years, with interest rates at 6% to 7% and unemployment rates less than 4%, there is little question that growers should purchase equipment to replace hard-to-find and expensive labor. Making the decision whether or not to automate and determining how to do it profitably cause constant concern.

The right answer for you depends on the vision you have for your company. I think of the saying, "What the mind can conceive and what you believe can be achieved." Ideas from science fiction films of the 1950s and '60s – going to the moon, operating without surgery, talking on a wireless phone – are common occurrences today. The bedding plant industry of the '50s and '60s was no different. Those growers were the dreamers that envisioned today's reality.

I recently rediscovered a Michigan Science In Action booklet from September 1969 titled *Michigan's Blooming Industry*. It contains a model drawing of how the author thought a bedding plant factory would work in the future. It is amazing how closely this 30-year-old diagram approaches an actual operation of today.

The pamphlet explains research that was conducted on consumer preferences, the size of the bedding plant market, flat fillers, slow-release fertilizers, direct seeding of petunias into the final flats, using chemicals to improve germination, adding light to hasten flowering, improving air circulation patterns for more uniform temperatures, and storing bedding plants in cold temperatures and light. Plug storage research was built on these first studies.

It has taken more than 30 years and the hard work of hundreds of people, but we can all agree that the plant factory is here. Certainly this can and will be improved upon, for the plant factory of the future depends greatly on the vision of today's growers.

It's interesting to read in U.S. and European trade magazines about new equipment and concepts being developed to improve production systems. Many of these innovations come from countries where labor rates are extremely high. In Denmark, for example, greenhouse laborers can make up to $20 an hour. To be competitive, Danish growers must accomplish a great deal of work to pay these costs. Not surprisingly, the Danes are working with robotics. One piece of robotic equipment is controlled by a joy stick a grower can maneuver to pick up an entire 10- to 15-plant row from one bench and move it to another.

### Do The Math

The decision whether to hire more labor or increase mechanization depends primarily on the economics of each greenhouse business. If one grower can operate one acre a year with a production labor cost of $1.44 to $2.16 per square foot without the equipment, and an automated grower can handle three acres at the same cost, then the equipment cost may well be justified. Smaller growers may have difficulty obtaining the necessary capital to finance these investments, but this may work to their advantage.

The question for both large and small growers comes down to the cost of substituting labor for equipment or equipment for labor.

Larger growers may invest $1 million per acre to automate the entire production process, so labor is needed only for placing, removing, and shipping crops. But these mechanized systems are most effective with large quantities of one crop, or a monoculture. With many different crops, the process becomes more complicated.

The most profitable large growers produce large quantities of fewer crops. Smaller growers may take the opposite approach and automate where they can, with computerized environmental controls, automatic watering, and seeding machines. Unlike larger growers, small operations are more likely to grow smaller quantities of more plant varieties. This doesn't justify spending hundreds of thousands of dollars on specialized planting or robotic equipment.

### Make A Plan

I couldn't agree more with the phrase, "The devil is in the details." The days when the entire production plan is in the owner's hands and trusty notebook are over. Large and small growers alike are spending time with their key employees to develop detailed plans for their operations.

No one in this industry can afford to lose large quantities of plants to production mistakes. Sales cannot be hoped for – they have to be made. Some growers start implementing vague thoughts and ideas immediately, and then have to make expensive changes to achieve the ultimate goal. Someone once said of this method, "Experience is the best teacher, but the tuition is higher."

The vision cannot be achieved unless all details are thought through and precise action plans are worked out. It's better to develop a plan on paper, have people review it, and make corrections with an eraser before you actually start to build it.

Being in business today takes much more skill than it did 20 or 30 years ago. You need to know what you want and follow the necessary steps to get it. As Bill Gates says, business now happens at the speed of thought. There is no doubt you will mechanize and need more labor. The laborers will be fewer, more skilled, and paid more, but they will do more work in less time, and provide consistently higher quality products that can be more successfully marketed to the consumer.

As one of my favorite clients' accountant always reminds us, "I don't care how much production labor you have, just keep it at or below the budget." Likewise, the accountant says, "I don't care what you want to automate, just keep it within our capital expense budget." At the end of our yearly discussion on labor vs. mechanization, the accountant has the final say – keep this business profitable.

*– May 2000*

# Family Business Succession: Have A Plan

*It takes as much time and effort to pass on a business as it does to start one. If a business is to survive, a plan for its continued growth is essential.*

When I first started working in Michigan, I visited many greenhouses. It was interesting to see the different stages that each business was in – some were just getting started, some had been in business for 10 to 20 years, and some were in business for more than 50 years.

Today, nearly 34 years later, those mature businesses are all gone. They didn't survive the transfer to the next generation and they weren't able to find someone who could buy and continue the business.

### The Life Cycle

A floriculture business is a cycle just like life. Someone starts a business and sees it through those struggling first years. If they're successful, they grow that business, waiting eight to 10 years before they reap some financial rewards. They continue to work hard every day, usually foregoing free time and vacation, to mature the business. After several years, the owners start looking for someone to whom they can leave the business – in most cases a family member.

It takes as much time and effort to pass on a business as it does to start one. Some would say more. Many people think they will live forever and don't want to face the fact that change will occur. If the business is to survive, a plan must be made to ensure its continued growth.

The government already knows how much of your business it will take upon your death. Your family, on the other hand, will be forced to make last minute plans for your business without you around to share your business knowledge and experience. In some cases, your employees may be put in a situation of having to run your business because you believed the end would never come.

### Lessons I've Learned

Let me share a few true stories about floriculture operations that were lost or the families that were ruined financially and emotionally because there was no concrete plan to pass on the business.

**Instant tragedy.** A young grower was building his business while working full-time as a railroad brakeman. His wife and family were helping care for the plants, making deliveries, and providing labor, but the grower never shared the production or financial information with them. Then one spring night he was killed in an accident while working on the railroad. There was no plan to hand down the business. His wife and family didn't know what to do, and the business shut down less than one month after he died.

**No one wants it.** A husband and wife worked side by side for 40 years. They built the business but had no children and were reluctant to take outsiders into partnership with them. They offered the business for sale, telling potential buyers it provided a living but was hard work. The owners even mentioned they hadn't had a vacation in 10 years. With that negative sales pitch, no one bought the business. The owners had to close their 40-year effort, dismantle the greenhouses, and sell the land to raise funds to live at a nursing home.

**Everyone wants it.** A husband and wife had four sons and indicated in a will that their floriculture operation should be shared equally among them. But each son wanted to be the boss and had different definitions for the word "equally." The sons hired lawyers and filed lawsuits for complete ownership, and the operation was in trouble. In the end, the business closed and the four sons no longer speak with each other.

**A family divided.** In this family business, the father had a close bond with their son while the mother had a similar relationship with their daughter. The father and son were managing the greenhouse when the daughter and her husband lost their jobs outside the business. The mother told the father to hire the couple to help them. After a month, the son told the father that neither were good workers and was advised to fire them. That night the mother locked the father out of the house, giving him an ultimatum to either hire them back or never come home. They divorced, millions of dollars were divided, and the business barely survived.

These stories are just a few examples of what can happen. The point is, it's tough to quickly transfer a family business and it won't happen by itself. The most successful transfers are well planned and almost always are done with professional help. Good lawyers, estate planners, and accountants are essential to making sure all the details are discussed before drafting the plan.

### Well Laid Plans

Developing a scheme to pass on the business is important, and it's just as important to make certain that those who are involved in the business know the plan's specifics. Recently, I helped a grower develop a fairly simple succession plan. We would put the two children on the company's board of directors and have them work in different positions within the business. We thought it was a good scheme.

When the plan was presented to the children, neither of them wanted the responsibility of running the business. The children said they had watched how hard their parents had worked, and feel it's more important for them to have free time to spend with their families than to have the constant pressure of the business on their shoulders. The grower is now searching for other individuals interested in the business and is hoping to develop a succession plan that will work.

This example shows the difficulty of running a family business. It's like having to wear three hats. When you wear the family hat, you try to do what's best for the family. The second hat involves doing what's best for the employees, who also may be family members. The third hat is doing what's best for the business, the owners of which also may be family.

If family members are not involved in the business, then they must be treated with your family hat on. But if a family member is also an employee, you must know which hat to wear and at what time. If that person also is an owner, there are three hats to juggle. At times, conflicts will arise among family members, employees, and the business. Which hat you wear will govern the decisions you make.

Finally, remember that not everyone may want the same end result. Some may want to sell the business, some may want to own it, and some may just want to work in it. As you can see, it's as difficult to pass on the business as it is to start it. Do you have a plan to hand it down?

*– June 2000*

# Developing A Sales Forecast

*A sales forecast is as dynamic as a production forecast – maybe even more so. Here are Carlson's calculations for potential sales.*

In the last 20 years, we have made great progress in developing production forecasts and scheduling plants for sale during any week of the year. Researchers have developed models that predict the time to flower for many crops. Great improvements also have been made in production media and fertility systems for reducing insect and disease damage. Twenty years ago it was common to have a 5% to 10% crop loss due to production problems. Today, these losses can be reduced to 1% to 2% if all the right procedures are followed.

When I was a graduate student, I developed an equation that stated the time to flower for bedding plants was based on many factors – not just one. Any of these factors could be the one that prevented the plants from reaching their full potential. For example, all factors can be ideal for plant growth, but if you don't fertilize the plants properly, a nitrogen or potassium deficiency can develop and limit plant growth. In my first equation, I listed more than 35 factors that needed to be controlled for proper plant production.

With this in mind, I talked with several growers about how they make sales forecasts. Many said they consider what they did the previous year and how much money they generated up to this point last year. A grower of a large greenhouse operation told me one of his major chain store customers makes its weekly decisions based solely on the accountant's figures of this year compared to last. The grower spent two hours trying to convince the store management the potential sales of his product are more dynamic this year than last.

### Figuring The Forecast

This May was not typical in many parts of the country. Trying to predict what would happen in the next week based on previous year's data might not have worked. A sales forecast is as dynamic as a production forecast – maybe even more.

Research money used to develop a valid forecast is minimal. Perhaps we should use the production model as a starting point for a sales forecast model. Let's consider all the factors that go into a potential sale, making another equation in which all factors must be in the appropriate range for the sale to occur.

### Carlson's Calculations

Plant quality + plant quantity + proper packaging + proper transportation + proper display + proper retail care + proper price + proper place + right consumer + proper weather + proper personnel + proper promotion + proper financial data + uncontrollable factors = Potential Sale. If we start with this equation and attempt to control each factor to the best of our ability, we'll have a better chance of making the sale happen.

Let's look at the factors we can control. If we have quality plants and a sufficient quantity, then these are major factors in making the sale. If our plants are poor quality or we have insufficient quantity to sell to make our sales forecast, we're finished before we start.

I visited one retail grower this spring who sprayed all his geraniums with an insecticide that caused phototoxicity. The damage was extensive, with 10,000 plants damaged and more than $50,000 in lost income before he even opened the door.

Another grower planted 20 unique baskets, which all sold in two days. There was a demand for 50 more, but insufficient quantities resulted in lost sales of $2,000.

On each item in our equation, we can determine how much we made or how much we lost because of how well we controlled each factor. For example, how much damage occurred because of improper packaging? How many plants were damaged when a rack fell over? You can total all the losses that occur because of each factor. Remember, each of these events decreases your total sales and your potential profit.

### Chain Store Plant Care

Proper care at the retail level is a major factor in potential sales, accounting for a loss between 10% and 15% of total sales. If you traveled with me on my visits to retail areas in the Midwest and East Coast, you would say it costs between 25% and 30% of total sales.

Most major chain stores are not designed to handle plants. They place the plants outside with little protection and have few people available to water them. The chains don't realize that 80% of the potential sales depend on how the product looks when the customer walks in.

I was at a large chain in Rehobeth Beach, DE, on May 15. It was a sunny, windy day, and I saw flats of impatiens, salvia, and petunias outside in the garden area with the wind blowing. All of these flats were completely dried out, had yellow foliage, and were close to death. All the flats were right next to the cash register with a sign indicating they were $12.95 a flat. I was so upset I went inside the store where the garden manager and two helpers were staying out of the wind. I asked, "Do you know all your plants need water?" The manager said nothing but smiled and shrugged his shoulders.

The major chains have great difficulty in handling perishable products. A grower friend said the only people he would hire as employees in a major chain garden center would be those who have experience in the produce department.

Most bedding plants sold in California are serviced by employees who are hired by growers. The chains are willing to pay 15% to 20% more as long as the plant material is maintained properly and the sales are made. Some East Coast and Midwestern growers also are providing plant-maintenance personnel. Grower-owned and independent retail garden centers are better equipped to display and maintain their product properly.

The only factor in the sales forecast we can't control is the weather. If we sell our plants from greenhouses or protected areas, we will see sales occurring even during rainy weather.

One retail grower I know has a 10% discount on all plant material on any rainy day in May and June. It helps sales. Weather is one reason why using only the accountant's figures is a very poor sales forecaster.

A sale is not a simple act. It takes as much time and money to sell product as it does producing it. I hope you will continue to improve your sales forecast and strive to make it more accurate each year. Once you have an accurate forecast you will become a true entrepreneur, predicting your business based on all the forecasts you need to make it profitable.

*– July 2000*

# Always Have Some Options

*Don't put all your eggs in one basket or you may end up out of business. Live by these five points to avoid bankruptcy.*

Ask the growers who have consistently sold more than half their production to Kmart or the employees of Enron if it isn't true. The old adage, "Don't put all your eggs in one basket" has again become advice to live by.

Many growers have put all their eggs in one basket and, as a result, have gone out of business. Whether they relied on only one source of supply, one crop to sell, or one customer to buy all of their crops, they set themselves up for failure.

In the old days, we dealt with people because they had integrity and we trusted each other. A handshake was our contract and we were as good as our word. Within the floriculture industry, everyone knew who they could trust and who needed to pay when the order was delivered.

As our industry grew, outside interests became involved. Big business people who ran large corporations became major players in our industry. They used all the business strategies that they thought would work – most were successful in other industries, so why not floriculture? But, over the last few years, we have watched many such groups flounder and fail.

### How Does Chapter 11 Affect Me?

In the 1990s, a word we seldom, if ever, heard in floriculture became well-known and today is very common in our business vocabulary: Bankruptcy. Chapter 11 bankruptcy protection is called a reorganization effort by failing companies to keep creditors from taking their assets, allowing them to continue their businesses under court supervision. However, once a company declares bankruptcy, it is also protected from the vendors to whom it owes money.

For example, those of you who sold your poinsettia crops to Kmart in December will probably not get paid, but if you do, your payment will be a fraction of what you are owed. According to the laws of bankruptcy protection, because it filed Chapter 11 in January, Kmart does not have to pay you for the product until it comes out of bankruptcy. Most of the time, the bill is settled for 10¢ to 20¢ on the dollar.

Bankruptcy hurts everyone – not only the company that files for it, but its vendors, employees, and customers.

### Scandalous Schemes

Although it was the seventh largest corporation in America, the Enron bankruptcy proves that bigger is not always better. Poor business is poor business, regardless of size. Enron tried to show if it made money on one business, it could start a few more and then try to carry all the debt from these businesses without disclosing the debts to its shareholders. You would think that its auditing firm would have stopped this less-than-ethical scheme. But if the auditing firm is also the financial consultant, there is a very large conflict of interest.

The simple lesson to be learned from the scandal is never get the people who audit your financial position to advise you on management decisions. If they get their hands into the cookie jar, it is hard for them to be fair about how to count the cookies.

### Yes, It Can Happen To You

You might think these problems only occur in big business, but that couldn't be farther from the truth. Such mistakes will destroy businesses of any size. Here are five points to live by if you want to avoid bankruptcy.

**1. Never conduct more than 25% of your business with one customer.** Some folks will say no more than 30% or 35%, but if you have more than 50% of your business with one customer, you have real potential for disaster. You may currently think it is much easier to deal with fewer customers, and granted, it may be easier. That is, until the day comes when your major customer decides to dump you and use another vendor at a lower price. While you may need to work a little harder to keep more customers now, consider it an insurance policy to protect your business in the future.

**2. Never expand faster than you can afford.** Quick, large expansions usually mean problems. Show me a company that increases its size by 25% a year for four straight years and I'll show you a company that will be bankrupt by the fifth year. Growers get so excited when their retail customers say they did a great job but that more product is mandatory. "I'll take all you can grow," say the big box buyers. "If you want to keep our account, you'll have to produce more product."

Sound familiar? Growers think their only choice is to increase production and thus, increase in size to keep their accounts. What is your alternative? Build your facility to the size you can control and produce the product quantity you can sell profitably.

**3. Never allow your business to be controlled by a single manager or employee**. If there is only one person who knows how to produce or sell your product, or how to control the business finances, you are in great risk. This situation may happen if you buy a business and the head grower, head salesperson, or controller comes with it. They may know everything but you're kept in the dark. There should be no smoke or mirrors in your business – you must know what is going on at all times. The bottleneck is always at the top and that's why company leadership usually changes five times faster than front line employees.

**4. Never give all your business to one supplier.** Just as one customer can control your business, so can one supplier. I've seen great supply salespeople who get the materials, get it delivered on time, provide production schedules, and are very valuable. But what happens if the salesperson doesn't have the product you want or is pushing company brands rather than the best product? Always order from at least two to four vendors. The additional input, price quotes, and competitive nature will keep everyone sharp.

**5. Always look for new accounts and new business.** The small or new accounts you sell to this year may become your biggest account in 10 years. All businesses start, have a growth phase, mature, and die. It's just that some take longer than others to go through each phase. Always inspect and work on your total customer list. A good list has some new accounts, some in the growth phase, and some mature accounts.

### The Golden Rule

In business as in life, the golden rule must apply. Do unto others as you would have them do unto you. Always work with vendors, employees, and customers who have integrity and whom you can trust. When you also show these qualities, do what you say, provide a quality product, and deliver it to everyone's satisfaction, price will not be the only factor and bankruptcy won't even be an issue.

Plants aren't the problem – people are. You must learn how to handle people and business as well as you handle your plants.

*– March 2002*

# CULTIVATING EMPLOYEES

Greenhouse plants can't grow without people.

As a graduate student, I once wrote an equation to predict plant growth (i.e., the number of roses a plant could produce per year). I came up with 35 to 40 different factors that affect plant growth. I thought if we could control all of those factors, we could produce the perfect plant. The fallacy of my equation, however, was that I left out the human factor.

How can we as an industry recruit and train people to be our future employees and managers and keep our current employees on board?

I remember with great fondness my first contact with floriculture.

After being discharged from the Navy, my brother moved to Westchester County, NY, to work as an apprentice to my uncle, who worked in landscape maintenance on estates in Westchester and Putnam counties.

When I was old enough to get a job, it wasn't hard to choose between working in the coal mines of northeastern Pennsylvania or working in floriculture with my brother. A few summers and school vacations learning landscape maintenance skills from him gave me the idea that floriculture could be my career choice.

I looked into colleges that taught the subject and found that Pennsylvania State University offered both two and four-year programs. It was hard to decide which was best, but I went with the four-year program and then for a master's degree and doctorate. And, as they say, "the rest is history!"

Because people are so important to the success of our industry, following are some of the columns I have written with ideas on how to nurture and grow your employees with the same care you give your plants.

# Success Related To Concerns For 'People Problems'

*A good starting point for finding and keeping employees is understanding what people need to succeed.*

Each year bedding plant growers face a big problem in obtaining good employees for transplanting, shipping, and the many other part-time jobs needed to produce and ship our product.

Many managers also face the task of hiring good, year-round employees for production, sales, maintenance, and other necessary operations. This fact is evidenced by a Bedding Plants Inc. questionnaire sent yearly to growers. The answer most frequently given to the question of the biggest problem in production and marketing is "finding and keeping" good employees.

### Management Is Key

If you were to travel to many greenhouses, you would find some operations with all the employees they need and a waiting list of those wishing to gain employment. At other greenhouses, the manager is short of help, can't find any new help, and isn't satisfied with the help he or she has. Sometimes, you can find both of these situations in the same town or even on the same street. Why? I believe the reason is management or lack of it!

There have been many books written on the subjects of motivating people, helping individuals achieve their goals, and treating people like people. There are probably more books written on how to handle people than how to care for plants, and this is most likely due to the fact that there are more problems with people than there are with plants.

In our business, people problems mean plant problems. For example, moisture stress in plants can often be traced back to someone neglecting to water on the weekend. Most plant problems can be traced back to someone forgetting to do a job or making an error in doing a task. Many times, the fact is that the manager forgot to ask an employee to do the task or he or she did not explain the job properly. Often the manager is so busy running himself that he or she is unable to communicate instructions to someone else.

If you want to obtain and keep good employees and run an efficient greenhouse business, the following outline of people's needs might make a good starting point.

• **Physiological Needs.** Your workers (anyone from a transplanter to a foreman) have fundamental physical needs (i.e., food, sleep, shelter, clothing). If these needs are not satisfied, they dominate the thoughts of the individual. For example, a thirsty man can only think and dream of water; therefore, his ability to work will be greatly limited. I'm sure most bedding plant operators pay adequate wages so that the physical well-being of the workers is cared for. But once the physical needs are met, there are also emotional needs to be satisfied.

• **The Need For Routine.** Most people need a system. They like to work in a familiar, orderly routine and, if this is developed, work can be accomplished faster and more efficiently. All one has to do is close his eyes and picture shipping season in a bedding plant operation. Ask the question, "Is work laid out in an orderly fashion or is there chaos – running here, shouting orders there, complaints about the help's inability to get the work done?" Perhaps this is management's failure to lay out an orderly work schedule and consistent routine.

• **The Love Need.** Once you meet physiological and routine needs, your workers will seek a group identity. This might be achieved by having friends at work or by associating with others who have a similar job occupation. It is important that the employee be accepted and made to feel like one of the group.

• **The Need For Esteem.** All people in our society have the need or desire for a stable, firmly based evaluation of themselves in order to achieve self respect, self esteem, and the esteem of others. This helps them to obtain a sense of achievement, strength, adequacy, independence, and freedom.

For example, an individual might be the best transplanter, the fastest loader, or the best grower in an operation and he should be aware of it. The self esteem he receives from knowing he is good at a job, or the best, will be all the motivation needed for him to continue his top-notch performance. Employees need to know where they stand and how well they are doing. If they are not doing well, they should be advised of this, along with ways to improve.

Most people have a desire for a good reputation, prestige, and recognition. It is important that when someone does a good job, you take the time to compliment him for it.

One greenhouse worker candidly told me, "I catch heck for everything that goes wrong. The boss gets credit for everything that goes well." He was actually telling me that he didn't get the esteem he needed and, therefore, probably wasn't happy with his work or a good worker for the business.

• **The Need For Fulfillment.** Everyone wants to have a sense of accomplishment. The owner or manager of an operation takes pride in the fact that he has produced so many flats or sold so many plants. A good manager doesn't use the pronoun "I" but uses the pronoun "we." The team, our team, accomplished this goal. He or she also lets every member of the team know how important their contribution is to the achievement of that goal.

### Some Common Sense

After you have read all of the books ever written on the subject of employer/employee relationships, you'll come to the common sense conclusion that the golden rule is still the best guide. "Do Unto Others As You Would Have Them Do Unto You."

If you pay an adequate wage; provide a job and routine which can be understood and performed; create a friendly atmosphere and make your employees feel wanted; compliment them on a job well done or constructively comment on a poor job; and allow employees to have a sense of purpose and accomplishment, you and your help can then go back to the job at hand – growing and selling bedding plants!

*– September 1974*

# Would You Want To Work For Yourself?

*Employees want to work for a manager, not a boss. What's the difference? A manager motivates!*

Recently, a student came into my office, inquiring about a particular greenhouse firm where he had interviewed. After making several positive comments about the operation and its owners, I asked him what his impressions were. I expected he would have been impressed by general things such as the size of the place or the quality of the plants, but the specific nature of his observations – and conclusions – surprised me.

He first noticed brown algae on the greenhouse walls. Had he spent four years learning about the importance of light to plant growth, only to work in a place that didn't let the light in?

Next, he noticed a group of plants wrapped for shipping that had been left to wilt and die. They were past the point where a good watering would save them. Didn't anyone care?

As he looked further, he noticed that general sanitation was poor. Tools, materials, and debris were strewn about, as if employees had no time to pick up after themselves. Where was pride in the workplace?

So what did my student conclude from these observations? Lazy employees? Understaffing? A busy season? None of the above. He suspected that management was the cause of the trouble.

His suspicions were confirmed when the manager gave him a tour. As they walked through the operation, the manager was very short with the employees – most of whom were high school students. It seemed that employees were motivated by fear, not reward.

In his interview with three members of the management team, my student heard many negative comments. The managers blamed the employees for doing sloppy work; blamed the customers for not paying enough so they could afford to hire good help; in short, blamed everyone but themselves.

"It was a depressing interview," he said. "I certainly wouldn't want to spend my life working in surroundings like that!"

## Interviewing Ourselves

If only we could see ourselves as others see...Those managers thought they were interviewing a prospective employee when, in fact, they were being ruled out as prospective employers. They thought they were in control, but they only succeeded in alienating a potential employee who was bright enough to recognize poor management as the source of their problems.

It is a common trap to blame employees or customers – but unless management takes corrective action, problems such as these can eventually kill a business.

The Danish poet, Piet Hein, says, "He on whom God's light does fall sees the great things in the small." To be successful, a manager must see great things in the small. Just as negative attitudes and sloppy work contribute to a business failure, so pride and attention to the small details of production contribute to the overall success of the operation.

In helping develop business plans for several greenhouse operations, I've discovered having a written plan is not universal. For many greenhouses, the only "plan" that exists is in the head of the owner and consequently it is neither complete nor communicated to the staff.

Often a greenhouse will call someone a "manager" when in reality that person never manages, but only grows the crop or owns the business. True management involves planning, goal setting, and employee motivation.

The purpose of motivation is to increase desirable behavior and to decrease undesirable behavior. It works by the following formula: *ability x motivation = productivity*. Ability cannot produce results on its own. Good managers must motivate the employees involved to work with them, not for them, to achieve maximum productivity in the greenhouse.

Motivation methods of management are more important today because of a general change in the ethics and values of today's workforce. In the post-Depression era, workers were motivated by fear, money, and the work ethic. These motives tended to de-emphasize the human element.

Today, the human element is a central motive. According to Daniel Yankelovich in a 1980 issue of *Compensation Review,* it can be offered as leisure time, opportunities, personal attention, status, coordination of work and personal values, and planned worker participation in the business.

The next time you interview a prospective employee, remember that you are being interviewed as well. Employees want to work for a manager, not a boss. What's the difference? A manager motivates.

### Ten Tips To Motivate Your Employees

Here are 10 tips to motivating your workforce:

1. Remember that performance is affected by both ability and motivation.

2. People will perform well if they believe that they are able do the job and that accomplishing it will result in rewards.

3. Participation and involvement increases commitment and motivation.

4. Together set specific, challenging, but realistic goals.

5. Forget the past; focus on the future and what can be done in the present to get there.

6. Set up systems for employee feedback; talk out problems.

7. Use planning skills to establish a realistic schedule.

8. Communicate your expectations clearly.

9. Take action quickly and follow through.

10. Encourage positive behavior by offering human rewards such as attention, status, recognition, work-time flexibility.

*– May 1987*

# 'I Could Do A Better Job If ...'

### How would you respond to this statement? Owners' responses differed greatly from those of employees. Understanding these differences can help everyone do a better job.

How would you complete the statement, "I could do a better job if ..."? How does your position at your firm affect your answer?

Last September, I had the opportunity to discuss this question with employees and owners at the Northwest Florist Association's convention in Eugene, OR. We talked about management, developing a business plan, and how to do a better job.

As a part of the program, I asked everyone to complete the statement: I could do a better job if only....

The owners' answers differed greatly from those of the employees. How did they differ and, perhaps more importantly, why did they differ? Understanding these differences can help everyone to do a better job.

### Education

Almost a quarter of the employees believe that they could do a better job with more education. Employers can provide flexible work schedules to allow employees to take classes at local colleges – or provide on-the-job training that relates to the specific job at hand. Employees do a better job when they understand why they are doing it. On the other hand, only 3.8% of the employers cite lack of education as a problem. This is probably due to the fact that many have degrees in horticulture; they do know how to grow plants. But if we take a second look at the survey, we can see a definite need for more education in the areas of management and time management.

### People Management

Both employers and employees agree that ineffective management is by far the biggest problem area. Managers believe that in half the cases this limits their ability to do a good job. All can agree that poor management results in poor performance, but what exactly do we mean by poor management?

Many owners are managers by default. They may have started the business and done everything themselves – and now that they have help, they don't know how to use it.

### Time Management

This problem is closely related to the previous one. Employers always seem to have more work to be done than employees can accomplish. They consequently complain about employee incompetence by saying "You can't get good help anymore."

Employees, in turn, complain the boss is disorganized and expects more of them than they can realistically accomplish. Many were frustrated by managers changing priorities in the middle of a job. This is a result of managers reacting to problems as they come up instead of planning ahead to avoid them.

### Personal Problems

Employees admitted that personal problems – their children, their car, problems at home, relationships – adversely affected their work performance 18% of the time. Employers must understand that employees are not machines. Anything a manager can do to help with personal problems will result in a harder working, more loyal employee.

Offering a limited number of personal-leave days, for example, is one way to help employees deal with personal problems. Often an employee can take an hour to solve a problem he or she would have spent days fretting about – and working less efficiently as a result.

### Better Facilities

Poor facilities were considered a problem by only 4% of the employees and only 9% of the employers. We all want better facilities, employers more so because they are aware of the improvements in equipment and structures that are available today. In most cases, however, facilities were not a major limiting factor in a successful operation.

### Product

It was interesting to note that neither employers nor employees considered this a major problem area. Everyone seems to agree we have a great product. Production techniques in our industry have progressed to the point where quality plants are not a problem. Most of us are in this business because we love plants. It may be one reason managers are spending more time growing than managing.

### Marketing

I consider it a problem. However, most employees and managers don't consider it a problem. Here again, people in our industry focus on the product and not the customer. Those 1.5% of employers who see marketing as a problem and find a way to solve it will be the successful growers and retailers of the future.

### Employers

Employers could do a better job if only…they were better managers. Eighty percent of all new businesses fail within the first five years due to poor management. Good management is essential to survival – and it involves a lot more than managing the plants. Managing people, time, finances, and marketing are all part of the management job.

It is ironic that educational sessions on management at industry conferences are so poorly attended. Management sessions draw roughly 20% of the crowd attending a production session.

### Employees

Employees could do a better job if only…they were better managed. Employees want to do a good job. If management can provide them with educational opportunities, teach them job skills and time management techniques, and also allow them some flexibility to cope with personal problems – they will do a good job. Employees perform best with specific goals and specific time periods in which to accomplish them. They need to know that the business is under control and that their employer knows where it is going.

Try our question out on your employees and yourself. How would you answer? Both the answers you get and the answers you give can help you make that "better job" a reality.

*– December 1987*

# Empower Your Employees

*The last four letters of enthusiasm stand for "I am sold myself." Help your employees be powerful, confident and enthusiastic by being powerful, confident, and enthusiastic yourself.*

While attending the New England Greenhouse Conference in Sturbridge, MA, I heard an excellent presentation on human resources by Richard Curran, president of Curran Association of Madison, WI. He specified three key ingredients for professional success.

The first is power or, more precisely, the power product knowledge can give you. Curran explained knowing your product gives you power. In floriculture, this involves knowing how to grow plants, how they perform in the home or landscape, what cultivars are available, and interesting facts about them. These elements of product knowledge are the batteries that power your job.

### No Knowledge + No Power = No Sale

I once walked into a garden center and asked the clerk for a philodendron. He smiled and led me to the tree lot, where he pointed to a rhododendron and said: "There it is!" In this case, no product knowledge and no power meant no sale.

All too often, those people with the least product knowledge are put on the sale floor to face the customer, only to lose potential sales because they are not empowered with product knowledge. A continuing training program is imperative if you expect your employees to do their jobs properly.

It's fun to watch knowledgeable employees help customers buy the product. They can determine the customers' needs and match them with the appropriate product. Once this link is established, the sale happens.

### Neutralize The Negative

Even negative customer beliefs can be neutralized with product knowledge. All too often, prospective customers complain that plants cost too much. A knowledgeable clerk might address this complaint by saying: "I've had a Christmas cactus like that for 25 years that has flowered every year. I paid $5 for it. I figure it cost me less than one hundredth of a cent per day to enjoy that plant. What a bargain!"

"But plants are too much work," the customer persists. The knowledgeable clerk replies: "If you use the self-watering pot – which we have here for $15 – you'll have to water the plant only once a week. It takes me only 10 minutes a week to water my collection of 20 plants."

Product knowledge can turn objections into positive statements that remove sales barriers and establish a need for the product. Once you have that product knowledge, you need the second ingredient: confidence. Confidence grows from practicing your presentation – speaking with customers and winning their trust.

Customers are loyal to businesses that seem to understand their needs and which are confident in this knowledge. Once you have satisfied their need, customers will look to you for help the next time they want to buy your product or service.

For example, I know a botanist who is very knowledgeable. If you ask him any question about a plant – what it is, where it is from, or what zone it grows in – he has all the answers. But he is so wrapped up in his work that he rarely sees people. Because he doesn't deal with people very often, he is shy and lacks confidence. Despite his copious product knowledge, he would not make a good salesperson because he lacks confidence.

You may have knowledgeable employees like this who need to build their confidence to be successful. Consider enrolling them in a course, such as Toastmasters, where they can conquer their fears and gain experience in speaking to people.

### 'I Am Sold Myself'

Enthusiasm is the frosting on the cake. Enthusiastic employees stand head and shoulders above the ones who are just doing their job. Remember the last four letters of enthusiasm stand for 'I am sold myself.'

When you think of all the possibilities your job offers and ways to expand your business, you become sold yourself. A sense of excitement about your work makes it easier and more fun – and it attracts others and makes their lives more exciting, too. This kind of energy leads to accomplishment and a sense of pride.

We need good employees. We need to attract them, motivate them, and keep them. Most of all, we must help them be powerful, confident, and enthusiastic. The way to start is by being powerful, confident, and enthusiastic yourself.

Give employees the necessary product knowledge. Express confidence in their abilities and potential. Communicate your own contagious enthusiasm.

Don't be one of those employers who complains there aren't good employees anymore. This attitude perpetuates the negative situation it describes – and it's just an excuse for not empowering the people who work with you.

Keep Curran's three key ingredients for success in mind – both for yourself and your employees. Ask yourself – and ask them – how you can help them improve their product knowledge and communication skills.

*– December 1990*

# How To Be A Better Manager

*Employees don't come fully equipped with all the knowledge they need to do the job. Assess the maturity and skill levels of your employees to determine how to direct them.*

Eighty percent of businesses fail within the first five years – and the major cause is poor management. It could be management of capital, human, or physical resources – but failure occurs because management couldn't move the business through a bottleneck in one of these areas.

While financial and physical management are certainly important, the tightest bottlenecks tend to occur with human resources. Managing employees requires a great deal of time, effort, and leadership.

Too often, growers who own their own businesses do everything themselves until the business gets so big they are forced to hire outsiders. Growers may know how to grow, but not how to train and manage people. Consequently, new employees don't know how to water, how to transplant – they often don't know anything. At some point, many growers complain: "You just can't get good help anymore."

To avoid this scenario, accept the fact that employees don't come fully equipped with all the knowledge they need to do the job the way you want it done. They require training.

Maturity has been defined as people's ability and willingness to take responsibility for directing their own behavior. We have all seen "immature" employees who are willing to work but lack the ability for the job at hand – or those who have the ability but are unwilling to perform the task. Either way, the job doesn't get done.

As a manager, assess the maturity and skill levels of your employees to determine how to direct them. There are four leadership styles you can use: telling, selling, participating, and delegating.

### Telling

Telling is effective for employees of low maturity – the people who are both unwilling and unable to take responsibility for a task. Because they lack competence, they lack confidence – and their unwillingness is often a result of this lack of confidence.

This style gives employees a clear set of specific directions. It is characterized by clearly defined leader/follower roles. The leader tells the follower exactly what the job entails, and when, where, and how to do it.

This is the only style many growers ever use. It has its place, but it prevents employees from developing and assuming responsibility.

### Selling

This style works on those with low to moderate levels of maturity, including those who are willing but unable to accept responsibility. It offers a great deal of direction along with supportive behavior to reinforce the employee's willingness to do the job.

This style is designed to get the follower to buy into the desired behavior. Although the leader still provides most of the direction, there is an opportunity for two-way interaction and explanation. At this level of maturity, followers go along with a decision once they understand the rationale behind it.

Selling takes more time than telling, but it results in a greater degree of employee cooperation.

### Participating

Participation is for moderate to high maturity level employees. People at this level are able but unwilling to do what the leader desires. Their unwillingness is often motivated by insecurity, which means that overcoming their reluctance is not so much a motivational, as a security challenge.

Here, the leader must open two-way communication to support the followers' efforts to use their abilities. A highly supportive, nondirective style is most likely to succeed. In this style, decision-making is shared between leader and follower, with the leader acting as a supportive facilitator.

### Delegating

This style is for employees with a high level of maturity, both willing and able to take responsibility. Delegating provides little in the way of direction and support, but recognizes capabilities and encourages individuals to use them.

While the leader may still be involved in problem identification, the responsibility for problem-solving and carrying out plans is left to the follower. The mature follower is permitted to run the show.

### Assessing Your Employees

The key to using the above information effectively is to correctly assess the maturity level of your employees so you can use the appropriate management style. The goal is to help employees grow to their highest possible level of maturity. Nurturing such growth requires continual reassessment of maturity levels so you can adjust your management style to increase employees' levels of participation and responsibility as they grow.

Of course, maturity can also skip backwards. As employees take on new tasks, their maturity level may slip until they have the competence and confidence to handle the new assignment. Managers must be ready to adjust their management style to provide appropriate levels of initiation, structure, and consideration. The important thing is that the maturity level of the employee is matched with the appropriate management style.

Having good help is a direct reflection of the quality of company management; poor help is a direct indictment of management. Since labor is the largest single expense of business, even a bottom-line-oriented view of success will point to the importance of acquiring the leadership skills to get the most out of your employees.

Remember: The bottleneck is usually at the top. If the leadership is effective in identifying the maturity level of employees and implementing the appropriate management style, work is fun, things get done, people are happy. If the leadership cannot identify the maturity level of employees and adopt the appropriate management style – work is long and hard, employees come and go, and good help will be hard to find.

*– January 1992*

# Employees: Your Greatest Asset

*Employee training is a business investment, not just an expense. Help your employees maximize their potential and they will grow in value.*

I saw a cartoon recently showing a California earthquake victim commenting, "I'm sure glad I'm not in the Midwest where it's 50°F below zero!" and a freezing Midwesterner saying. "I'm sure glad I'm not in the earthquakes of California!"

Needless to say, these past few years have been eventful for Mother Nature – hurricanes in Florida, phenomenal flooding in the Midwest, record-breaking low temperatures in the eastern half of the United States, and earthquakes in California. I'll bet no greenhouse operator planned for any of this – not to mention the array of smaller-scale disasters that appear every year. How can we deal with these events?

Most of us just pray such things won't happen to us. It still makes sense, however, to take steps to protect ourselves in case they do happen.

### The Power Of Good Employees

How do we survive such crises? It helps to have good employees. Let me give you some personal examples. In mid-January, the East Lansing, MI, area, where Michigan State University (MSU) is located, experienced five days of temperatures below 0°F. I was concerned about the 100,000-square feet of research greenhouses at MSU. During those five days, the steam pressure from MSU's power plant dropped to half its normal strength, and it was rumored the people running the power plant would go out on strike. I talked with Dave Freville, the person in charge of the day-to-day operations at the greenhouses, about what could happen and how we could cope. As a result, we acquired a back-up kerosene heater, developed a plan to move the research plant material if necessary, and determined how long the plants could survive under such conditions.

Dave was the one who handled the situation as it played itself out. For four nights, he lived at the greenhouses while checking temperatures and moving heaters. He kept the plants alive even while the temperature outside reached -22°F with a wind chill of -50°F. Thanks to his dedication and loyalty, 50 scientists still have their research plant material. I can't tell you how proud I am of Dave's efforts.

Some managers say you can't hire people like that anymore. If there's any truth to that, it's because hiring is only half the picture. Training is the other half. I had confidence that my greenhouse manager had things under control. I'm sure many of you have experienced the same sort of situation.

Isn't it great to have responsible people working with you?

Most of us in the horticulture business, however, don't put enough effort into training our greatest assets – employees. When we hire people, we may check their technical skills and train them to perform the basic tasks of growing plants, but we don't train them in other vital skills such as working well with other people, creative problem-solving, and gaining a business perspective to see that company growth is just as important as making sure plants grow.

How can we help our employees to develop skills like these? Send them to a grower meeting every year to hear a few one-hour seminars. These kinds of experiences broaden their industry horizons and give them valuable information to use in your operation.

### Make The Investment

I view employee training as an investment in business development, not as an expense. Here are some examples of training that certain folks at MSU chose to undertake last year:

• A secretary/data manager took a community college course in Fox-Pro software to improve her computer skills.

• A creative services coordinator took a weekend seminar on a new computer illustration and design program.

• An information specialist took a class on how to handle a difficult boss (me) so she could run the office despite my interference.

• A full-time conference manager takes one week a year to work on her MBA at Notre Dame University.

• A greenhouse manager annually attends the major industry meetings and trade shows.

The point is you must continue to develop each employee or you may lose an important asset.

### Maximize Management Skills

Samuel Certo in *Modern Management* suggests tips to enhance management skills. One is to train your own replacement so you can perform jobs besides basic growing functions as soon as possible. In this way, you can free yourself to learn different skills.

Rare is the greenhouse manager who follows this advice, however. How many of us have heard a manager say, "I'm the only one who can water the crop." It may, in fact, be true that the manager is the best grower at that operation – but that doesn't make him or her a good manager.

Effective managers must overcome their fear of change and dare to step out of the security of being the best grower at an operation. They must learn to be a grower of future success – for their business' and employees' sake.

Here are four points that can help you maximize employees' potential:

**1. Have yearly goals for each employee.** The most important part of being a manager is to help each key employee formulate goals so you both agree on what should be accomplished in the next year. While there's nothing more discouraging to employees than not knowing what a boss expects, there's nothing more encouraging for them than knowing that boss shares their vision of purpose and progress.

**2. Prioritize your list of company goals.** You could have five or six goals on your list – but two or three may have to be accomplished for your company to survive. My employees appreciate a list of priorities so they know what I think is most important.

**3. Develop an action plan for each goal.** Have each employee list the step-by-step procedure for accomplishing a goal, including what must be done, who will do it, and when it will be done. Managers must check to see that each small step is finished on time. The old saying,"Inch by inch, everything's a cinch," is plainly true.

**4. Evaluate employees annually – appreciate them daily.** It's important each year to discuss frankly with employees how they're doing. Encourage them along the way by appreciating the daily jobs done well, so they know you're aware of their efforts.

Spend as much time on your employees as you do on your company. Remember, they represent the largest portion of your production costs – 25% to 30%. Treat them as the assets they are, and they'll grow in value.

*– March 1994*

# Help Wanted

### Take these tips to finding and keeping good help.

Times have certainly changed. In the old days, labor was relatively cheap and there was plenty available. If an employee didn't work out, he or she could be replaced easily. Today, many greenhouse operators say one of their biggest problems is finding, managing, and maintaining labor. The reason, of course, is that times have changed.

### Sign Of The Times

In the last 10 years, the national unemployment rate has dropped from around 10% to 4.1%. Also, the cost of labor has increased, making minimum wage no longer the norm.

High school students are working part time for fast food operations for $6.50 to $7.50 per hour. High wages for easy jobs make it tough to compete. For growers, it's almost impossible to offer minimum wage. In many cases, there are no people available who can or will do the job.

Last month, I was in Benton Harbor, MI, having lunch when four people from a local factory entered the restaurant. They sat in the booth next to me and talked shop.

One of them said the labor situation was getting a little better. Another asked him to explain. He said, "At least we can keep all the production lines open."

Apparently, he had 40 production jobs open last summer and had to reduce output. Today, he has 11 jobs available, but all the production lines are open. The jobs pay $10 to $12 an hour.

All you need to do is drive down any main street to get a sense of today's job market. You'll see the signs – now hiring, help wanted, full- or part-time jobs available – posted everywhere.

### Tis The Season-al

Floriculture is in a difficult predicament. More than half our employees are part time. In many areas, it is difficult, if not impossible, to find a U.S. labor source. Our industry is depending more on migrant labor to satisfy labor needs.

Finding and maintaining migrant workers is no easy task. I know of one floriculture operation that needs more than 300 seasonal employees. Rounding up this force is a full-time job. The business is even working with the government to develop programs that provide transportation to and from the workers' homes outside the country each season; housing while they work; transportation to and from work; and hourly wages.

### A Few Good Growers

Floriculture has high-value crops, perhaps the highest value agriculture crop per acre that can be grown in the United States. If you lose one acre of vegetables, it would cost $2,000 to $3,000. One acre of fruit may be a loss of $5,000 to $8,000. If you lose one acre of greenhouse flower crops, it could cost $300,000 or more.

We must have well-trained full- and part-time employees to avoid catastrophic losses. The shortage of well-trained, full-time employees is critical. The number of calls I receive from greenhouse owners who say, "I need a grower" continues to increase. I've estimated that our industry has a shortage of about 300 assistant growers in the United States.

Michigan State University's remedy is the Floriculture College of Knowledge. This is a course for people who are already in our industry. Many run small family operations or they are reliable workers for larger greenhouses, and they have not had formal training in production procedures.

The college has 12 courses and each four-hour class costs about $150. Students receive the class materials, read them, and discuss them with other people in their businesses. Once they feel comfortable with the materials, they take an exam. When they pass it, they get certificates of completion for the course.

Once they complete the 12 courses, they will receive their certification as assistant growers. Presently, they will be certified by the Western Michigan Greenhouse Association and the Detroit Metropolitan Flower Growers. The first four courses are now being taught; the next four will start in November; and the final four in November of 2001. Approximately 90 people have enrolled in the program. One section of each course is taught in Spanish, and more than 20 people are enrolled in that section.

### Mixing People With Plants

When I was working on this article, I had an opportunity to discuss labor issues with Fran Johnson from the marketing department of The John Henry Co. Fran also was chairperson of Bedding Plants Inc.'s (BPI) marketing committee and helped develop BPI's point-of-sales leaflets.

She has a unique perspective on this subject because she has managed people and also has seen many managers and vice presidents come and go. She has observed many different styles of management – the good and the bad.

Fran listed 15 points that greenhouse operators should consider to be successful in dealing with their employees and maintaining them:

**1. Plants are predictable, people are not.** If you grow 100 plants and treat them all the same, they will all perform similarly. If you have 100 employees and treat them all the same, they will not all perform similarly, You have to get to know how to treat each one for the best results.

**2. Plants produce profit if people function effectively.** A good-looking greenhouse and quality plants are directly related to how well your employees are performing.

**3. The key to getting employees to function effectively is communication.** You must constantly tell people what they need to know to do their jobs effectively and efficiently.

**4. If your employees were mind-readers, they would all be wealthy.** Because they are not mind-readers, and, if they and you want to be wealthy, you must communicate.

**5. They need to understand what's expected of them and how they fit into the total scheme.** You must show them that they are important to your business's health.

**6. People respond to words and attitudes that show them respect.** If people feel good about themselves, they will perform better than if they think they are of no value.

**7. Give them responsibility and provide involvement.** Reward them for a job well done, not just with money, but personal recognition.

**8. Good communication is a two-way street.** An employee and an employer must communicate, but each also must listen to the other.

**9. Managers owe employees clear direction.** Give employees clear goals, clear methods to accomplish those goals, and discuss the chosen systems and schedules.

**10. Employees need encouragement in understanding their roles.** They need to know their own personal responsibility and their importance to the organization.

**11. Never assume that people, managers, or employees understand.** That is why communication is so vital. The statement, "I thought you took care of that," is an indictment for poor management.

**12. Help people feel good about themselves.** Compliments go a long way, but give them fairly.

**13. Employees who want or expect the most rewards need to seek ways to contribute the most.** The people who are of greatest value to the company should be the most rewarded.

**14. Plants thrive on tender loving care, or "TLC." So do employees.** Treat your employees as well or even better than you treat your plants.

**15. Remember communication flows not only through talk but by listening.** Greenhouse owners must be good listeners when employees offer suggestions. They usually have reasons for doing so. Many times they can make companies stronger.

The bottom line is that we know people are creative. Instead of trying to mold them into our ideal employees, we must isolate their talents and help them achieve their professional goals. In turn, this will help your company profit greatly.

*– February 2000*

# 'If It Is To Be, It Is Up To Me'

*To be profitable, a company must be able to plan, organize, influence, and control its assets – both money and people.*

Making changes to a business, like expanding facilities, hiring new employees, or growing new crops, can add stress to the job. We are currently experiencing some of these changes at Michigan State University (MSU). We are searching for a new dean of the College of Agriculture and Natural Resources, a new extension director, and a new horticulture department chairperson. While the administration has asked faculty members to temporarily serve in these positions, it will take 12 to 18 months to find full-time replacements. In the meantime, the daily and yearly work must go on. There are experiments to run, students to teach, and extension activities to complete.

At some point, everyone who works knows that, if a job needs to be done and you are the one responsible for it, only you can make it happen. In any profitable business, many capable people do their jobs and accept their responsibilities to help contribute to the company's success. They know, "If it is to be, it is up to me."

### Accepting Responsibility

Each person is responsible for his or her own destiny. Whether or not you survive in a business will depend on how you handle your responsibility and authority. Foremost, you must be good at what you do. You must have the knowledge, skills, attitudes, and actions that distinguish excellent performers.

It is fun to work with a group of people who know what they want to do, can work together, and get the goals accomplished. Each person may have a part of the responsibility and authority to make it happen, but each realizes, "If it is to be, it is up to me."

My greatest lesson to prove we must take responsibility for what we do in life came from my mother, who lived to be 94 years old. When she was about 80, her doctor told her how to take care of herself and prescribed some medicine for her. She disagreed with him and said, "I'm not going to take these pills!" The doctor said, "You're going to die if you don't take them." She looked him in the eye and said, "Don't worry, I've already buried five doctors." She knew, "If it is to be, it is up to me."

To be a profitable business, a company must have proper planning, organizing, influence, and control of its assets – both money and people. While most businesses think primarily of money, developing people is an important part of success.

### Invest In People

At the 2000 Seeley Conference, a speaker from the cranberry industry said if you can increase the educational grade level of your employees by one grade, you can increase profitability by 8% in comparison with increasing automation, which averages a 1% increase. He indicated educating your workforce is the most productive factor in increasing your profitability.

Let me give you an example. I manage nine staff members at the university. Each year I allocate between $1,000 and $2,000 to each for professional improvement. I send them to conferences, short courses, or tours at other production facilities or universities. I also have given them time to take courses for advanced degrees. Once I've shown them I'm interested in their future, they become very interested in our project's future. They also become much more interested in their responsibilities and feel more comfortable with their authority.

Once a year I do a planning session with each employee. The university's human resources department encourages us to have a written summary of each employee's responsibilities and priorities. We then compare the employee's responsibility with his or her accomplishments. Most employees take great pride in their work. I try to act as their coach, counselor, and evaluator and identify areas needing added support for their development opportunities. My job is to help them succeed. Here are some of the areas we discuss with each employee:

1. Employee's performance in primary responsibilities and priorities during the last year. We look at the written areas of responsibility and the time the employee spends on each.

2. Employee's strengths and/or areas for growth.

3. The barriers to effective work performance and job satisfaction.

4. Work process improvement needs.

5. Employee development over the past year, future needs for the job, and long-term career goals.

6. Whether the employee continues to grow to meet the employer's needs.

7. Employee's feedback/constructive suggestions for the supervisor.

8. Anything else the employee or supervisor would like to address.

9. Each person writes any extra comments.

10. Determine whether the employee meets or exceeds current expectations.

11. Both the employee and the supervisor signs the document.

We spend about an hour together, and then fill out the paper work. After we sign the report, we both feel we've had the opportunity to talk and listen to each other. We know what the employee's responsibilities and authorities are, and that the employee will be evaluated on these tasks next year.

This is one of the best tools I've seen to make sure the employee accepts and realizes ownership in his or her responsibility and authority. The employee then becomes one of the building blocks of your company and knows, "If it is to be, it is up to me."

In the three major areas I manage in the department of horticulture at MSU with a total budget of $1 million, I evaluate nine employees this way. In turn, they manage 30 part-time employees. Once these nine people know their responsibilities and authority, they control their part of the program. Then my job becomes merely monitoring the overall planning, organizing, influencing, and controlling of the three areas. Monthly meetings with each group and the use of action plans provide the framework to make the plan happen. This way we all know, "If it is to be, it is up to me."

### Carpe Diem

One of the major concerns within our industry is labor, and there is a severe shortage of growers, assistant growers, and knowledgeable people to fill jobs. Because of this it is critical that you develop a system within your company to keep, evaluate, train, and motivate the people you have. It is less expensive to provide training and education to the employees you already have than to attempt to hire new employees and have a large turnover of personnel.

Within our industry, technology helps get the job done, but it takes people to make it work. I hope you can develop your company so every employee will say and feel, "If it is to be, it is up to me."

*– January 2001*

## Let's Grow People

*If you can't grow people, you probably won't grow plants for long. Follow these five steps for hiring, training, and keeping good employees.*

From using better plant genetics to installing the latest automated equipment, our ability to produce successful crops has greatly improved over the last 50 years. These developments have helped us create "factories" that produce plants at a 90% to 95% success rate, from seed to sale.

While we should pat ourselves on the back for these accomplishments, we should also ask ourselves, "What have we done to help grow the people who run these factories?"

I believe we take better care of our plants than our people. For instance, let's equate a new employee to a seed. Have we identified the four stages of initial growth of that person's career in our business? For a seed, it's simple. We know we have to germinate it, give it moisture and proper temperature, and check it regularly to ensure it's progressing properly. Essentially, we are giving the seed tender, loving care. Do we treat a new employee the same way? Do we keep them under close supervision and show them step-by-step what needs to be done and how to do it?

### Steps In The Right Direction

I recommend the following five steps for hiring, training, and keeping good employees:

**1. Recruitment.** Effective recruiting begins with a written job description. Most small businesses never write a job description; they just expect the new employee to do everything.

Advertise the position in local newspapers and trade magazines, or contact a placement firm that specializes in our industry. Solicit as many applicants as possible. Whether a family or nonfamily member, choose the most qualified person for the job. It will take you more time and effort to train the weakest candidates to be the best employees than to pick the best and train them to a greater skill level.

Also, comments like "I can't afford to hire good help" are a surefire way to disaster. The old saying, "you get what you pay for," is certainly true. Large companies and universities realize the importance of attracting the best people. This takes time and money, but if this investment is made properly, you will have 80% of your problem solved.

**2. Orientation and basic training.** Even if you lure the best candidates you will still need them to become familiar with your business. Many companies provide a manual, video, Web site, or CD that highlights the organization's history and gives basic facts. Just because you may have been with the company for 20 or 30 years doesn't mean new people will have the same experience and knowledge. Don't assume that the new employee knows everything.

Remember the analogy to a seed. You must spend the most time and effort in nurturing new employees early in the growing process. Make sure they have all the information they need to do their job. Encourage them to work well and compliment them when they successfully complete a task.

**3. Guidance.** After new employees have finished training, you will need to guide them into the area where they are most needed. This is when they start to contribute to your company. Perhaps they have computer skills your company needs or they learned new strategies to produce pest-free crops. This is the fun part of hiring new employees: finding out their talents or skills and influencing them to use those skills.

**4. Professional development.** In our business, we can never stop learning. There has been more information made available about our business in the last year than there was in the previous 10 years. Just look at the number of new varieties introduced in this last year. One of my friends told me there were 174 new varieties introduced at the California pack trials this year. Most growers can't name all the new varieties let alone know the cultural requirements to produce them.

In the old days, we grew eight or 10 species of bedding plants, which represented 80% to 90% of our business. Almost all of the product was grown in flats. Today, only 38% of all bedding plants are produced in flats, and the number of species and cultivars are mind-boggling.

In the past, it was fairly simple to develop 10 to 15 action plans on how to grow the major crops. Today, 50 to 100 plans are needed and, in some cases, there may be more than 250 different items that have to be produced. While computers help keep track of the information, the growers with experience and a "personal" computer (i.e., the computer between their ears) is the most critical part of the entire greenhouse operation.

Likewise, sales managers must also not only understand the products but use their skills to sell the product to the wholesale and retail customers. Remember, it takes as much time to properly sell a product as it does to produce it. Good salespeople aren't just naturals. They need the training and development to make them an effective part of your team. They must know their products and customers, how to negotiate, and be able to deliver what they promised. It takes time to develop quality people. We have to realize that just like plants, people go through different phases in their careers: the germination stage, the growth stage, the maturation stage, and the end stage.

**5. Replacement.** For a business to survive, there must be people in the organization who can replace those who will retire. This is a major problem in small businesses. Owners either feel they can't be replaced or don't want to be replaced. This is why it is difficult to take a business to the next generation and, even more difficult, to take it to the third generation. Of the tens of thousands of floriculture businesses started in the United States in the last 100 years, fewer than 100 have made it to the third generation.

It takes as much planning to leave a job as it does to start a job. The best retirements and job replacements occur after one to two years of planning. If you want to be the least disruptive to your operation, you will need to make certain that your replacement is ready and able to fulfill all of your responsibilities.

### Making People A Priority

Within the last month, I've worked with interns who are just starting to work within our industry. I've helped develop training systems for new employees and worked with companies on how to influence new employees to help them develop their potential. I have also worked with a company on replacing a top manager.

All of those experiences reaffirm that it takes as much or more time and effort to grow people than it does to grow plants. It also proves that if you can't grow people, you probably won't grow plants for long.

*— September 2001*

# Growers Never Stop Learning

## Ten ways people have gained the knowledge needed to pursue careers in floriculture.

When I started my training 45 years ago, floriculture was a fairly simple field of study. But in today's competitive market, keeping qualified employees satisfied is one of the most challenging aspects of our industry. With constant adoption of new technology in the floriculture industry, the process of producing commercial crops continues to grow more complex. That's why it's important to find and keep educated, skilled workers who have a good work ethic, the motivation to continually seek new knowledge, and the ability to get along with your company's staff and management.

### Floriculture's Levels Of Learning

Throughout our industry's history, there are at least 10 ways in which people have pursued careers in floriculture. Let's look at each of these methods, indicating the level of knowledge obtained, time involved, and cost to both the knowledge-seeker and the employer.

**1. Self-taught.** Often, amateur entrepreneurs start from scratch, build a small greenhouse, and try to produce their first crops alone. This is the most difficult method and takes the longest time to learn the basic knowledge. In many cases, such a novice will kill the plant before he or she learns how to properly grow it. Such lessons are hard to learn but growers never forget them. Many of these folks fail in business but can make very good employees with the proper supervision.

Many others have chosen floriculture as their second career, coming from such fields as engineering, business, education, the military, and more. Basic college or military training has proved to be an excellent base for learning the technical information needed in floriculture, allowing them to do well in our industry.

**2. Greenhouse Laborer.** Some people pursuing a career in floriculture will work for someone else, see how it is done, and try to work their way up to more responsible jobs. This type of work pays a lower wage and it may take many years until one advances to an assistant grower position. Although an advantage is earning money while learning, this is a slow and costly way to learn.

**3. Grower Apprenticeship.** One excellent example of this type of education is the European system, in which a student works directly for a grower who teaches the student all the necessary steps in crop production. In return, the student performs much of the manual labor. Students can learn a lot from growers willing to share all their experience but apprentice wages are usually low and sometimes the learning curve is steep and slow.

**4. Vocational Agricultural High School.** In the 1970s and '80s, these programs were thought to be the answer for training workers in the basic skills needed as a laborer in a greenhouse. As greenhouses became more sophisticated and more mechanized, many programs did not have the proper facilities. But the schools provided a basic level of knowledge while being a resource for introducing our industry to potential employees.

**5. Continuing Education.** Examples of continuing education include extension programs, short courses, and seminars. These events serve as a way to introduce new and potential employees to our industry, providing both technical information and product knowledge at a relatively inexpensive cost. They are also great industry networking opportunities.

**6. Correspondence Courses.** In the 1930s and '40s, some growers provided independent tutorial courses. Written materials and tests were completed by the student and graded by the grower-instructor. The cost was reasonable and students could continue working while learning the necessary information. These courses provided contacts to industry personnel and updated information yearly. In the early stages of our industry, correspondence courses were one of the only ways to obtain basic information on a formal basis.

**7. Certification Programs.** In 1998, Michigan State University developed a 12-course program called the Floriculture College of Knowledge. Available in both English and Spanish, each course has a student notebook and textbook on the subject discussed. Students take four-hour courses from professional floriculture instructors and then return home to read the materials and discuss them with others from their class and in their places of employment. Michigan's Metropolitan Detroit Flower Growers and the Western Michigan Greenhouse

Association certify the completion of all 12 courses and issue the Greenhouse Grower Certificate. All 12 courses cost about $2,400 and can be completed in six contact days.

**8. Associate Programs.** Several U.S. universities offer two-year technical floriculture courses. Programs take one year to 18 months on campus and six months to one year in a work experience off campus. These courses offer basic technical information, along with practical greenhouse experience. The program can cost from $10,000 to $15,000 and take two years of study to complete. Once completed, the student usually finds employment as an assistant grower.

**9. Internships.** At some universities, two- and four-year students are required to have a working experience for college credit at a greenhouse in the United States or in a foreign country. Several countries have developed exchange programs. The experiences last three months to two years and many employers provide housing and a stipend to cover expenses.

**10. Professional Degrees.** There is no substitute for a college degree. Providing a well-rounded, general education in the first two years, students spend the next two years studying a specific subject in depth. College is expensive. It usually takes at least four years to receive a bachelor's degree, typically costing a student $40,000 to $60,000. However, college is a great investment in one's future and usually accelerates earning potential, allowing college loan repayment within five to 10 years.

In addition, college graduates advance faster than self-trained individuals. Starting salaries for holders of B.S. degrees are $30,000 to $40,000. A master's degree takes about two years to complete and provides advanced courses to specialize in an area. It can cost $40,000 to $60,000 but starting salaries range from $35,000 to $50,000. A Ph.D. usually takes another three years and $60,000 to $80,000 to accomplish. Candidates learn to conduct in-depth research, as well as how to identify and solve complex problems. Ph.D. holders start in the $60,000 to $70,000 salary range.

*Fuel For The Fire*

Any company that wants to remain competitive in our industry must provide regular and ongoing training programs, not only within the company but by taking advantage of the many industry meetings, short courses, and topic seminars. Employers keep good people by giving them a sense of achievement. Employees need recognition, meaningful work, responsibility, advancement, and growth opportunities. If you provide this environment, you will keep your employees. But, if you provide poor supervision, poor company policies, or inadequate working conditions, salaries, wages, or benefits, your workers will look elsewhere.

It is important to produce the right environment so your human resources can be utilized to their full potential. People who are happy want to do well and will usually help make the company profitable. It is simple to say, "Hire the right people, train them properly, evaluate them fairly, and reward them for their performance." It is much harder to do. Remember, it takes much longer to grow a quality employee than it does a quality plant.

*– September 2002*

# CONNECTING WITH CUSTOMERS

It's time to change our focus. The industry is often manufacturing oriented: the focus is on production. We are basically order takers with our profits tied to production efficiency. Some growers have progressed to a sales orientation. They are still interested in production, but they realize that they have to sell the product to make money.

A marketing orientation goes beyond sales, focusing on the customer. Production is geared to satisfying the customer's wants, and profits are tied to customer satisfaction. Everyone involved in marketing bedding plants is constantly looking for ideas to increase sales. What will the customers want this year? What is a new idea that will catch their eyes? What size plant do they want? How much are they willing to pay?

When we focus on customer satisfaction, we not only build sales this year, but encourage customers to come back again next year, to expand their gardens and to inspire their friends to start gardening, too. When we tie our profits to customer satisfaction instead of manufacturing efficiency and sales volume, it promotes the health of our whole industry.

Most growers I know are very good at taking care of details. They know every aspect of how to produce a specific crop. These growers consider themselves shepherds of their crops and often refer to particular crops as if they were part of their families. But while most growers have great technical skills, many do not know how to educate customers.

Connecting with customers is an important part of every operation's plan for success. Following are some of the columns I have written that provide ideas for how you can make these connections.

# Finding A Market

*Before you plant one plant, know your market!*
*Determine what is selling, why it is selling, and how*
*much more can be sold.*

Many bedding plant growers think finding a market is the last step in a bedding plant operation, but nothing is further from the truth. Finding a market should be the first step in a successful operation. Industrial manufacturers would go bankrupt if they did not first determine how much material and what specific type they need to produce to meet market demand.

Could you imagine a company like General Motors or Ford merely producing one car after another at full capacity with just the hope that they would sell? It is a sure-fire formula for bankruptcy – in automobiles or in bedding plants. Before you plant one plant, know your market.

### Why People Buy

A 1968 study by Ernest Dichter indicated people buy bedding plants for three reasons: creativity, excitement, and therapy. With the rise in food prices, perhaps necessity could be added as a fourth factor for producing vegetable transplants. When we attempt to promote or sell our products, we must establish a need for our product. The need can be established by appealing to one of these four reasons why people buy our product.

With the tremendous increase in gardening and the avid ecological movement, our product has enjoyed a steady and ever-increasing rate of growth. But remember, consumers must be successful in growing our product if this growth rate is to continue.

### Your Place In The Picture

Everyone in business must have an objective. It can be stated in solely economic terms, such as "I want a 10% return on my investment." Or it could be solely in noneconomic terms like "My family and I like this way of life!" In most cases, however, it is somewhere in between – being both profitable and enjoyable.

It is important, however, to list your objectives so you will have some way of measuring your degree of success. Merely having more money in the bank this year than last year doesn't indicate a great deal about what's happening to your business. And if you have less money in the bank, it will be difficult to determine why if you have no records.

### Market Feedback

To service a given area, it is necessary to determine what your customers want and need. To be successful in retailing, one must determine what is selling, why it is selling, and how much more can be sold. This can be done by formal surveys or just informally talking to retailers and customers.

Surveys have been conducted to determine consumer purchasing patterns. For example, one 1969 survey in Michigan showed 78% of the families interviewed bought bedding plants within the last year. Generally, the wife or female head of the household made the actual purchase.

An independent garden center was most often mentioned as the retail outlet where plants were purchased. Expenditures for bedding plants increased as the average income of the family increased. Homemakers 30 to 44 years old were the biggest buyers of bedding plants.

Responses given for not buying plants included: 1) not interested in gardening; 2) preferred to grow them from seed; 3) unfamiliar with growing them; and 4) they were too expensive.

This is what we call market feedback. To increase sales, we must solve these problems. As individual producers, you must survey your area, determine the strengths and weaknesses of your market area, and plan accordingly.

### Trends Evident

From my discussions with many growers, some trends become evident. First, petunias are accounting for a smaller percentage of total sales than a few years ago. Their decrease represents perhaps as much as 10% in the last five years. Second, begonias and impatiens are increasing in popularity. This is due to new varieties and great acceptance by consumers. Third, vegetables are showing a tremendous increase in popularity. They now account for 12% to 15% of the total bedding plant market.

It might be a good idea to get out your old records, if you haven't already done so, and see if you can observe trends that will lead to your goal of selling every flat you produce this year. Remember, planning on paper is cheaper than planting large quantities of flats that will not sell.

### Finding Your Niche

Not every grower can grow all things for all people. Not every grower can meet his competition head-on in all respects. What you can do is find a niche. Become a specialist in one area where you can earn a good return on your investment and an adequate net profit on your merchandise.

Perhaps you can grow hanging baskets better than the competition, or you might grow different varieties in different containers than the competition will grow. Some producers have made a profitable venture out of growing potted annuals – three- or four-inch material for late spring or early summer sales.

But do what you do well! If you're a small retail grower, it would be very unprofitable to attempt to compete with large mass producers on the same item they produce. By observing what is needed in the market place and filling this void (finding your niche), there are many profitable areas to be filled.

### Salesmanship

You have to sell confidence in yourself first. People deal with people they can trust and who deliver what they promise. If you can grow a quality product and provide the service that is needed at a competitive price, you will have no problem selling. You have to respect your profession, your company, and yourself, and base your expectations of sales on a solid foundation of service rendered.

If you ask people why they buy where they do, it boils down to price, location, variety of selection, quality, service, and sales personnel. Even if you have all these items, you have to communicate this to your potential customer. If you're a good grower, you need to tell other people how good you are. The whole "thing" of merchandising is built around how to communicate your story so someone to whom you want to sell will eventually buy what you sell.

Remember, 1% of learning comes by way of our sense of taste, 1.5% through our sense of touch, 3.5% through our sense of smell, 11% through our sense of hearing, and 83% of our learning comes through our sense of sight. The sense of sight is almost eight times as powerful as the sense of hearing. Therefore, you not only have to tell people you are a good grower, but it is eight times more effective to show them you are a good grower. Showing your potential customer the plants you want to sell will work much more effectively than just talking about them. Quality is remembered long after the price is forgotten.

Once you've established this market information and have developed a plan on how you are going to sell your product, you need to develop the following market description:

    A. Market analysis

        1) Where is your market?

        2) Number of accounts?

        3) How will they be serviced?

        4) When can you start delivery?

        5) List specific accounts?

    B. Sales forecast for next five years

    C. Type of market you're after

Once you have answered these questions, you may proceed to grow the plants you need to fill this market demand.

*— June 1975*

# Know Your Customers – And Increase Sales

*See your business as your customers see it. Tune in to what your customers want in plant material and service.*

Ah! If we could only see ourselves as others see us, not just in our personal life, but in our business also. Too often we may not take the time to understand what our customers want in the way of plant material and service.

This fact was again brought home to me in two recent studies conducted at Michigan State University. The first study was conducted by Janet Spence, my graduate student, during her Master's thesis. Some 2,000 Michigan consumers were asked to evaluate five different chrysanthemum types, noting which type they liked best and which ones they would buy. Janet also asked a group of commercial growers and retailers which types they perceived the consumer wanted.

While consumers liked Incurved mums best, retailers and growers thought they liked them least. This is quite a gap between consumers' wants and growers' and retailers' ideas of what they want.

In the industry today, you hear retailers and growers saying the customer has been "mummed" to death. They are tired of the same old mums. But in Janet Spence's study, only one out of two consumers recognized all five plant types to be chrysanthemums. Therefore, because growers and retailers don't really have an understanding of consumers, they are missing sales, losing dollars, and overproducing certain types of mums.

In the bedding plant industry, we also need to be in tune with our consumers. We hope that we are not as far off consumer demand as the chrysanthemum industry seems to be. Because our sales have been increasing steadily each year, it seems we are on the right track.

This past season, Dr. Roy Mecklenburg's class at MSU surveyed 12 garden centers in Michigan and Ohio and interviewed 100 customers at each garden center. One of the questions asked was "What did you plan to buy when you came to the garden center today?" Of those interviewed, 48% said: "just plants," 40% named a specific type of plant, such as petunias, while 12% mentioned a particular variety such as 'Comanche.'

This seems to confirm that about nine out of 10 sales are impulse type sales. The petunias that look the best or the plant species that is in the best condition will be the first one sold. Thus, it is important to keep the display area in tip-top shape at all times – not to do this would mean lost sales.

### Questions Offer Insight

Another question asked these garden center customers was, "What do you consider the most important reason you shop here?" For garden center operators, this should offer a great deal of insight into what the customer wants: a variety of merchandise to choose from. The old peddler always said, "You can't sell from an empty wagon." Neither can you sell from a poorly stocked garden center.

Customers are looking for knowledgeable salespeople and their presence will increase sales. The customers also want plant care information, prices that are in line with the value of the product, and a good display of merchandise.

First-time customers were asked if there was enough information available on choosing and caring for their plants – 60% said yes, while 40% would have liked more. When repeat customers were asked this same question, 70% said there was enough information, while 30% requested more.

The customers were asked where they got the information they needed to care for the plants they purchased. Labels are perceived by consumers to be the best source of information. It is interesting to note that between 80% and 85% of all bedding plants in the United States are labeled. This has been done because it is good business; the progressive grower and retailer realizes this. And the government didn't force us to do it!

We like our customers; they like us. In fact, they come back every year and buy more because we have helped them be successful. They even bring back their friends.

*– April 1976*

# Ideas For Retailing Bedding Plants

## How do customers choose a garden center?

Recently, a survey was conducted at 12 retail garden centers in Michigan and Ohio by students taking a Horticulture Merchandising class at Michigan State University. More than 1,200 consumers were questioned in this survey.

There were five main reasons why a consumer shopped at a specific garden center.

**1. Variety of merchandise.** According to the survey, most consumers rated variety of merchandise as the main reason they shopped at their favorite garden center. This seems logical as today's consumers want a choice. They like to look at a lot of different plant material before making a decision. The diversity of material is also a big drawing card and you may want to advertise this fact (i.e., "Area's largest and most complete bedding plant selection," or "100s of varieties from which to choose").

**2. Display of merchandise.** Create eye appeal with the material you have to sell. Bedding plants are great items for impulse buying. If they are displayed to attract attention, you have a tremendous sales opportunity.

**3. Price.** Consumers are price conscious and they want a good buy for their money. Bedding plants are one of the best buys in our society. What else can you purchase to get so much beauty, life, creativity, and therapy at such a bargain!

**4. Plant care information.** The typical consumer wants to keep their plants in a healthy condition. They want and appreciate proper care information and it is a good business practice to supply it. Customers who are successful with our product will buy again. If they are not, they will probably spend their money on something else.

**5. Good sales help.** Customers go where sales help is courteous, friendly, and knowledgeable. These qualities are very important in any business. Nothing can turn off a sale like a sales clerk who doesn't care about the product or the customer.

Another question asked in this survey was, "What is your primary source of information on growing the plants you purchase?" Of the people surveyed, 45% indicated the label in the pot or flat was their source of information, followed by sales help (28%), garden books (27%), handouts (10%), and other sources of information (6%). (This adds up to more than 100% since some indicated more than one source.)

But the point I want to make is that the label in the flat, pack, pot, or basket is the most used source of information. Make certain all the plants you grow or sell are labeled with the plant name and care instructions. We don't need the F.T.C. (Federal Trade Commission) to force us to do this. It is good business and to our own marketing advantage to label.

A third question asked was, "When you entered the garden center, what did you plan to buy?" The responses indicated 48% planned to buy just plants, 40% wanted a certain plant like petunias, but only 12% mentioned a specific variety. Therefore, most people entering the garden center are just looking for plants! It depends on you, your salespeople, merchandise display, variety of merchandise, and price to help that consumer decide what to buy. That's a tremendous challenge for any retailer.

### Making The Sale

Here are some guidelines to help you make those bedding plant sales.

**1. Upon arrival, check to see if plants need water.** When plants do need water, water them thoroughly so the soil is completely moist. Avoid, if possible, splashing water on flowers as this may cause spotting. Watering the flats thoroughly at soil level is best. If flats must be watered overhead or by sprinklers, do it early in the day so that all foliage is dry by nightfall. This will help prevent diseases.

**2. Display in a protected area.** Modern garden centers have protected display areas. It is important that either well-lighted or greenhouse-type structures shield plants from wind and rain. Also, this type of display area accommodates customers shopping on poor weather days. If plant material is displayed outside, it is subject to complete loss at any time, and customers don't like to stand in line to buy in rainstorms.

**3. Place plant material off ground.** It is inconvenient to have people bend over to pick up material. Display at a comfortable height to accommodate ease of selection and never on asphalt parking lots, which absorb the sun's heat and dry plants quickly or where people may drive over them.

**4. Label plants with name, price, and planting exposure clearly visible.** If you or your help don't know the name of the plant or how to care for it, find out!

**5. Build interesting displays.** "How to" or "What to do with it" displays are great. With vegetables, for instance, you might show a great display of tomato fruits with transplants around them. Use your imagination, give people ideas. Show them unusual containers and creative plantings. People love to copy interesting ideas.

**6. Maintain area daily.** Make a daily check for watering needs. Remove yellow leaves and wilted blossoms, and eliminate any plant material you wouldn't personally buy. Remember, it takes good material, well-kept, to create that impulse sale. Poorly maintained material discourages the sale.

**7. Keep only top quality stock.** Keep only fresh, top quality stock, consolidating it often so it doesn't look picked over.

**8. Provide care and planting information.** If plants are labeled and handouts available, you can cut down the time spent on answering questions. You can't afford to spend five, 10, or 20 minutes on one customer on a busy Saturday in May to answer a general question. Yet, you can't ignore that person. Make certain they can get the information they want without taking all your time.

**9. Keep sales area attractive.** When products look good, sales are good. When you finish selling annuals, clean up and remove all remaining material. Dead plants discourage sales.

**10. Success builds success.** If you look successful, act successful, and follow these guidelines, you will find annuals are a blooming, booming item for sales and profit.

*– May 1977*

## Develop New Customers

### Increase sales by looking for future markets – especially when times are good!

This year will go down in bedding plant history as one of the best sales years ever. The spring weather conditions in most parts of the United States were the best in the last 20 years. Weather is the most important factor in the selling of bedding plants.

A great deal of our product is sold from parking lots and open areas where there is little protection from poor weather (wind, rain, etc.). If a retailer buys plants early and puts them in the open to display them, he is totally at the mercy of nature. If it is wet and cold, the plants will deteriorate. If they don't look good, they won't sell; if they don't sell, the retailer won't buy anymore. I've said for years we must have all our product under cover. Use double poly greenhouses as display areas so we don't have to worry about the weather, and the plants will be at their peak for selling.

Because every year will not be as good as 1985, let's look at some areas where we can increase the sale of bedding plants.

**Increase sales to golf courses.** About 15 years ago, I started giving one lecture a term to students who were studying to be golf course superintendents. At that time, few bedding plants were used on golf courses. Since then, little by little, the use of bedding plants has increased. Each year I've had the opportunity to visit several of the courses in Michigan and see how some of these former students have used bedding plants on the courses. I've asked the students to send me slides of the flowers on their courses. You would be amazed to see how the use of annuals has increased – flower beds around the clubhouses, beds near the tees, hanging baskets on the yard markers.

Last month I visited with the golf course superintendents of Southeastern Michigan. I would estimate there are between 30 to 50 flats of annuals used on each course in Michigan. Here is a market that took 10 to 15 years to develop. Now, it could mean the sale of a significant number of flats. This type of relationship should be developed in every state. If you have a golf course near you, visit them and see if you can book their order for next year. Help develop this market.

**Industrial clients could develop new markets.** More and more bedding plants are being used by commercial businesses. Last month I traveled to Columbus, OH. As I traveled on Route 23 into Columbus, I was delighted to see the large number of commercial businesses using bedding plants. Those companies that take time to keep their grounds beautiful are usually those that take care of their employees and business as well.

This can be a tremendous market. If it were actively developed, one could meet with the companies in the fall, help them develop their landscape plan, and grow the planned varieties for next year. We have not begun to develop the potential for this market.

**Work with landscape contractors to ensure sales.** There are not many landscape contractors who design new buildings or homes to include bedding plants. Usually 10% of the cost of a house is spent in landscaping, yet with all the costs for trees, shrubs, and lawns, little or nothing is spent on flowers. Many times this is because the architects are not familiar with the plant material and do not know which annuals will do well in their designs. This could be a great market if you are willing to work with architects and show them what can be done.

**Work with a realtor.** One of the most novel ways to sell bedding plants was done in France. One garden center actually had model homes built on its grounds, filling the landscapes with shrubs and annuals. When someone buys a house, they also buy the landscape that goes with the model, including trees, shrubs, and annuals. What a great way for customers to see what they'll get – and what a great way for us to sell plants! Why not work with a realtor in this country? Maybe you could get the realtor to provide five or 10 flats of bedding plants with every house he or she sells. If we could do that, we could increase sales five to 10 million flats per year. This would be a great market to develop.

**How many annuals does your town use?** Gale Arent did a survey of Michigan cities and found 70% of the towns used bedding plants. Most used them in parks or in shopping areas. Recently I was in Marlette, MI, where a one-mile stretch of their streets are lined with petunias. The Kalamazoo community group has planted town parks and public areas with hundreds of bedding plants. This is a tremendous market.

Why don't you contact your park commissioner? See what is needed for next year. Many towns put their needs out for bid. If you are interested in increasing sales, develop this market. It can mean even more than the actual municipal plant sale – because once the public is exposed to these plantings, they will be inspired to plant themselves.

This was a great year with great sales. But don't just sit there and expect it to happen again next year. It won't unless you work to increase your sales. Bedding plant sales have increased 10% a year for the last 30 years. With your help we can make it 31.

*– September 1985*

## Community Beautification Means More Bedding Plant Sales

*Tourism, beautification, and bedding plants go hand in hand. Promoting the use of flowering annuals can increase sales and beautify your community.*

The first week of September my wife, Barbara, and I decided to take a week off – away from business, without the kids, to rest and relax. For the first time in about 10 years, we headed to Northern Michigan. Once we got off the expressway at Grayling, we started to see plantings of annuals in many of the towns. Some were spectacular displays. For example, the town of Charlevoix had planted each side of the road for two miles in petunias. We nearly had an accident while I tried to count the number of plantings.

Next, we traveled through the small town of Alanson and stopped to see its flower display. There were small plantings in other towns along the way to Mackinac Island. The town of Cheboygan had a particularly outstanding display of petunias. When we got to the Grand Hotel on Mackinac Island, we found more 200,000 annuals on display.

Needless to say, I got excited about these displays and spent most of the week calculating what is the potential of this market. Not wanting to spend all of my vacation thinking about business, I played several rounds of golf at different courses in Northern Michigan. But instead of worrying about my golf game (which is not worth worrying about), I found myself counting the number of tees adorned with hanging baskets and the number of flower beds on each golf course.

When I got back from vacation, I started a phone campaign to find out who is responsible for these projects. First, I called Rod Cartwright, the county extension director in Charlevoix County, MI. He told me some of the details of the "Keep Charlevoix Beautiful" committee. Each year they organize 600 to 800 volunteers to plant the four miles of petunias (50,000 plants) in 1½ hours. They actually close the city's main street for the period of time they plant the flowers.

The beds are treated beforehand with a herbicide and soil tests are done to evaluate the nutritional requirements. Rod is responsible for most of this. The beds are weeded by inmates in the local jail and watered by the people living along the route. Many other towns have similar stories, indicating bedding plants play an important role in these towns.

Last week, a person from the Michigan Department of Transportation visited me to discuss plantings. All Michigan rest areas will plant annuals next year, using a total of 1,500 to 2,000 flats. In addition, the state government has appropriated $20,000 to plant annuals on the grounds of the Capitol building to celebrate the Sesquicentennial.

Tourism, beautification, and bedding plants go hand in hand. Many people in Michigan, from the highest state and city officials, to service and garden clubs, and to ordinary citizens on the street are beginning to realize that.

I estimate bedding plant sales to communities and local and state governments will soon exceed 10% of our total sales. This is not even considering those plants used by private businesses and corporations in their own company beautification programs.

Promoting the use of flowering annuals will not only help you sell more bedding plants but will help beautify the community in which you live.

*– November 1986*

# Selling To Supermarkets

## Follow these keys to success in selling floral products in supermarkets.

I recently had the pleasure of presenting a lecture to the Produce Marketing Association Floral Seminar in San Antonio, TX. It was interesting to note the challenges and opportunities these people encounter as they deal with floral products.

### Supermarkets Want Quality

"Quality" was a word I heard frequently at this seminar. But what does quality in floral products mean?

Everyone would agree quality plants should be insect- and disease-free, have good flower and foliage color, and strong, healthy stems and foliage – but other aspects of quality are more difficult to agree on. What is a quality height? What is a quality flower size? As beauty is in the eye of the beholder, quality is in the eye of the grower, the mass merchandiser, and the consumer – and varies with each interpretation.

Supermarkets would love to adopt grades and standards for all floral crops they handle. They stress repeatedly their desire to know exactly what they are buying. But the specific components of quality create controversy over grades and standards. Consistent uniformity and quality may be difficult to determine, but that is what supermarkets are looking for in floral products.

All you have to do is look in the newspaper to see that supermarkets advertise by price. Therefore, the floral buyers must be continually aware of the competition's selling price. If one buyer pays $1 more than his competitor for a six-inch poinsettia and then advertises it in the paper for $1 more, you can be sure he will be called on the carpet and severely reprimanded for his "mistake." This is what makes supermarket buyers so price-conscious.

Part of this problem can be traced back to the difficulty in defining quality. All we can define effectively is the size of the pot. Because we cannot communicate the difference between a "quality" six-inch poinsettia and a "regular" six-inch poinsettia, floral buyers and consumers expect equal prices.

### Supermarkets Need Employee Training

There is frequent personnel turnover in the supermarket floral department. The departments are usually run by assistant produce managers. If these assistants do well, they are quickly promoted to other positions. The result of this frequent turnover is a continual need for training. But who will provide it? Sometimes the grower will conduct training sessions, but usually it is the supermarket – or no one. Unfortunately, not all supermarkets acknowledge the need for training. Some believe the producer or wholesaler should package the plants so care is unnecessary at the retail level.

Successful floral marketers have found a way to have their floral department run by a trained staff. If they do not have a training program of their own, they subcontract the department to a knowledgeable group that handles the entire floral operation.

The supermarket floral department can be profitable when it is run by trained personnel. One operation has reported between $500-$600 gross per square foot, primarily in cut flowers. That is certainly proof that flowers can be popular and profitable items.

### Proper Displays

Most supermarkets started selling flowers in makeshift displays or in areas designed for other products. These soon proved inadequate as the plants and flowers were easily damaged. New fixtures and displays especially for flowers are currently being developed, with protective features to preserve that undefinable "quality."

More work is needed in this area. The challenge is to provide good visual displays and at the same time offer protection for the flowers and plants. These two functions are not mutually exclusive, but can be a challenge to combine. It is not impossible. Just as supermarkets have developed attractive, functional displays for meat, bread, vegetables, and delicatessen items, they must also develop special displays for flowers.

### Cooperating With Suppliers

In supermarket floral marketing, there are usually no formal, written contracts. Sales are made on trust. This necessitates a high degree of mutual trust among growers, wholesalers, and supermarket buyers. They must reconcile their definitions of quality and concerns over price competition to agree on a given quality at a given price. Working together, they can bring floral products to the consumer with profits for all.

### Your Potential Market

As you might expect, about 80% of supermarkets handle cut flowers, while only about 50% handle pot plants and foliage plants, and less than 20% handle bedding plants. Where do they get these products?

In most cases, the small, local grower is not involved in supermarket selling. Large growers and wholesalers have captured most of the business. Occasionally, a small grower will sell a specific crop to the manager of a single store. One reason this happens infrequently is the red tape involved. In many stores, the grower must register with the main office and acquire a seller's number before dealing with the store.

Even though small growers have not participated heavily in marketing to supermarkets to date, they can't ignore the fact that nearly 50% of total U.S. flower sales are made through supermarkets. There is no doubt that potential sales in this area are even higher.

*– December 1986*

# Buyers Vs. Growers: Questions To Help Both Win The Game

## Here's what buyers and growers need to know to promote quality, cooperation, and fair profits for all.

The object of the game: to provide quality plants and flowers to the consumer at a profit. The players: the grower, wholesaler, and retailer – each trying to produce, buy, or market the plants for as little as possible and sell them for as much as possible. Playing the game involves finding a price that is mutually acceptable in light of this competition. As a smart buyer, you need to ask more than, "How much?"

### You Get What You Pay For

"How much are your six-inch, pinched poinsettias?" This question could receive a variety of answers depending on plant quality, packaging, and shipping methods. A meaningful answer requires a more specific question. "How much are your six-inch, pinched poinsettias with five to seven blooms, 15 to 18 inches tall, with dark green foliage and red bracts, free of insects and diseases, with the cyathia just starting to show a yellow center, in foil-covered pots, individually sleeved and packaged eight to a cardboard box and delivered to a central warehouse in groups of 12 boxes?" Obviously, the price of a six-inch, pinched poinsettia can vary greatly, depending on these specifications. You not only get what you pay for, but you pay for what you get – and you get more than just the plant and the pot.

Quality and service are more important than price. You can pay very little and still lose money, if the grower can't provide quality plants in the quantity you need and deliver them at the time your customers are ready to buy.

### A Matter Of Timing

"When should I buy?" This is another question buyers must ask. While low-price deals can sometimes be found at the last minute, the buyer who waits runs the risk of having no plants to sell.

As a buyer, you want to make sure that the right plants are in the store at the right time to meet consumer demand. The best way to achieve this is to order plants well in advance. This system benefits both grower and buyer, because it allows for maximum control of the grower's schedule and efficient use of resources to fill your order on schedule.

You must remember, however, that you are dealing with a biological product that is affected not only by the well-laid plans of grower and buyer but also by the whims of Mother Nature. For example, the crop could be a week late and the weather could turn cold, leaving the retailer with no place to hold the quantity of product ordered. Mother Nature can be the opponent in this game.

Growers and buyers who play the game in a spirit of cooperation and trust get further ahead than those who play for the short-term advantage.

Growers who dictate unfair prices and conditions in a season when plants are scarce can be the victim of a buyer's retaliation in a season when plants are plentiful. Neither grower nor buyer ultimately wins with this adversarial relationship – and the consumer winds up a loser, too.

As a successful buyer, you must build a network of growers you trust to deliver the quality and quantity of plants you want at the time you want them. This cooperative working relationship between buyer and grower helps build a "green team" that can win the game for both sides.

Our industry needs to promote this teamwork in matching supply with demand. Woody ornamentals have availability lists within specific states or regions, but bedding and potted plants do not. It's frustrating to see a buyer searching fruitlessly for a certain plant when 50 miles away, there's a grower trying to unload a surplus of the same plant. I see a real need for a central communications system to get these people together.

### Strength Begets Strength

To maintain a position of strength, the grower must receive a price that covers production and marketing costs plus an acceptable profit. This strength supports the ability to supply the quality and quantity of plants the buyer requires. Likewise, to maintain a position of strength, the buyer must receive a price that allows a proper markup with a competitive selling price. This strength supports the grower's ability to move more product.

### Low Price Alone Won't Sell

Of course it's possible to compromise on production techniques to reduce costs. Tighter spacing and scrimping on materials can produce plants for the lower prices demanded by some buyers. But what is the end result? Poorer looking plants with shorter shelflife, more waste, and dissatisfied customers who won't be back to buy again.

### Buyers Ask Growers

Here's a checklist of questions for buyers to ask growers to make sure other vital elements of the sale are taken into consideration before price.

1. Can you deliver the specified plants when needed?
2. Do you have the facilities to produce the specified quantities?
3. Are your employees qualified to grow and ship the plants?
4. What is your previous experience in this area?
5. Do you have the flexibility to increase or decrease orders as needed?
6. Do you have a system to help train store personnel?
7. Do you provide any point-of-sale information, signs, or displays to help sell the product?
8. Can you consistently produce the plants to the specifications required?
9. What is your policy on claims or damaged material?
10. What is your price?

When both buyers and growers step back and look at the entire marketing process and how it affects our industry as a whole, they can see beyond the short-term, price-conscious deal to the long-term benefits of promoting quality, cooperation, and fair profits for all.

*– February 1988*

# Customers Make Your Business

*Even if you are on the right track, you can get run over if you move too slowly. Keep looking for new customers and run a customer-oriented business.*

I recently heard some interesting reasons for not advertising: "We have all the business we can handle." "We don't want any new customers." "We don't need any new business." It seems many growers won't advertise because they already have all the business they need. These people are in trouble, but they don't know it.

One of my first bosses gave me this advice: "Be happy, but not content." Even if you are on the right track, you can get run over if you move too slowly. It's important to keep looking for new customers – and to run a customer-oriented business.

### Most Important Part

If a business is not sensitive to customers' wants and needs, it is doomed to failure. When you plan what plants to grow, what varieties to buy, what size containers to use, and when to make them available for sale, you must do so in light of what your customers want.

My favorite example of not knowing what customers want is the geranium color controversy. We surveyed 1,000 customers and asked their favorite geranium flower color. The customers were mostly female and their responses were mostly pink and salmon.

We subsequently surveyed 50 growers, mostly male, and asked them what they thought their customers' favorite geranium flower color was, and they said, "red." In fact, one grower grew red geraniums exclusively to avoid the possibility of confusing colors during shipping. Growers may have saturated the red geranium market, but not the pink/salmon market. Are they listening to the customers? I don't think so.

### How To Treat Customers

Customers want the most courteous and attentive treatment you can give. Why do you shop where you shop? Of course, good selection, reasonable prices, and convenience are important, but customer service can override these reasons. Many people will drive a little farther and pay a little more to shop where they get individual attention from employees who know what customers want.

Delivering what is promised is part of customer service. Have you ever gone to a restaurant where the hostess greets you and announces "Sam will be your waiter," only to wait 10 minutes before Sam finally shows up? This is like a salesperson making the sale, and promising delivery by such-and-such a date – only the flats don't show up on time. Do you feel like returning to that restaurant? Do you place another order with that grower? Courteous, attentive treatment goes a long way toward keeping customers.

### Best Material

Customers want the best plant material available. Whatever store I go to, I expect the owner to have reviewed all the products available and chosen only the best for me. I expect these owners to attend trade shows and conferences, read their industry trade press, do everything in their power to become knowledgeable to help me make my best buy. If I get the impression that they've chosen products based only on what's convenient for them or what will make them money, I shop elsewhere.

Customers expect the same from you. They want to be able to depend on your expertise to offer them the best plants available. When you do this, you build your reputation not only as a plant seller, but also as a plant expert. A plant that performs at a reasonable price is worth more to your customer than a cheap plant that dies. Selling the best gives you the advantage over the grower who doesn't know or doesn't care.

### Lifeblood Of Your Business

Customers are the lifeblood of this and every other business. Think of your customers as you develop all aspects of your business. What do your customers want? When do they want it? Can you fulfill those wants so customers are satisfied – no, ecstatic – about what you do?

I spent last Saturday looking at 1990 seed catalogs, planning my vegetable garden. The detailed descriptions of each plant were great. I thought, "If only bedding plant growers could promote their material this way." Why can't we go beyond the 50-word label telling how to grow a bedding plant, to include information about how it performs and how it compares to other cultivars?

Such information is part of what customers want from you. It's no longer enough to just grow the plants. You have to grow the best – and provide information that explains why yours are the best – to help customers be successful with their gardens.

### Who Pays Your Wages?

If you don't keep your customers satisfied, sales decrease, income falls, and you have to reduce your labor force. If this cycle continues, you'll soon be out of business.

I know one grower who thinks only of himself. He always complains about his customers. He tells people how dumb they are, how they don't know what to buy, and how they expect more than anyone could provide. His negative attitude has spread to his employees and the result has been a cycle of "bad years." This grower is a disaster in progress. His fatal mistake is failing to realize that customers pay his wages and help his business survive.

### Not An Outsider

At a recent fruit and vegetable meeting in Springfield, IL, I spoke to a group on farm marketing. What a great program! Several farm operators gave talks about their operations and told how they involved customers in their business. They hold tours for school children, have a clown meet the bus, and let the kids pick an apple, visit the witch in the orchard, and go to the pumpkin patch – and charge $5 a head for the experience. They realize their customers love not only their products but also the whole farm experience, and so they make the customers feel part of their business.

Enthusiasm is contagious. People like to feel like winners; they like to deal with successful people. It's up to you to develop that winning team, but be sure to make your customers the stars of your team. That way, you will be the winner.

Have a great spring season. With the help of your customers, you can make it happen.

*– March 1990*

# Insights On Today's Customers

*Pre-Boomers, Baby Boomers, Baby Busters, and Baby Boomlets – categorize your buying public to appeal to the customers who can build your business.*

You know about demographics – the process of grouping people according to factors such as age, sex, area of the country, etc., in order to determine potential markets.

But have you heard of psychographics? It's the process of grouping people by the ways in which they think and act – and can be a helpful adjunct to demographics in determining who your customers are and how to reach them.

Recently, I attended a two-day session on Association Management by Glenn Tucker of Glenn H. Tucker, Consultants, Trenton, NJ. He divided the population not only by age demographics, but also by psychographics.

His observations struck home with me, and I'd like to share them with you. I believe they can help you categorize your buying public to make you better able to select and appeal to the groups that can build business.

### Pre-Boomers

Pre-Boomers are the people born before 1945, sometimes called World War II babies, Depression babies, or the 50-plus Generation. Within this group are three subgroups:

**Vitally Actives.** They are hard-working, involved, trying to succeed by their own efforts.

**Adapters.** They are people who have had to make changes, shift jobs, perhaps retire, and take part-time jobs – or make other concessions to their situations.

**Society's Dropouts.** These people are overwhelmed, unable to cope, and have given up on the world.

As you can probably guess, the first two subgroups are big users of our products, while the third subgroup is not.

### Baby Boomers

Baby Boomers were born between 1946 and 1964 – the largest generation in history. Because of its size, this group has pushed society to adjust to its needs and has generally gotten whatever it wanted.

This group contains four distinct psychic subgroups: Innovation-Driven Secure, Innovation-Driven Insecure, Tradition-Driven Secure, and Tradition-Driven Insecure.

Achievers are the Innovation-Driven Secure subgroup and represent about 10% to 15% of the Baby Boomers. These are the people who want the newest things, the fastest cars, the latest computers.

We can attract this sub-group by advertising the newest cultivars, tissue-cultured plants, and the latest advances in our industry.

Contented Traditionalists are the Tradition-Driven subgroup and represent about 30% of the Baby Boomers. They hold family and country in highest regard; everything revolves around their families. They can often be found in Ford or Chevy vans, with the kids and family dog strapped in for a family picnic. This group holds the same values as the Pre-Boomers.

Of all the Baby Boomers, the Contented Traditionalists are the most responsive to our product. To appeal to this group, emphasize the effect of our product on family well-being and how it improves the quality of life in our communities. We need to make sure we identify with all the values of the home.

Discontented Traditionalists are the Tradition-Driven Insecure subgroup, representing about 30% of the Baby Boomer population. These are the people who worry about everything. When everything is all right, they worry that there is nothing to worry about. If plants look good, they worry that they might die.

The insecurities of these people cause them all sorts of problems, real and perceived, but these very insecurities can make them good customers. They can be a good market for garden gloves, insecticides, fertilizers – anything to combat a worry. To sell to this subgroup, we have to reassure them that everything is okay. They need to be told that our product is fine, they can be successful with it, and there are no hazards involved in handling it.

About 10% of the Baby Boomers comprise the Innovation-Driven Insecure subgroup. These people are removed from the mainstream. They may have a 1960 VW van and spend most of their time working on its motor – yet have a hard time holding a job.

This group may appreciate our product as part of the "flower power," back-to-nature movement of the '60s, but they don't have the capital or the dedication to make much of an impact on our market.

### Baby Busters

Baby Busters are people in their early 20s, born between 1965 and 1975. Because this group is much smaller in population, it has had a less competitive experience growing up than did the Baby Boomers. They're in the high-tech, high-touch group.

While the 50-plus group works because work has meaning and is an integral part of their lives, the Baby Busters work as a means to an unknown end. This group is more inward-looking, but less reflective.

One important factor about the Baby Busters is that some are well educated and some are poorly educated, and the gap between these segments is growing. Our industry must relate to both segments, because they represent significant parts of our market. The well educated know growing plants is an important part of life, but the poorly educated must be taught the importance of plants.

### Baby Boomlets

Children of the Baby Boomers, the Baby Boomlets, were born between 1971 and 1987. We have a great challenge to work with this generation. We can teach them how plants help us lead more fulfilling lives – that we need plants for such basic necessities as eating and breathing, as well as for the aesthetic and emotional qualities that make life worth living, the pride in creation, the appreciation of beauty, and the expression of feelings throughout life's journey.

Keep these demographics and psychographics in mind when you're researching the market for your plants.

Could reassuring "We will help you" advertising bring in more Discontented Traditionalists? Could a spread on new and unusual cultivars attract some Achievers? What can you do to help educate Baby Boomlets on the benefits of plants? School tours? Kiddie garden kits?

The more you know about your customers – and potential customers – the more you can expect your market to grow.

– *August 1990*

# Get Smart About Retailing Plants

*Attention to detail is a main ingredient of producing and selling quality bedding plants.*

As another bedding plant season winds down, many growers look back with disappointment and thoughts of what might have been. A late winter and almost nonexistent spring wreaked havoc with schedules and plants. On the bright side, there seemed to be someone selling bedding plants on every street corner, as consumers tried to brighten their own little corner of the world. On the downside, there seemed to be someone selling bedding plants on every street corner, increasing competition and cutting into already thin profits of a slow season.

The number and types of retailers of bedding plants has expanded over the years. Now, in addition to traditional outlets, plants are marketed through discount stores, grocery stores, home centers, gas stations, and even the back of pickup trucks. This provides a great advantage by exposing our product to many more people than before, hopefully increasing sales.

### Attention To Detail

Most growers do their best to produce a quality product because their livelihood depends on it. But what happens to that flat of petunias or impatiens after it goes out the greenhouse door? Weeks of hard work to produce a quality plant can easily slip away after only a few days at the retail level.

Many retailers do a fine job during the spring season. They try to offer good plant material and other supplies, guarantee their product, and provide various customer services. Master gardeners or other knowledgeable people are made available to answer homeowners' questions. But when we move beyond the experienced plant person, the use of an untrained employee all too often results in loss of quality at the retail level.

A main requirement in producing a quality plant in the greenhouse is attention to detail. Experienced growers recognize that the plant material they produce is actually very fragile. Small mistakes quickly compound into major disasters. This attention to detail is all too often forgotten at the retail level.

### Pseudo Greenhouses

A few mass merchandisers try to maintain a level of plant quality by erecting small greenhouses in their parking lots in the spring. On the surface, this seems like a good idea. The plants are placed in a protected environment and are still readily available to the customer. But as in production, a momentary lapse in attention to detail and problems quickly develop.

Those retail greenhouses go up with the first delivery of pansies, snapdragons, and the cole crops. Soon, plants overflow the doors. When later crops such as impatiens and geraniums arrive, room is usually made on racks or tables around the outside of the greenhouse. As a result, the pansies labor in the warm sun during the day and the impatiens do their best to tolerate frosty nights. Some advance planning and knowledge of warm and cool crops can eliminate this problem and keep plants in top form.

A couple years ago, a local store of a well known grocery chain decided to offer bedding plants and small shrubs for spring sales. The manager didn't want to go through the expense of erecting a greenhouse. A canvas tent was put up for protection instead. Several incandescent bulbs provided light, and a fan at the doorway provided some ventilation. Under these dark, hot conditions, plant quality quickly vanished. The tent and plants were gone within a week.

### A Call To Order

Very important but frequently ignored at retail is maintaining a neat, attractive display of plants. After the Saturday morning rush of customers subsides, a jumbled mess of broken plants, missing labels, and half-full flats remain. If some retailers maintained the rest of their store like they do their garden center, they would quickly be out of business.

With only a little effort, pots can be stood upright and dead or broken plants removed from the display area. An orderly, well-stocked display indicates to consumers they are purchasing healthy, vigorous plant material. Racks of dead and dying plants under a big sign that says "Reduced For Quick Sale" encourages them to shop elsewhere.

Plant quality is hard to preserve under the best of conditions and almost impossible when retailers seem to work against themselves. Research at the University of Georgia showed high levels of ethylene and carbon monoxide from the exhaust of passing cars quickly accumulate in plant displays near the parking lot. Simple things such as a regular watering schedule or checking temperature go a long way in keeping plants in prime condition. Large chain stores display a tremendous sense of humor as they plan their marketing schedules. We are told we need to buy winter coats in July and bathing suits in January. Thanksgiving is ignored because Santa Claus shows up before Halloween. The idea is to always get a jump on the competition.

But this marketing technique does not work as well with bedding plants. On April 18 of this year, many retailers had already set up displays with impatiens, peppers, and tomatoes, and beautiful baskets of New Guinea impatiens. The catch was these retailers were in Detroit, not Atlanta or Dallas as one might expect for this time of year. If we grow these plants in a heated greenhouse protecting them from the elements, how can the consumer be expected to have any luck with the plants outside?

A student in a greenhouse management class defended her family-run greenhouse's practice of "selling early, selling often" by saying that if the customer was dumb enough to put out plants to freeze, they deserved paying to replace the plants two or three times. Fortunately, this wasn't the mindset of the entire class. Most were able to grasp the concept that it would be better to educate the customer and ensure sales for years to come than to lose these sales because the home gardener becomes discouraged. The problem of early spring sales is hard to solve because most growers are reluctant to delay these early sales knowing the retailer will just find another grower.

### Get Plant-Smart Employees

Most problems resulting in reduced plant quality at the retail level are usually traced to lack of plant knowledge and experience. Retail outlets with plant-smart employees have far fewer problems than those that don't. Retailers need to pay that same attention to detail that the grower does. This includes educating their employees. Something as simple as bringing in a Master Gardener for an employee seminar can go a long way to ensure the high-quality plant received from the grower will be sold to the customer in the same condition.

*– August 1996*

## *Calling On Customers*

*Customer input is important! Know how to collect it and use it to determine your opportunity for success.*

Over the years, several methods have been utilized to obtain consumer feedback. Often, retailers write their own customer questionnaires and then try to determine what to do with the information. But most of the time, little is accomplished here because:

a) the questions may not be properly worded;

b) surveyors don't ask for the necessary information; and

c) very few people respond to mailed and/or in-store questionnaires.

### *Gathering Information*

Before you create a questionnaire, you need to know what kind of information you want. Developing the questionnaire or "instrument" is the most important step in the process. If you know what information you want, hire a professional poller to develop the instrument so it will be short enough that your customers can answer it in less than three minutes. But keep in mind that if you want to know all the demographics about the customer, keeping the questionnaire short and simple becomes a nearly impossible task to accomplish.

Consumer focus groups are another way to discuss customer expectations. Some feedback may have merit and some may be off the wall. Over the years, I've found consumers don't often know what they want. But they continue to be a valuable source of information that can inspire new products and services if you know how to listen and condense the information, and find out their most important concerns and how satisfied they are with what is presently available.

Let me give you examples of horticultural success using information gathered from customers.

### *Foliage Plant Customers And Plant Care*

In the early 1970s, when the popularity of foliage plants began to increase, the question that emerged from talking to consumers was how to make them successful with the plants they bought. Consumers liked all the new plants that had become available but didn't know their names or how to grow them. This information was collected from question-naires and focus groups asking the question, "What is your biggest problem in growing foliage plants?"

We did not ask our participants for a solution – we just wanted to identify the problem. As an industry, it is our job to translate the information we collect into opportunity by developing potential products or services that will help answer our customers' concerns.

When we talked with potential buyers of foliage plants, they indicated whatever was developed needed to be simple. "We don't want to have to take a botany course to buy a plant," was one consumer's response.

After studying and digesting the data, we went to the research and development (R&D) group of a horticultural printing company and said, "Here is a tremendous opportunity. Give us a simple way to identify the plant and explain how to grow it – and don't make the instructions too complicated."

A week later, we met with the R&D group. They had several suggestions, one of which was a color-coded plant tag and a foliage plant guide that categorized the plants by light, temperature, and moisture requirements. The tags were coded yellow for high light, orange for medium light, and blue for low light; and each included a plant photo, common name, and suggested moisture level and temperature range. This simple system, providing all the information the customer requested on one tag in each pot, was the start of the great expansion of the plastic labeling business. Today, billions of tags, featuring very elaborate yet simple information, are used by growers worldwide.

### Consumer-Friendly Displays

In the late 1970s, the former trade association Bedding Plants, Inc. (BPI) investigated plant display problems at garden centers. A focus group including garden center retailers, retail growers, allied tradespeople, and consumers was formed. We asked retailers and growers to tell us about their plant displays and we asked consumers to tell us how easy or difficult it was to shop at garden centers. The outcome of these meetings indicated garden centers were not well organized and no two were alike, making it difficult for consumers to understand whether to plant material in sun or shade, and how to take care of it. In addition, industry participants in the focus group insisted that any solution must be affordable to all businesses.

We took this information to BPI's R&D group, where a committee was formed to solve the problem and thus, the idea of color-coded garden center signs was conceived. We printed yellow annual signs for sunny annuals and blue annual signs for shady annuals, as well as appropriate signs for perennials, vegetables, and other products. This idea allowed retailers to group all plants by type, while communicating whether plants were to be planted in the sun or shade.

Color-coded garden center signs were the best product ever developed by BPI. Thousands of sets were sold and the price was affordable for all garden centers.

### Getting Into Grasses

My last example is a plant, purple fountain grass. In the last five years, consumers have become more interested in ornamental grasses. Based on this increased interest, we saw tremendous potential for purple fountain grass, a grass that is striking in color and bears flowers. The plant has a deep red to purple color foliage with gray flower stalks that also turn pink to purple. At the time, fewer than 3,000 plants were sold each year in Michigan, and most were not sold in flower. The plants flower naturally in Michigan in August and September, but the grass is killed by frost and does not overwinter in zones 4 or 5.

Research at Michigan State showed we could flower purple fountain grass for Mother's Day if we gave it 14 hours of light a day for 10 to 12 weeks before selling the plant. Thus, we had a new product: A flowering, colorful grass for Mother's Day and Memorial Day sales.

Today, there are more than one million purple fountain grass plants grown and sold annually, and it has become a staple annual grass in botanical gardens, horticultural gardens, and home landscaping.

The bottom line is, customer input is important. Know how to collect it, understand what consumers' expected outcomes are, and then organize the information you've obtained.

*— June 2002*

# MARKETING YOUR PRODUCT

You've heard the old saying that there are three types of people: those who make things happen, those who watch things happen, and those who wonder what's happening.

As more and more greenhouse plants are being grown, those of you who are watching and wondering will be left behind. It is becoming increasingly important to spend as much time marketing your product as you do growing it.

I once spent some time with a leadership group, talking about how we can help growers market their product. Some thought marketing should be left to private companies. Others thought everyone should get involved. Still others thought our product can sell itself. It seems everyone has more opinions about marketing than about how to grow a quality crop of begonias!

If we want to reach higher sales goals and make a profit, we must realize that our planning does not end with the finished product. We need to have a marketing plan and the strategies to make it happen. It involves keeping up with what is new and unique, defining our products and services, identifying our customers, and promoting what we have to offer.

Marketing involves more than just what's written on paper. It's an attitude! What does the front of your greenhouse or commercial building look like? Do you display plants and flowers? Does it send a positive image? Also, what does your home look like? Are there plants and flowers? Do people stop by on their nightly walks to talk with you about how beautiful your yard and landscape are?

As I said before, and I will say it again and again, it's all about finding the right product for the right customer and getting it to the right place at the right time for the right price!

# Interesting Products To Increase Sales

*New ideas and new products will continue to make the bedding plant industry dynamic. Find your niche, select your products, and grow them well.*

Visiting many greenhouses this spring, I noticed an increased diversity in products being grown for consumers. A few years ago, bedding plant growers grew everything in flats and the entire industry had an attitude that if it couldn't be grown in a flat, it couldn't be used.

While large wholesale growers will probably remain primarily in flats, small and medium growers are finding it more profitable to diversify. Thus, three- and four-inch potted annuals, five-, six-, and eight-inch combination pots, pots of mixed-color garden mums, hanging baskets, and seed geraniums in flats and pots are increasing tremendously.

**Potted annuals.** Many 2¼- or three-inch potted annuals have been grown by retail growers who want to sell large, established plants or for use in cemetery urns or other "made-up" annual planters. There are also customers with window boxes or patio planters who look for this type of product so their planters will look great the same day they are planted.

**Combination pots.** With the increase in container gardening has come a revival of mixed containers of annuals. Growers who plant these five-, six-, or eight-inch containers may find this a profitable venture.

Usually four different annuals are planted in a five-inch pot, such as one geranium, one petunia, one ageratum, and one salvia for a sunny area or one coleus, one impatiens, one begonia, and one dusty miller for a shady area. For a six-inch pot for sunny locations, one geranium plus four annuals are used, and for an eight-inch container for sunny locations, one geranium plus five or six annuals. For shady areas, substitute a coleus for the geranium.

These colorful pots are outstanding for patios and many are sold for Memorial Day as cemetery flowers. It is evident there is an increasing demand for made-up planters and many smaller retail garden centers are finding it profitable to develop these items.

**Garden mums.** Primarily a field-grown, fall item in the past, they are now being sold as a spring-flowering plant that can be placed in the garden after Mother's Day and reflowered again in the fall. A very colorful way to sell this item is to place cuttings of three or four different colored varieties in the same container. I saw an entire greenhouse with this material this spring and it looked great. Also, it had been entirely presold to a large chain store.

**Hanging baskets.** Hanging baskets are now found in all shapes and sizes, usually between four and 12 inches in size. While four-inch baskets look cute, customers will probably be disappointed in the results because it is difficult to keep the small basket adequately watered. Usually eight-, 10-, or 12-inch baskets are used – the bigger the basket, the more moisture it will hold, and the better chance for customer success.

Growers are finding more and more annuals can be grown in baskets and look good. Most growers use one species of annual per basket. Usually it is ivy geranium, impatiens, fuchsia, petunia, or begonia. Two annuals that look great are Reiger begonia and a pink, trailing verbena. Both are propagated from cuttings, not seed.

With great frequency, combination baskets are being sold because of their colorful and unique appearance. A striking combination is a highly colored coleus with dusty miller, variegated ivy with begonia, or ivy geranium and asparagus fern.

Also, don't forget fruit and vegetable baskets like strawberry baskets, tomato baskets, or even cucumbers in a basket. A small quantity of these items are not only conversation pieces, but they will sell.

**Geraniums.** Ten years ago, the potted four-inch geranium was usually grown by the florist and not by the wholesale bedding plant grower. Probably the most revolutionary change in the bedding plant industry in the last 10 years has been the increased production of geraniums from seed.

Carl Dietz of Vaughan-Jacklin Corp. estimates in 1976 more than 10 million geraniums started from seed will be sold. Seed-grown geraniums are primarily grown by bedding plant growers. Dietz estimates three million plants will be sold as four-inch pots and more than seven million will be sold as conventional bedding plants in packs and flats.

The seed geranium is making inroads into cutting type geranium sales, and, if the trend continues with seed geranium gaining more of the four-inch market, it will be the primary geranium sold in the United States.

An interesting concept is now being tested where seed is started in Florida, grown for 40 to 45 days, and then shipped north as 2½-inch plants where they are finished in six to eight weeks. This can be done at a cheaper cost per plant than for a cutting.

Watch those seed geraniums. They have only just begun.

New ideas and products will continue to make the bedding plant industry dynamic. A small grower must have new ideas, techniques, or products because it is impossible to compete head-on with larger, wholesale growers. Whatever your size, find you niche, select your products, and grow them well!

*—June 1976*

## *Only YOU Can Make Sales Happen*

*Our industry may be great in production planning, but marketing often takes a back seat. Use this outline to develop your own marketing plan.*

All growers have developed their own plan to produce a bedding plant crop. They know what dates they must sow their seed, the date they will transplant, how many flats they need, how many labels to order, how much soil to mix – all the details that go into producing their crop.

Most growers figure that if these details are worked out, the weather, the product, and the customers will all come together and their product will sell. Our industry may be great in production planning, but it doesn't do half as well in marketing planning.

I've often asked growers or retailers, "Where is your marketing plan?" The common answer is, "We don't have one." Many times it exists in the owner's head and is not revealed to anyone else.

I thought it might be of interest to go through the different steps involved in preparing a marketing plan. You might want to use this outline to develop your own. Remember, it takes as much time, effort, and creativity to market a product as it does to produce it.

**1. Define the market.** How many plants are grown nationally? How many are grown in your state and trading area? How many potential customers do you have? How many plants do they buy now and how many will they buy next year?

**2. What is your history?** When did you start in business? How did you progress to your current status? What kind of background do you and your key employees have? How is your business expertise?

**3. What are the general statistics?** What is the total population of your area? Number of households? Income per household? Amount spent on floriculture?

**4. What is your sales history?** How many plants did you sell 10 years ago? Five years ago? Two years ago? Last year? What market percentages did you have each year? Is the trend increasing, remaining the same, or decreasing?

**5. What are your strengths?** List those points that are strengths in your organization and that will help you succeed.

**6. What are your weaknesses?** What are the negative aspects of your business? Improve those areas to make marketing your product easier.

**7. What is your purpose?** Do you want to make as much money as possible? To have a good way of life? To produce the highest quality plant?

**8. What are your objectives?** To be the best grower? To have the most satisfied customers? To have the widest selection of material?

**9. What is your marketing mix?** How will you handle your product, distribute it, and communicate through sales promotion and advertising to sell it? To get the proper mix you must have the right product quantity, sufficient transportation, and the proper amount of advertising to sell that much product.

**10. List all your opportunities.** For instance, capitalize on an expanding market, quality product, or improved packaging.

**11. What are your major problems?** Do you need to improve product facilities? Do you need to hire salespersons? Should you spend more money on effective advertising and promotion?

**12. List all your goals in specific detail.** For example, 1983 goals for a fictitious company might be: (a) to sell 10,000 geraniums; (b) to sell 20,000 flats of bedding plants; (c) to create a good image of reliable service to customers; and (d) to find five new accounts.

**13. List your strategies for accomplishing those goals.** Using the goals listed above: a) to sell 10,000 geraniums, an effective advertising program must be developed; b) to sell 20,000 flats, another retail center is needed; and c) to create a good image and reliable service, a new truck should be ordered.

**14. Tactics.** How will the strategies be carved out, by whom, and when? Tactics for the fictitious company would include: (a) advertising every week with a local paper and selecting a person to be responsible for developing these ads for the paper by April 1; (b) opening another selling area in the parking lot of the local mall, and choosing an individual to be responsible for this project and signing the lease on March 1 for three months; and (c) getting quotations on trucks from dealers, picking an employee to make the decision, and purchasing the truck by March 15.

**15. Budget.** Develop detailed costs, income, and expenses for the entire marketing plan.

**16. Evaluation.** At the end of the season, make certain you evaluate your plan. Was it done correctly? Did it happen as you had planned? What needs to be changed? What worked right? Who did their job? Who didn't? Did you make your budget, your goals, your profit?

Use all this information to develop next year's production and marketing plan.

*– April 1983*

## Get Out There And Market

*For years we have been selling our product, not marketing it. Marketing is finding a consumer's need and filling it. Five keys are important to unlocking the door to success.*

Within the last several months, there have been signs that all is not well "down on the farm." The overall economy is making it difficult for people in agriculture to survive. Some economists predict that 10% to 20% of the farmers will go bankrupt in the next two years. With, high interest rates and the strong dollar on the world market, it is more and more difficult to compete.

Within my home state of Michigan, the extension service plans to hold many meetings in the next several months to address the questions of how to handle the economic situation. In discussing what should be presented to help farmers through these difficult times, the main area that seems to need attention is improved marketing systems. This also happens to be the biggest problem in the floriculture industry as well.

At the Ohio Florists' Association Short Course last July, "Floriculture's Biggest Problem Is Weak Industry" was the topic of a very interesting and excellent presentation by W. Wayne Talarzyk, chairman and professor of marketing at The Ohio State University. He actually presented a whole course in marketing in a fast 1½ hours. Here are some of Dr. Talarzyk's major points.

"A simple definition of marketing is finding a consumer's need and filling it," he said. "Also you must do this better than your competition."

A good business finds consumers' needs and satisfies them with a quality product or service that makes them feel the transaction was worthwhile.

For years in the bedding plant and container plant area, we have been selling our product, not marketing it. Many greenhouse operations produce a product first, then go after a market to sell it in. What should be happening is that operation should determine what the consumer wants and needs, then produce a product to fill those needs.

A main point of Dr. Talarzyk's talk was the keys to future success. He listed five of them and I think they are very important for a bedding plant grower to survive.

**1. Understanding the changing business/technological consumer environment.** What effect will the high interest rates, strong dollar, plug culture, computerized environmental control, more quality oriented consumer have on your business? Do you know what changes are occurring nationally or internationally and how to react to them?

**2. Developing products (goods and services) to respond to the environment.** Are you growing what the consumer wants? Are you producing it in the right container, at the right price? What new products are you developing? Changes occur in products continually. Over half the major items sold today were not even on the market 10 years ago. What's new? You better find out!

**3. Pricing those products to meet consumer wants and provide an adequate return on your investment.** One grower I know goes to his accounts and says "How much do you want to buy it for?" Then he goes back and produces a crop that will be profitable to produce in that size container at that price. Why grow $10 pot mums if the market will only buy $5 pot mums? But remember you can't grow the $10 pot mums for the same price as the $5 pot mums!

**4. Distributing those products at the right places at the right time.** Our season for the sale of bedding plants is short. Therefore, we have to be where the people are and be there when they are there. The first sunny weekend of spring when they want to plant, the product must be there. Also, the right place means a physical place to put the product. It can't be on the parking lot asphalt – we can't expect people to stand in the wind and rain to buy our product. When we provide covered shopping areas, retail level sales will increase and our losses will be less.

**5. Communicating to the consumer that your business has the product that will satisfy their wants and lifestyles.** Promoting the product is everyone's job. If we were to do the job properly at least 3% of the total value of the crop should be spent on communication. The industry should spend more than $15 million a year just on bedding plant promotion and probably close to $30 million on a combined potted and bedding plant effort. Many wholesale growers do not spend a cent on promoting our product. You will not be successful in the future if this continues.

Two marketing questions are always asked:

**1. Are you doing things right?** Do you have a good quality product, a good organization, good service, and an adequate supply for your customers?

**2. Are you doing the right things?** Are you producing the right crops, right varieties, the right new products?

I hope you will realize it takes as much time to market a product as it does to grow it. Lay out your marketing plans now and get to work on accomplishing them. Good luck in the 1985 season.

*– December 1984*

## *Take The Competitive Edge*

*Picture this: a well-maintained operation with quality product, courteous sales staff, and plenty of customers enjoying their shopping experience. How does your business take the competitive edge to create such a picture?*

"What this industry needs is more marketing!" This battle cry rings out at trade association meetings, conferences, and trade shows. But its impact diminishes when a meeting on marketing draws only a third of the attendance as the one on crop production.

"We need to spend more money on marketing." In a recent PPGA survey, an overwhelming majority of respondents wanted a marketing program, but most indicated they would be willing to contribute no more than $100 to such an effort. Another battle cry is extinguished by reality.

### What About Marketing Annuals?

Some people believe we have reached the saturation point with annuals. Are we ready for the traditional agricultural overproduction blood-letting ceremony?

Not yet. Even as our attention is diverted by these alarmist claims and battle cries, we are ignoring simple, common-sense marketing tools and techniques that can keep us well ahead of that saturation point. Consider the following observations:

• **Pick the best cultivars for consumers.** All-America Selections evaluates thousands of cultivars at 33 sites throughout the United States and Canada and publishes the results. At Michigan State, we offer our own list of great performers to anyone who requests it, yet this year not one retail outlet in the state offered all of the cultivars on our list. The best any retailer could do was offer about a third of the list. It's not difficult to find out which cultivars will perform best for the consumer; the least we could do is offer them for sale.

• **Display is for protection as well as for show.** Late spring frosts, heavy rains, high winds – Mother Nature can wreak havoc on annuals placed outdoors, unprotected, on retail display lots. I know of one retail outlet that lost $10,000 worth of inventory to a record low temperature of 23°F the first week of May. Protected display areas are a must. They will more than pay for themselves in the product they save.

• **Proper retail maintenance is vital.** No amount of marketing will sell a wilted plant, yet on all too many of my visits to chain stores this year, I found plants that were wilted, picked-over, and generally in need of attention. A regular employee training program is needed badly.

• **Prices vary widely – and so does quality.** This past season, I saw flats selling at retail for as high as $12.98 and for as low as two for $5. Both were priced appropriately – an example of the old adage, "You get what you pay for."

• **Are you growing the product for yourself or for consumers?** Be honest. Don't you grow the cultivars that looked good in the flat? That are compact and therefore cheaper to ship? That will last well on retailers' shelves?

These observations prove there is room for improvement in marketing areas that don't require complicated strategies or big budgets. It is time to take the competitive edge by applying customer-oriented marketing principles.

I recently visited a garden center that has done just that. The operation was a picture of success: well-maintained, quality product; knowledgeable, courteous sales help; and plenty of customers enjoying shopping.

How does a garden center take the competitive edge to create such a picture? It takes effort. This particular operation has field representatives that visit growers to see what they are buying and to ensure they get the very best for their customers. When they buy at the local farmer's market, they make sure they're the first ones there – again, to snap up the very best quality for their customers.

It is this type of operation that will survive and thrive, getting top dollar for top quality in spite of the supposed "saturation" of our annuals market. At the same time, the complacent garden center down the street will have trouble selling poor quality at two flats for $5.

*– August 1989*

## Let's Not Be A Part Of The Recession

*Recession changes the market. With the proper selling strategy, you can make the changes work in your favor.*

Recession was the message carried by various events and economic indicators as 1990 became history. The big freeze in California severely damaged citrus and vegetable crops and raised retail produce prices – just as gasoline prices soared after the Iraqi invasion of Kuwait. Bank failures, savings and loan bail-outs, the threat of war...suddenly no one wants to spend any money. It seems as if everyone is trying to talk each other into a recession.

This reminds me of the story of the man who sold hot dogs on the street near the Capitol in Washington, DC. His business was successful and he saved enough to help his son get a business degree from an Ivy League university. After completing his studies in marketing, the son graduated and came home to warn his father of impending recession. "Sales are going down, father," the son cautioned. "Don't order as many hot dogs, and while you're at it, you'd better cut down on your business hours and reduce the size of the hot dogs to reduce your costs." The father followed his son's advice and sure enough, there were fewer sales – and soon he was out of business.

### 'Business Is Great!'

As growers consider the effect recession will have on their businesses, they must also consider how the manner in which they conduct business will affect this effect. I visited one grower who has a big sign on his door announcing, "Business is great! If there is going to be a recession, we are not going to be a part of it." This attitude is not wishful thinking.

Historically, the greenhouse business has been recession-proof. When consumers cut spending, it is generally for high-priced items such as a boat, a car, or a two-week family vacation. Then what do they do? They stay home and fix up the house – planting flowers and vegetables to combat those higher produce prices I mentioned earlier.

*Take The Bull By The Horns*

The point is recession will change the market, but with the proper selling strategy, you can make changes work in your favor. Here are some suggestions that may help:

• **Advertise ways in which your product can save customers money.** Growing your own vegetables is one way to beat high produce prices. Gardening is also a low-cost recreational activity. It's good exercise, offers artistic expression, and can involve the whole family. Flowers also enhance the value of your home – a fact that can pay off at resale time.

• **Advertise how your product can improve the environment.** The "air-conditioning" effects of plants and trees have been well documented. Inspire your customers to make their home environments healthier with the addition of flowers and plants. Teach them about composting, natural mulches and fertilizers, and recycling. Get on the "green" bandwagon.

• **Show customers how they can create a little paradise.** The fact that the economic environment is beyond our personal control can be depressing. It helps to be able to control and improve one's home. Provide customers with information on how to prepare garden beds, how to choose plants that will thrive under their specific yard conditions, and how to plant and maintain their personal paradise.

• **Sell benefits, not plants.** People don't buy plants for plants' sake. They buy plants because they believe the plants will improve their lives in some way. It's up to you to tell them how. Sell natural beauty, clean air, a healthy hobby, homegrown produce, an impressive yard, or a thoughtful gift. Look at your product from a customer's point of view.

It's ironic to see growers spending so much time and effort to grow a product only to have the recession-mongers tell them no one wants it.

Just last Christmas, I visited a grower who told me no one wants poinsettias any more. He said this with a greenhouse full of 100,000 poinsettia plants. He sold his number ones for only $2.75 and his number twos for only $2.25 even though the plants looked great. Because he spent time growing them – and bad-mouthing them – he probably lost $25,000 to $50,000 of his own money.

The moral of this story is: If you don't think you can sell it, don't grow it – and if you are going to take a risk growing it, you'd better put some effort into selling it, too.

The first rule of salesmanship is to be positive. If you're not positive you can sell it for the price you want, don't grow it. If you have the right product at the right place at the right time, you will make the sale. With bedding plants, you already have the right product, the right place, and the right time. It's up to you to make sure the price is also right – for you, the grower, as well as for the buyer and the consumer.

Don't let people beat you down on price. The goal of a successful grower is to grow the crop for as little as possible and to sell it for as much as possible. The goal of a successful buyer is to buy it for as little as possible. Remember, you have a say in what's possible. By trying to beat you down on price and telling you times are bad, the buyer is just doing his job. If he can convince you that your product isn't worth what you're asking and you give in, give up, and walk away, that buyer is doing his job – and you are not doing yours.

There's no doubt in my mind that the recession mentality will make selling more difficult. The pressure will be on to get a cheaper price, but the result will be that we will still sell our product. Whether you make a profit or not depends on how well you sell.

I believe spring 1991 will be great and our product will sell. It's up to you to make it happen.

*– February 1991*

# Thriving Without Mass Merchandisers

*The advice "find a niche and fill it" can help many small to medium-sized retail floriculture operations succeed and profit in spite of chain store competition.*

Smaller retailers' advantage is the great number of different products they have to offer – more than mass merchandisers can handle. Just look, at bedding plants: more than 400 petunia and 200 seed geranium cultivars are available to consumers. Of the top 10 bedding plants, smaller retailers could offer more than 2,000 different cultivars.

### You Can Compete

Here are tips to help retailers compete successfully with "mega stores."

**1. Produce items the mass merchandiser can't or won't handle.** Larger items, custom-made planters, standard tree-type annuals, and taller flowering items too big for a flat would make shipping costs prohibitive for mass merchandisers, so they are reluctant to carry them. Look for new, unusual types of containers in different sizes and shapes. Sell the entire package, not just the plants. Get new items first. Be an innovator so you have the product before the mass merchandisers can get it into their systems.

**2. Specialize in many cultivars.** The large chain stores are reluctant to use cultivar names. There is not enough room in their computers to list all the cultivars separately, so they only want "red" petunias or "yellow" marigolds. Many consumers want to know cultivar names so they can stick with those that have performed well. Also, garden writers usually suggest cultivars that do well in a given area. It is discouraging to look for a cultivar at a chain store that offers only red.

At Michigan State University (MSU), Dr. Lowell Ewart has compiled a list of the best-performing cultivars. We promote these to the gardening public, only to have them tell us they can't find them in stores.

This problem could be a real plus for the independent retailer. Get a list of the best-performing cultivars in your area from your extension office, trial ground, arboretum, or botanical garden, and let them know that you plan to carry these cultivars.

**3. Show people how plants grow.** Did you ever go to Hershey, PA, and see Hershey's display on how chocolate is made? It's a 15-minute free tour that ends at a gift shop. Guess what? The average person who takes this "free" tour spends $10 to $15 on chocolate in Hershey's gift shop.

If you want to feature certain species or specific cultivars, why not make a display featuring them? Show the customer how they grow.

At the MSU Horticulture Gardens, we grow "hyacinth bean," an annual vine that can grow up to 25 feet in one session. It produces beautiful blue flowers and develops large, dramatic bean pods. So many people asked about the plant and wanted to buy seeds that we had to stock the seeds in our information center. Once the customer sees the plant, the desire to buy is developed and the sale is easy.

**4. Offer a wide variety.** About eight years ago, I worked with a former student on developing a business plan for his 10,000-square-foot greenhouse. He was a retail grower with about 20 acres of land on a major highway. How could he compete with retailers at better locations? How could he compete with mass merchandisers?

At the time, his total sales were about $150,000 per year. When we analyzed his competition, we found an area that he could capitalize on: His competitors all had very narrow product lines.

Perennials were starting to become more popular with the gardening public, so he decided to take a three- or four-acre plot and grow perennials from A to Z. He started with about 100 different species and he advertised this fact: "We have the largest selection in town; if you need a particular plant, we are the plant people that have it."

People were pleased with the selection and that they could get their plant questions answered. Each year he broadened his plant line, and today he handles 300 to 400 different perennials as well as bedding plants, pot plants, cut flowers, and nursery stock.

When a superhighway was built right past his business with no exit nearby, the location became less desirable, but his sales did not decrease because people knew he probably had a particular plant they wanted. Wide selection made his business. Today his sales are more than $1 million a year.

**5. Have better trained and more knowledgeable salespeople.** People love to talk about plants and to learn how to grow them. This year, I planted my front yard with New Guinea impatiens in Magic

Planters and they turned out great. Now, every night when I walk my dog, people stop me to ask the cultivar name of the New Guineas, how they were planted, and how they were watered and fed. As a result, several people have bought New Guineas and planted them.

In garden centers, customers talking with knowledgeable salespeople increases sales. Consumer surveys show an important source of information for consumers is knowledgeable sales help. Remember, people want to be successful with plants.

In large chain stores, the salespeople responsible for plants are not trained in product knowledge – or if they are, it is the bare minimum – and turnover at these stores is tremendous. I used to give yearly seminars to one chain of stores; in a three-year period, 90% of the personnel changed.

One of the competitive strengths of the small- to medium-sized retailer is a better trained and more knowledgeable staff. This can relate directly to increased plant sales. I know of a number of nurseries and garden centers that send their employees to extension-sponsored Master Gardener programs to make certain they all have good basic plant knowledge.

**6. Provide excellent service.** If you have a great product, knowledgeable staff, a real interest in plants, and provide excellent service, you can survive the threat of any chain store. But if you don't have the service, you won't make the sale.

Welcome people when they enter your store. Ask if you can be of help. I know of one store that gives first-time customers a tour of the retail area, showing them where everything is and making them feel "at home."

Whatever your technique, it's important to make people feel welcome and that they are getting the product they want at the right price, with the information they need to be successful. This will lead to future sales. These customers will be back many times with their friends because they were well satisfied with your service.

The old saying "Find a niche and fill it" can make many small- to medium-sized retail floriculture operations succeed and profit in spite of chain store competition.

*– October 1994*

# Secrets To Sell Your Plants

*As one grower said to me, "Selling all boils down to the Golden Rule: Do unto others as you would have them do unto you."*

The goal of a grower is to produce a plant for the least amount of money and to sell it for the highest price. The goal of a buyer is to buy it as cheaply as possible and sell it for as much as possible. Therefore, there is a conflict at the interface between the grower and the buyer. This area is where selling and marketing occur.

You don't have to be in this business long before you hear horror stories about deals made – great ones, good ones, fair ones, and poor ones, or deals made between growers and buyers that were never completed. "Buyers always try to beat the grower down." "They try to make you sell below cost." "They know every technique in the book." "They must train them to kill any vendor."

All these statements and hundreds of others can be heard when growers meet. I'm sure that buyers feel growers can be a problem as well. "They don't deliver on time." "They didn't deliver what they promised." "The plants were too short." "The plants have too few flowers."

### Create A Win-Win Situation

Some growers say they will never deal with chain stores because it is too time consuming, the buyers are too difficult, and it isn't worth their effort. Likewise, some chain store buyers will not deal with smaller growers because their supply is too small, and it isn't worth their time and effort on such a small supplier.

After all the griping is over, everyone must realize that 70% to 75% of the product is sold through mass marketing outlets. To make certain that a quality product is produced for the consumer at a fair price, both the grower and the buyer must work together. I believe both parties must have a similar goal, perhaps "to provide as many flowers to as many people at as fair a price as possible."

Both parties have to remember that the best deals are win-win situations. That is, the grower can sell the plants and make the profit necessary to stay in business and the buyer can buy the plants at a price where his company can make a needed profit and still provide the product at a price the consumer will perceive as a fair value.

After talking with many grower salespeople, here are a few of their secrets on what leads to a successful win-win sale:

**1. Be honest.** If you have a quality product, good quantity, and excellent service, being honest is easy. The problem occurs when the product is not excellent, the quantity is low, or there is a problem with service. You must be straightforward with the buyer. One grower said, "We always deliver better quality than the buyer wanted." Understating your product is definitely better than overstating and then delivering something less.

**2. Be consistent.** If one time you have a great product, but the next time you have a poor product to sell, the buyer doesn't know what to expect. The same goes for service and quantity. If you set a standard and the buyer knows that's what will happen each time, then you have a much stronger chance to make a sale and to make it every time.

**3. Know what the buyer wants.** Too often the price is the first item everyone wants to discuss. The salesperson gives the buyer the price list, and the battle begins. The buyer tries to lower the price (that is the buyer's job), and the salesperson tries not to lower the price, and the conflict rages. I've had grower salespeople relay stories of arguing with the buyer for more than four hours for less than 5¢ per pot. Before either can establish a price, the exact product, service, quantity, packaging, or time – a method of payment must be known. Let me give you an example.

### What Not To Do

The salesperson met the buyer and handed out a price list for Christmas crops. The six-inch poinsettias were listed at $3.25 per pot. The buyer immediately started doing a buyer's job. "Well, I'd like to buy 20,000 pots. What is the quantity discount?" The salesperson, seeing the size of the order, showed that for the quantity, they could be provided for $3.15.

The buyer stated that the price was still a little higher than expected and $3.05 would be more in line. The haggling continued, and finally the salesperson, anxious to get the sale, suggested splitting the difference at $3.10. The buyer agreed.

After establishing the price, the buyer stated the rest of the terms of the sale, saying "I'll pay $3.10 for 20,000 poinsettias as we agreed. I assume this will be in pot covers, cased with eight to a box, delivered at weekly intervals to my 20 stores with 200 per store per week, and we will pay you within 60 days after Christmas." The salesperson said, "Okay," and left.

The question is how much did the salesperson really sell the poinsettias for? The salesperson had pictured a pot with foil, not a pot cover which costs at least 15¢ more. The salesperson thought they would ship them all to a warehouse, not to 20 different locations at a time, which adds 10¢ per pot. And the salesperson thought the company would be paid within 15 days. The additional 45 days could cost another 5¢ per pot so the bottom line could be $2.80 per pot. What a sale!

The salesperson walked in with a $3.25 price, negotiated the sale, and actually got $2.80 per pot. That is a 45¢ difference per pot. Was the price list any good? Did the salesperson do the job? The buyer knows how to treat the salesperson from now on. Beat that salesperson down. The buyer knows how to get 40¢ to 50¢ on each pot. The buyer made $9,000 in one hour. What a great employee.

**4. Stick to your price.** In the example, the price list was $3.25. The grower calculated a break-even cost of $2.90 but actually lost 10¢ per pot, so for the privilege of growing 20,000 pots of poinsettias, this grower lost $2,000. If buyers realize sellers are honest, considerate, and know what they want, then price is not negotiable. If a lower price is needed, then find the product to fit that price.

### Profits For All

Being a buyer is tough. You have to find all the products your company needs, get them to the stores when they're needed, sell them at a price customers are willing to pay, and make a profit. Buyers need good sources of supply – people they know can provide a quality product in the quantity they need, when they need it. If you help them do their jobs, there should be money in it for everyone.

If we can continue to build the business so that the grower profits, the retailer profits, and the customer profits, it will continue to grow.

*– December 1996*

# Grow Some C.R.A.P.

*C.R.A.P. stands for Consumer Requested And Profitable.*
*Read the market, try something new, develop the product*
*details, establish a marketing plan, and make it happen.*

Retailers, wholesalers, and most importantly, consumers are looking for something new. As we all know, there are trends that occur, and most of the time growers in floriculture have to be receptive to producing what customers want.

As production people, growers want to be the best at what they produce. They spend a great deal of time, effort, and money to produce that perfect product.

It also takes a great deal of effort to learn how to grow a product so that it will be the best for consumers. I know of growers who grow 10 or fewer products per year, but they produce the best possible product. You can spend a whole week with them discussing in detail all the steps involved in the production for the product. They have more details in their head about the infinite details of production than anyone else in the world.

### Drawing Comparison

This reminds me of Henry Ford and the production line. He developed a system to produce more cars faster than anyone in the world. But they were all the same type and the same color so he saturated the demand for that type of automobile.

Using this example, I suggest floriculture may be hitting the market saturation point on some of its products. Our industry might be in the same position as Henry Ford in that we can produce unlimited quantities of a narrow product mix.

The product mix in our bedding plant industry has greatly narrowed. More than 80% of our sales are in 10 or fewer species. Some growers have 40% of their crop in impatiens, 10% to 15% in petunias, and, if we consider geraniums (seed and cutting), 50% to 70% in this species.

We have taken these products and built an assembly line to produce large quantities in the shortest period of time possible. We can brag about producing flats of impatiens from plugs in 17 days, petunias in 17 days, and seed geraniums in 28 days. Cutting geraniums can also be finished in 28 to 35 days. Henry Ford would be proud of us. I kid people by telling them if we make the same progress of reducing the time to flower in the next century as we did to this century, we will be able to plant the plug in the morning and have it ready for sale that night.

### The Meaning Of C.R.A.P.

This is where C.R.A.P. comes in. C.R.A.P. stands for Consumer Requested And Profitable. Trends like wildflower gardens, butterfly gardens, ornamental grasses, combination planters, the newest varieties of the most popular annuals, and forced perennials fall into the C.R.A.P. category.

The common statement by large production growers (the Henry Ford production type floriculturists) is, "I don't want to grow that new C.R.A.P." I believe it is important for every grower to produce new products every year. Learn how to grow them and try to sell small quantities of them, just in case they change from C.R.A.P. to the main line of large production.

Here are five steps that every production operation should take each year to have the ability to adapt to trends or changes quickly:

**1. Read the market.** Know consumers. What C.R.A.P. do they want? What do they like? Discuss with your retailers and salespeople what they think will happen next year. What plants and ideas should be test marketed? You would be surprised how your retailers and salespeople would respond if you asked them to be part of a new idea or a test to see if the new product would sell. People like to be part of the excitement. Don't leave them out.

**2. Always have something new.** We all know there is a lifecycle on each product we produce. There is an introductory phase, a growth phase, a maturation phase, and the demise of the product.

Take the example of the black and white television. In the early 1950s, it was in its introductory phase. I remember seeing television for the first time by watching network programs on Friday nights at a friend's house. There were 15 to 20 people from the neighborhood who watched in amazement. By the late 1950s and '60s, everyone was buying a television. I didn't have to go to my friend's house to see it anymore.

The growth rate of sales was tremendous. Then the market matured until a new product – the color TV – came into being. We purchased one in 1967. What a difference! The black-and-white TV became obsolete. Realize this point in your production of floriculture crops. Where are each of the products you now grow on this product lifecycle? Make sure you don't have all mature or dying products.

**3. Develop production plans for new items, even if you don't grow them.** You or your production manager should be able to write a step-by-step production system for the potential crops you wish to grow. You need to know what all the proper steps of production are and that they are executed in the proper order. You also need to know what the potential problems are and what the proper control is for each one. Remember, it is much easier to write this information on paper before the crop is started than it is to make a mistake on the crop and try to correct it.

**4. Develop a marketing plan.** If you can tell your salespeople how much product they will have and when they will have it in advance, then they can develop their plan to sell the product. It is fun to be a salesperson if you know the products you have and when you will have them.

I'll give you an example of our student flower shop. We have a yearly budget and at the end of August we needed $24,000 to reach our yearly goal. This money provides our student labor and helps defray student lab fees. So we had four months to get $24,000 or $6,000 per month. We have the products to do it – roses for Sweetest Day, poinsettias for the December open house, and butterfly plants from our new Butterfly House.

When the plan was done, our students knew exactly how many roses, how many poinsettias, and how many butterfly gardens they had to sell. They are now working on their promotion and advertising programs. Their goal will be accomplished because they know what they have to do.

**5. Make C.R.A.P. happen.** Try new products every year. Remember that one out of 50 will probably be a winner. The secret of success is to fail quickly. Try the new product, make sure it is grown properly, marketed properly, and then see what happens.

If it's a winner (profitable), build up production accordingly. If it's a dog, drop it quickly. It is up to you to make certain that what customers want can be provided by you. If you can't do it, your competitors will. It has been said, "Lead, follow, or get out of the way." The same is true with new products.

*– November 1997*

# Create A Gardening Experience

*Meet some growers who are great entertainers. They turned their businesses into theaters and put their products on stage.*

I recently read *The Experience Economy – Work Is Theater And Every Business A Stage* by B. Joseph Pine II and James H. Gilmore. The authors equate a business to a theater. They say products and goods are like props, service is like a stage, and employees are like entertainers. They contend goods and services are no longer enough to survive, but companies need to create experiences to ensure economic growth.

For example, coffee can be sold as a commodity or an experience. The greater the experience that coffee drinkers have, the greater the price that can be demanded of them.

If you buy coffee as a commodity, you can have a cup for 1¢ or 2¢. If it is ground, packaged, and sold in a store it may cost you 5¢ to 25¢. If you buy a cup of joe in a restaurant it might cost 50¢ to $1, but if you buy it in an upscale coffee shop, it can be between $2 and $5 per cup. If you go to the finest cafe in Venice, Italy, and sit looking at the sights of an old world square, watching people pass by, and enjoying the whole atmosphere, your steaming cup of coffee will cost you $15.

Is the experience worth the added cost? Different environments create different experiences and their worth is perceived by consumers.

### Lead By Example

An example of someone with an innovative mind is George Todd, who grew cauliflower in New York and Florida in the late 1960s. He turned the seedling into a speedling when he created a flat with separate cells for each seedling. With this idea, he and several other inventors gave birth to the plug industry.

In 1965, there were no plugs produced in the world. Today, more than 50 billion plugs are produced worldwide. With the plug, Todd created an experience for consumers and growers. This new concept gave us a faster growing, healthier plant that has made consumers more successful gardeners.

Another grower who has created experiences for his customers is Bruce Bordine. Not only do his two retail stores in Michigan have a great assortment of varieties, but they have them when others don't. Bordine has adopted the forcing perennials technology and has extended his two- to four-week sales window to eight weeks.

Bordine also is a very visible part of the experience. Whether he's ringing a cash register in his famous short pants, driving his 16-wheel semi-truck with a big Bordine Nursery ad on its side, or attending meetings across the world, he has definitely created a horticultural experience for consumers and fellow growers. People visit Bordine Nursery for the plants and for the experience. It is a gardener's delight.

### All The World's A Stage

If small growers are to survive, they have to sell the gardening experience to their customers. They need to set the example and realize they can't grow everything for everybody.

In floriculture, we are blessed to have hundreds of thousands of potential products to grow and sell. If you want to sell a plant, you should know everything about it. What are its strong points? Where does it normally grow? What is its history? What are its uses? When does it flower? What can you do with it? Learn how to grow and exploit your plants.

Great entertainers get excited about their work. They know what it takes to provide the audience with an unforgettable experience. These performers follow the adage, "If it is to be, it is up to me."

The same is true in floriculture. Once you know the script (sell 10,000 flats and hanging baskets), you'd better work with the other performers (employees) because there will be millions of spectators (customers) who will be watching you perform.

The Experience Economy is an interesting book and may change your life. It will certainly have you considering that theater and business are similar and to do well in either, you need to be a great performer. I hope this spring will be a great performance for you and your company.

– April 2000

# Shrink The Shrink

*The "shrink" isn't a psychiatrist or a shirt that's too small. It's the more than $300 million in sales lost each year when product is "killed" before it reaches the consumer. It's time to play detective and find out who is killing the plants.*

More than $4 billion worth of annuals, perennials, vegetables, and other crops are sold at garden centers each year. Yet, that sales total is low compared to what it could be.

While growers realize the time, effort, and attention to detail it takes to make these plants acceptable to the retail market, others do not. Greenhouse owners know how to care for plants. But once the plants are placed on the truck and shipped to retailers, their fate is often left in the unskilled hands of people at the other end.

Nearly $300 million of product started at greenhouses in North America is killed and never reaches the consumer. That value is unfortunately deducted directly from retailers' and growers' profits.

Most growers I have spoken with don't know where this shrink occurs. How much happens at the greenhouse? How much during transportation? How much at the retail level? Are the losses associated with a production problem, a transportation problem, or a sales problem? Sure, computers can keep track of sales through the cash register, but they don't indicate why plants didn't make it to the consumer.

### Who Is To Blame?

It's about time we play detective to find out who is killing the plants. The quality and performance of potted and bedding plants can be decreased by everyone along the path to the consumer. Mistakes made by growers will seldom be corrected or improved by retailers or consumers. Fortunately, however, the percent lost at the production level is usually only 1% to 5%. But if problems occur, it's a difficult decision to destroy the plants or sell them at a cheaper price.

Both growers and retailers need to understand the consequences of selling an inferior product to consumers who don't know the problem and will only see the poor results and death of the plant. You may fool the retailer or consumer once, but you will also lose the sale the second time around.

Every year, many retailers offer a training program for their store managers prior to their spring sales season. Often growers, sales managers, and academics like myself are given a chance to tell the store managers how to take care of and handle the spring flowers the chain will sell. Because turnover in personnel at these retailers can be more than 50% each year, these training sessions should be given every year and in a way that a beginner will understand what to do.

Because the loss of money hurts the growers, wholesalers, retailers, and the entire industry, I think it is everyone's responsibility to shrink the shrink.

### Desperate Times Call For...

Despite the attempts to educate retailers about plant care, we still have more than $300 million in lost sales each year. So, when all else fails, try my tongue-in-cheek technique to get your retailer's attention regarding bedding plant care. Then, after you have told them how to kill the plants, provide them with information on how to do it right.

**1. Buy cheap material.** Plants don't have to have quality – that way when you kill them, it won't cost as much as killing the quality plant material. Then order some more plants.

**2. Never water the plants.** If they can't stand drought at the store, they will never stand it in the customer's yard. Then order some more plants for the customer to kill.

**3. Display in an open area, preferably where it is extremely hot or cold, dry or windy.** This can be a quick death for the plants, usually two hours or less. If they die fast, you can order more.

**4. Place flats in the parking lot, either under very hot or cold conditions.** Asphalt is a good absorber of heat so don't water the plants. If they don't die in several hours, have customers drive over them with their cars – then order more plants.

**5. Don't label plants.** Labels only confuse the cashiers and customers. Most of the time neither wants to know what the plant is, and, if no price appears on the plant, the cashier can ring up any price he wants. This system can also help screw up the inventory control and, therefore, no one will know if the plant died in the store or not.

**6. Never tell your employees what the plants are or how to take care of them.** If they don't have that information, they can kill them faster so you can order more plants.

**7. Build interesting displays.** The closer the plants are to death, the closer you should put them to the cash register. Remember, as they move closer to death and closer to the cash register, lower the price. Even if a plant is dead, don't take it out of the display. If the price is low enough, someone may want to buy the dead plant just for the pot and soil.

**8. Don't clean or straighten up the sales area.** Make it look natural. Remember plants love dirt, weeds, diseases, and insects – that's nature's way. If you can keep all of these problems in your display area, plants can die faster.

**9. Don't provide any information on plant care.** If customers want a plant, they should figure out how to grow it themselves. And if they don't know how to take care of the plant, they can kill it faster.

**10. After holiday weekends, stop all care of your plants in the garden center.** No one wants plants after that time and you can use the space for outdoor furniture, hard goods, or boating equipment. Keep dead plants in a pile so all your customers can see what a favor you did for them by killing the plants at the store so they won't have to do it themselves at home.

### But Seriously, Folks

In summary, kill plants quickly, then order more. This technique will help keep your shrink at least 20%. We know this system works because it has been done many times before.

I showed one of my grower friends "Ten Ways To Kill Bedding Plants." He said, "Heck, don't give them 10 ways, it only takes one way – don't water them."

The bottom line is we have a major problem with shrink both at the greenhouse and retail level. Let's work on reducing the $300 million loss. It would be much better to put that money into your profit, the retailer's profits, and research development for new products that will lead to more enjoyment for our customers.

*– March 2001*

# 'I'm Not Lying, I'm Selling'

## Making a good deal is both an art and a science. It takes a lot of effort!

Growers often share with me the frustrations they have from negotiating plant sales with the big box stores. These discussions beg the question: Where do chain store buyers get their training and how do they know how to handle growers who negotiate a price for their product?

To help answer this question, I recently took a negotiation course offered by Chester Karass in Grand Rapids, MI. I was among 30 other students – all of whom were buyers or sellers. For two days, our instructor taught us the basics of negotiating. We also participated in case studies and role-playing games. Buyers had the opportunity to be sellers and vice-versa.

By the end of the course, I had a greater appreciation for the art and science of what it takes to make a good deal. I also realized that good deals don't just happen. They require a lot of effort from both buyers and sellers.

People with excellent negotiating skills use several techniques to get what they want. They are trained to know what strategies work best for any given situation and how they can use them. For people who don't possess good negotiating skills, it is extremely difficult to make a deal that is satisfying.

### Seller Beware

Here are four tactics trained buyers will use during a negotiation, according to Karass.

**1. The bogey technique.** When buyers compliment sellers on being great growers, they are probably using this strategy. The buyer might say: "I love your product, but you are asking $6.50 per flat. I only have money to pay $6 per flat, and other growers are offering me their material for that amount."

Buyers want sellers' product but don't want to pay their price for it. To make matters worse, they may only offer sellers an hour to negotiate the deal, giving a "take it or leave it" ultimatum. Buyers probably use this technique more than any other.

**2. The crunch technique.** In this scenario, a buyer has bids from four other growers. They are $6.05, $6.10, $6.20, and $6.30 per flat. You are the highest bidder at $6.50 per flat, prompting the buyer to say, "You have to do better than that." Buyers want to see how much sellers are willing to reduce their price. Sellers may think "better" means a lower price. But it may also mean better service or better terms.

**3. The nibble technique.** This technique is also widely used in floriculture. Buyers will agree to a grower's price, but then might say, "The price I quoted included pot covers, delivery to each store, and a free greenhouse for the spring and summer."

Buyers work at nibbling away at the quoted price. I've seen cases where growers thought they got $3.50 for a pot of six-inch poinsettias, but by the time the buyers were done nibbling, they only received $3.

**4. The "bear in the back room" technique.** One of the most effective ways to negotiate is to not have the authority. Buyers will listen to sellers, ask them questions, and try to agree on a price. They then tell the sellers that they can't make the final decision on the deal because their boss has to approve it.

In this situation, a buyer might say, "I really like you and your product and hope we can work together, but my boss (the bear in the back room) makes the final decision and you know how difficult he can be."

Buyers will ask sellers if they are offering the best price they can. "I want to work with you, but I don't know if my boss will accept this price," they'll say. Sellers will tell the buyers they have already lowered the price as much as they possibly can. Then, buyers will wait a day, ask the sellers again to lower their price, and, if they get the price they want, will tell the sellers that their boss (the bear in the back room) has agreed to the deal.

These are just some of the techniques used by buyers during negotiations. As you can see, in many cases buyers or sellers aren't always truthful. When I took the negotiation course, one of the students said, "I'm not lying, I'm selling."

### Developing A Win-Win Situation

As buyers and sellers get to know each other, they usually try to develop a situation in which they both can win. Both parties want to make the deal better for everyone. For this to happen, they have to know what each other needs and when the price is acceptable to each.

Buyers and sellers also have to stop "dumping garbage" on each other. In other words, they have to stop mentioning every problem they've had with each other in the past (i.e., "your delivery was one day late at Mother's Day" or "you rejected a load of plants because the fork lift was not available").

I've found price negotiations shouldn't be a half-hour discussion. Usually, quick deals are bad deals because all of the details can not be discussed in 15 or 20 minutes. This leads to misunderstanding, confusion, and disappointment.

A win-win situation often has to occur on a personal level. Each party must trust the other's ability. They both must be able to deliver what they promise. Once both buyers and sellers know what to expect, deals become easier to make and positive results occur.

Despite the personalization of today's transactions, technology is equally important for buyers and sellers. Every sale is now tracked by computers, bar codes, and scanners, giving buyers an instant financial profile of every seller. It is no longer just impressions on how the product looked or how it sold. The financial information, the bottom line, is known. Therefore, buyers don't continue to buy from sellers who can't make them money.

Likewise, sellers don't sell to buyers who can't make them money.

### Everyone Negotiates

Even buyers who say, "make me your best deal, I never negotiate," are, in reality, negotiating. If the offer is disappointing to them, they'll become unhappy and tell others that your price is to high.

One of the best negotiators I've met uses this technique with me. I reassure him that he doesn't have to negotiate. Yet, his technique is just a combination of all the negotiation techniques I've learned. I hope you will realize that if you don't learn the basics of the negotiation skills, you will lose a great deal of money and you will be at a great disadvantage.

I'd strongly suggest you take a two-day course in negotiating. It may cost $1,000, but you'll make many thousands more in future sales. Remember, "I'm not lying, I'm selling" is a shaky foundation for building a business.

*— June 2001*

# Meet Your Customers In Gardens

*So many new varieties are introduced each year that it is hard for growers – and consumers – to know what's what. Public gardens are hidden treasures where we can meet our customers where we should – in a garden.*

Never before have there been so many new products coming into the garden plant market. There were more than 700 new varieties and cultivars introduced at this year's California pack trials alone.

At the Ohio Florists' Association's Short Course, I gathered literature from every propagator and breeder and spent several days just reviewing all their material. I also visited a few trial gardens to look at more than 1,000 varieties being tested in the field. Without a doubt, there is no shortage of material from which to choose.

I then asked several grower friends what they were going to grow. Even at the end of August, many were unsure of their product mix. Some said they are waiting for requests from the big box stores. Others said they were variety weary from last year's promotional efforts, with some stores requesting almost 100 different species and cultivars (e.g., Martha Stewart mix, Proven Winners).

Because there are so many new varieties introduced each year, it becomes extremely difficult for growers to decide what to grow and how to grow it. Putting a new species or variety into production and taking it from 0 to 1,000, 5,000, or 10,000 flats with no previous experience is no easy task. Likewise, growing planters, hanging baskets, or color bowls with several different species and trying to get them to flower at the same time can be difficult.

### Less Work, Less Confusion

As you can see, growers and retail growers face a big dilemma in choosing what to grow based on consumer demand. Statistics indicate only 38% of our garden plant products are grown in flats. There is no doubt consumers, made up of more than 60% dabblers who spend only one or two hours a week in the garden, prefer plants that require little or no work. As a result, they are buying more containers.

One of my neighbors actually bought more than 30 hanging baskets, took the wires off them, and planted them on both sides of his driveway entrance. When I asked him why, he said they need less work and look great as soon as they are planted.

All the names of plants that we have introduced have confused everyone, as well. No longer is a verbena a verbena. It can be a Temari, a Babylon, or a Tapien. In 2000, there were five new Temari and five new Babylon. This is a species that represented less than 1% of bedding plant sales five years ago, now sold under three different names with 10 new cultivars introduced in one year.

It is not surprising consumers visit garden centers and ask for particular brands (e.g., Proven Winners) because that is the only thing they remember about the plant they bought the previous year.

The average gardener only spends an hour or two gardening a week. On the flip side, it would take a 10-week course just to learn the names of the new varieties and cultivars introduced into our industry in the last year. Therefore, I believe our industry has a great opportunity to inform the general public about the new products that are available for the next planting season.

### Tapping Botanical Gardens

One avenue that could be much more developed and provide a great viewing area for our new products is the botanical gardens. They are untapped goldmines for developing new, more informed customers.

Most botanical gardens were started by rich philanthropists, universities, governments, or foundations to study botany (i.e., plant classification, genetics, and plant physiology). Private botanical gardens like Longwood Gardens and the Missouri Botanical Gardens were developed to please the interests of the benefactors. Therefore, most plant collections were used to study the classification of plants and economic botany, that is plants that were grown for economic use (i.e., dye plants, medicinal plants, plants used for fiber). These gardens were also used to train gardeners who could work in them or in the gardens of large estates. Catering to the general public was not one of the original intentions of these facilities.

Several years ago, I visited the Royal Botanical Gardens in

Copenhagen, Denmark, and had the opportunity to visit with its director. I asked him who funded the gardens, and he indicated it was funded by the government. Some graduate students from the University of Copenhagen used the gardens as a laboratory. There was no admission charge for visitors.

In contrast, many botanical and horticultural gardens in the United States charge an admission fee to visitors to see what plants can do in the their own gardens. These gardens have become of interest to young people, and many school systems use this resource to teach young children from kindergarten through sixth grade the importance of plants in our everyday lives. Some botanical gardens offer children's gardens and butterfly gardens.

As these gardens now relate more to the average homeowner and to the general public, the number of visitors continues to increase each year. For instance, in Michigan, with a population of about nine million people, between one and two million people visit these facilities in the state each year. Where else can we directly contact 15% to 20% of the public who use and buy our products.

### Making Our Gardens Useful

With this great opportunity, we are still missing the boat. While the gardens display and identify the new materials, consumers who like what they see still don't know where to buy the product.

One of the most asked questions in our gardens is, "Where can I buy this variety?" While we can tell visitors the company that provided the seeds or plants, most of the time we don't have a list of local retailers that sell the product. Perhaps it's time for the industry and botanical and horticultural gardens to work together to satisfy consumers' wants and needs.

Some botanical gardens, such as the Niagara Parks Botanical Gardens in Niagara Falls, ON, display new varieties and cultivars from only six to eight major companies. The beds are 30- by 60-feet and contain six to 12 new items. Visitors can see how the plants look by themselves or in combinations with other plants. All items in each display bed are from a single company, and there is a plaque describing and identifying each plant. The plants in the bed are identified by number, and the information can be easily read from the plaque which is at the center of the bed standing about three feet off the ground. Some of the plaques refer to Web sites that list places where the plants can be purchased.

At Michigan State University, we have started a similar approach with hanging basket material. Four Star Greenhouses in Carleton, MI, provides us with about 100 hanging baskets each year, which are displayed on all the pavilions and lampposts in the gardens. Each container has an identification tag along with a Web site address where more information can be obtained about the plants and where to order them.

There are now many botanical and horticultural gardens with industry advisory committees that help the gardens in identifying what material to obtain and display. The committee works with the gardens to ensure visitors receive information that will help them in their own home or landscape.

### Building A Network

Our industry should become more involved with these botanical gardens. They are hidden treasures that can help provide new varieties and cultivars of garden plants. A network can be built to introduce new material and have it directly available to consumers.

Check out your local botanical or horticultural garden, and see if you can be part of this process. Then we can meet customers where we should, in a garden.

*— October 2001*

## Torment Your Customers

*Meet three people who have a talent for selling. They could sell a refrigerator to an Eskimo!*

Each month, I enjoy reading the *Harvard Business Review's* great business management articles. While most are pretty technical and require a lot of concentration to digest the content, the articles are of great value.

After reading this publication for several years, I was shocked by an article in the October 2001 issue written by Stephen Brown, a professor of marketing research at the University of Ulster in Northern Ireland. It was entitled "Torment Your Customers (They'll Love It)." While everyone tries to get their customers to love them by working together and doing everything the customers want, Brown suggests we should use a retro-marketing technique. He contends people want to want your product.

For example, Volkswagen has reintroduced the Beetle. I remember buying my first Beetle in 1965 for $2,000. Today, a design that looks a lot like that old model sells for $20,000. Brown indicates in his article that some suppliers make sales by saying, "If you want it, you can't have it," or "If we have one available, we might call you. But don't call us – we'll call you."

### Talented Trio

Some people just have a talent for sales. They can sell a refrigerator to an Eskimo. Webster defines talent as the facility for effective performance along certain lines, and superior intelligence and ability as in business or artistic pursuits. In our industry, I've been privileged to know some of the greatest salespeople. They were personalities who sold themselves first. Let's look at three of these folks. While you may not have heard of them and they may not have made the most sales in terms of dollars, they definitely possess the talent.

**Si Randolph.** When I first came to Michigan, I met Si Randolph, a salesperson for George Ball. Si knew everyone, their family and children, and their birthdays. He would talk to all his accounts weekly and when he came to visit – not sell – everyone would just have to be with him. At a time when growers were looking for someone to offer help, guidance, and products, Si provided it all. His customers loved him – except for a few – and whatever Si said, happened. He helped Detroit vegetable growers get into the bedding plant industry and make money. He was a great salesperson and he knew how to dazzle people with his personality and performance.

In the end, everyone prospered and made money. If a grower wanted a product, Si would deliver it no matter what it was. Often, he would tell people they couldn't get the product – it was too late to order it – but only Si could make it possible. All the growers thought he controlled and maybe owned the company because what Si said, Si made happen. We could argue over whether these were skills taught to Si by his company or if it was a talent Si possessed from the beginning.

I recently had a discussion with my boss at Meister Publishing Co., GG's parent company, about how we hire and train people at Michigan State University. After several sparring rounds, Dick Meister sent me a book, First, Break All the Rules by Marcus Buckingham and Art Coffmore, with a note – "Read it and you will see what I mean."

The bottom line of the book and of Dick Meister's point is: "You can teach skills but it is very difficult to change talents." I believed this statement before but after these reinforcements, I believe it more than ever.

**Hank Engh.** Another super salesperson who used retromarketing was Hank Engh, the self-proclaimed Petunia King from Utah. One spring day, he was stuck with 4,000 flats of petunias. The weather was bad and he had no place to sell them. Hank bought time on his local radio station and advertised that he was the Petunia King. He said in his honor, there would be a parade through the center of town that Saturday morning. He then hired the local high school band and a couple of fire trucks, and got a permit for his parade. The procession started at the town hall and ended in front of his nursery. It attracted about 1,000 people and he sold all the flats. From that time on, he has been known as the Petunia King.

I've often thought of Hank as the Music Man of horticulture. In the movie The Music Man, Robert Preston shows the talent he has for selling, even if in the end he does not have the skill to accomplish his goal. In contrast, Hank, the avid salesman, used his skills to create demand and excitement for his petunias.

While many industries, including floriculture, have spent millions of dollars on national campaigns to buy flowers, the most effective efforts have been made by companies, individuals, or groups that have supported consumer information on how to grow or use our product.

**Princess.** The third example of a talented salesperson in our industry is a woman who sells cut flowers to supermarkets and big box stores nationwide. Because she is still actively involved in the business I won't use her real name but I'll call her Princess. Because Princess sells only one major item, she realizes her competitor is not only the other people who grow her product, but also any other floral or nonfloral product that can be provided at an equal or lower price and provide customer satisfaction. Princess controls a large percentage of the market, and therefore she can set the price and provide service and quality over the whole country.

The key to her success is developing a win-win situation. Princess has the same talents as Si Randolph because she knows everyone, is truly interested in their welfare, and will do all that's necessary to make them successful. She also has a little Hank Engh in her, using her skills to create an event whenever she wants.

### A Gift For Sales

The interesting point about these three individuals is that none of them were trained in horticulture and only Princess has a college degree. But they all possess talent and skills that allowed them and their companies to prosper.

Si Randolph had a unique product. It wasn't the seed or the supplies. Si's product was what he produced – service, information, and concern for his clients.

Hank Engh's product was petunias. While not a unique product, Hank had the advertising and promotion skills that helped him become the Petunia King. He will always be remembered for his showmanship.

Princess can deal with the powerful buyers because, not only does she represent a low-cost producer, she also possesses the service, information, and concern for her clients. Princess also has the skill to generate the excitement, advertising, and promotion she needs to sell her product.

While I've only singled out three people to serve as examples of sales genius, there are thousands in our industry who work everyday to sell and market our products. While they all work to satisfy customers, many do well by understanding they should torment our buyers. It is only with mutual respect between the buyer and the seller that an industry will survive.

*– December 2001*

# Will Branding Help Floriculture?

*The right plant, the right service, and a great grower can make the right brand for floriculture. A washer is a washer, but a lonely repairman says "Maytag!"*

Brand names are not a new idea. A form of branding was found in prehistoric cave paintings, where marks were used as a sign of ownership of bison. It also can be traced back more than 4,000 years to Egypt, where cattle were branded to prove ownership. In 500 B.C., the Romans marked bricks to prove ownership. Around 1200 A.D., the Italians used watermarks to identify their paper.

### Brand Functions

Identification is the first reason for branding. Trademarks have always been used to identify individuals' work and, as mass production became more prevalent, companies used brands or trademarks to identify their products and services, as well.

But as more and more competition occurred and product variability decreased, certain products became commodities and branding was a way of product differentiation. This was a way to obtain loyalty between the company and the consumer. Therefore, a popular brand became a valuable asset for a company. It allowed the company to separate its product from all other companies.

As identification became common, some companies used their brands to be communicators. For example, Maytag Appliances uses its brand to tell people that its products are trouble-free. Maytag advertising always depicts a lonely repair man, instilling in consumers that the company produces quality products that never need servicing.

Within our industry, brands like Bordine's Better Blooms suggest that Bordine's plants are better than the average. Relating such messages to product brands can be a powerful tool in communicating a product's worth to consumers. A third function of a brand is as a protector. As a company's legal property, developing strong product loyalty among consumers can make a brand a valuable competitive asset.

Finally, brands are enablers in that if they are strong enough, they can play strong roles in a company's strategy for future growth while discouraging competitive companies to enter a particular market.

Because of these advantages, it is standard for companies to brand their products and services. In 1998, there were 106,129 trademarks, brand names, symbols, and words issued – 21% more than in 1997 and 300% more than in 1988. Interestingly, in 1905 when the trademark act was established, 16,000 applications were filed. Of this group, only 400 brand names are still in use today.

### Lettuce Vs. Salad

In horticulture, branding has also had a great effect on how a product is sold. Let's take lettuce as an example. Head lettuce is a commodity. Sold both in crates and by the head at retail, its price fluctuates greatly from 29¢ to $1.50 a head. But with added value, lettuce has grown into a brand name commodity. Two companies, Dole Fresh Vegetables Inc. and Fresh Express, now use 40% of the lettuce grown in California's Salinas Valley to produce bagged salads. While head lettuce prices widely fluctuate, the price of bag salads is fairly stable, ranging from $1.50 to $2 per one-pound bag. More exotic lettuce blends can retail for closer to $3 for a little as a five-ounce bag. In addition, bagged salads prolonged shelflife due to creative packaging makes the product last up to two weeks, while fresh head lettuce usually lasts a week or less. The added value has helped grow the bagged salad industry to a worth of more than $1.7 billion annually in fewer than 10 years.

Thus, as consumers' tastes and preferences evolve, so do their needs. Rather than settling for the head of lettuce, from which they would traditionally make their own salads, time constraints and expanded purchasing power have changed their perceived and desired quality of life, making the value-added product a necessity. The consumer now knows the bagged salads last longer and are convenient to use and they know that Fresh Express or Dole provide the products that satisfy their salad needs.

### Making Our Mark

In floriculture, we are still in the "head of lettuce" stage of brand development. For instance, one has only to look at the last few issues of *Greenhouse Grower* to see all the new varieties, products, and trade names currently on the market or in development. More than 500 new varieties were introduced at the 2002 California pack trials alone. How do we as growers know what to grow and what will sell? How can we possibly know what prices we can ask for products that are flooding the market? How can we expect consumers to know the difference between one red petunia and another if retailers can't tell them? Usually, a plant's identity is lost by the time the plant leaves the wholesale grower.

Although flats of bedding plants account for only 36% of total sales, we still go to our major accounts and quote a price per flat. Retailers continue to sell flats at the same price. That's why they have become commodity items – year after year, growers undercut each other and produce flats at the lowest price to get the business. This is the "head of lettuce" mentality. Conversely, if you can add value and differentiate your product from a commodity, then you can sell it for more than a commodity. This is the "bagged salad" mentality.

Most consumers still rely on a retailer or product with which they are most familiar. I asked a number of average consumers to name a horticulture company they were familiar with and they said Kmart, Home Depot, Wal-Mart, Lowe's, Scotts, Burpee, and their local garden centers or greenhouses. Yet The Flower Fields, Proven Winners, Simply Beautiful, and several other companies and campaigns are working hard to develop brand identities to communicate their products' messages and differentiate them from the 500 new varieties that will eventually reach the consumer. Millions of dollars will be spent on generating consumer awareness of the values of these new products and, ultimately, these initiatives will contribute to the greater good of our industry.

### The Future Is In Our Hands

In the baking industry, it is the dough that makes the difference in the bread. In the floriculture industry, it is the plant that makes the difference. Regardless of the brand of plants you grow, the quality you produce will be the protector of your business. It alone can be the brand name of your company and its legal property.

Three growers can grow the same variety three different ways. Thus, your name is your trademark. The plants you grow certainly will determine what the end product will look like, but you, with your skill and knowledge of how to grow them, will make the difference.

Produce the quality that will separate your products from others.

Buy the varieties that perform best in your region – those you would grow in your own garden. Package the plants so they will save the customer time in planting and make it easy for them to use. Grow healthy plants so gardeners can be successful with them and enjoy them in their gardens. The right plant, the right product and service, and a great grower can make the right brand. Good luck and happy branding.

*– September 2002*

## Knowledge Can Mean Money And Power

*You may not be an inventor or implementor of new knowledge, but you can be a plant exploiter. Use knowledge of new cultivars to build your business.*

In 1985, Peter Drucher wrote a classic article entitled "The Discipline Of Innovation," which listed seven sources of innovation: 1) unexpected occurrences; 2) incongruities; 3) process needs; 4) industry and market changes; 5) demographic changes; 6) changes in perception; and 7) new knowledge.

While all of these are sources of new ideas that can lead to new, profitable products or processes for your business, the area of new knowledge has never been riper for development than it is today.

Here are some data that will prove this point. The U.S. patent office was created in 1802 and will be celebrating its 200th anniversary this year. It took 100 years for the first one million patents to be issued. From 1900 to 1960, between 35,000 to 50,000 patents were awarded yearly. Then from 1960 to 1990, between 60,000 to 90,000 a year were issued. In the last 11 years, between 90,000 to 187,000 patents were awarded each year. All of these patents represent a wealth of new knowledge that is only a small portion of the total knowledge available for use. In addition, many profitable ideas are left unused and are collecting dust on bookshelves of libraries. It takes as much time, effort, and creativity to commercially develop this new knowledge as it does to discover it.

It also takes time to take the idea found in the research and adapt it to your specific need. Here are a few stories (or jokes) about this process:

**Story No. 1:** There was an inventor who tried to invent a new soft drink. He worked on it for a long time and finally tried to introduce it into the business world as 1-Up. Critics thought the product could be improved, so his second attempt was developed and called 2-Up. This continued on through versions 3-Up, 4-Up, 5-Up, and finally, on the last attempt, the product was tried as 6-Up. The inventor became so discouraged that he gave up on the product and sold the whole project to another inventor. The new inventor worked on the project for less than a month and introduced the world-famous soft drink 7-Up.

The moral of the story: If at first you don't succeed, try, try again.

**Story No. 2:** An inventor introduced what he thought would be a new toothpaste, but it tasted so bad that the test panel told him what he could do with it. So he did and that was how Preparation-H was developed.

The moral of the story: Make sure you have the right use for the product.

**Story No. 3:** When an inventor introduced Novocain, he thought the major market for its sales would be for surgery. To his surprise, surgeons wanted their patients completely sedated, while dentists thought Novocain would be perfect for local anesthesia. He spent the rest of his life giving lectures to dental groups all over the world about the use of his product.

The moral of the story: Know your market.

### Be A Plant Exploiter

While you may not be an inventor or implementor of new knowledge, you can be a plant exploiter. Thousands of new varieties have been introduced into our industry within the last five years. While several growers and companies are trying to exploit specific cultivars, many of these great cultivars will never have an impact on the gardening public in this country. Yet, many varieties would have great value and be enjoyed if only gardeners were exposed to them. Because of this situation, I am seeing more wholesale and retail growers building their own trial grounds. This is a great sales tool to show people what is available and then take their orders for the next growing season.

The Dutch bulb industry has successfully used this technique for years. Each spring, you can visit gardens in Holland where there are tremendous displays of all types of spring flowering bulbs. You can choose the ones you prefer and then place your order so you will receive the bulbs in the fall and have them flower in your yard the following spring. If it can be done with bulbs, it can and should also be done with annuals and perennials.

The major problem with U.S. public gardens is that they showcase all the new materials but when visitors ask where they can buy them, no one has the answer. You need to use this problem as an opportunity to attract customers to your business by providing solutions.

*Create The Demand*

Here are 10 steps to using new cultivar knowledge at your business:

**1. Identify the best cultivars for your area.** Get the information from local trial gardens or seed companies.

**2. Collect information about the plants.** People like to know not only what the plant is, but also information about it. What are its significant attributes? Also, tell them stories about the plant and make them personal. For example, did you see it in Europe? Do you know the breeder? Create interest.

**3. Develop your test garden.** Make it part of your retail display or use it as a center point of your wholesale greenhouse grounds.

**4. Let as many people as possible view the gardens.** Have them vote on the plants they would most like to have in their gardens or, if they are wholesale buyers, which they think their customers would prefer. Use different colored garden stakes to distinguish gardeners' votes from growers'.

**5. If customers want to order cultivars for next spring, let them fill out the order form.** Mandate a minimum order required to grow the cultivar.

**6. Provide everyone with the yearly summary of which ones were voted the best.** Keep those cultivars on a best varieties list for at least five years and make sure you offer them each year.

**7. Promote the winners.** Display pictures of the winners in your retail store or catalog during the fall and winter months.

**8. Advertise the winners and your business.** For example, adopt a slogan like, "Our customers pick the best, we do the rest."

**9. The best product and cultural practices produce the best quality product.** If the old saying, "Quality sells itself" is true, then the best plant plus the best production techniques equal the best sales.

**10. Get excited about your work.** Enthusiasm about your products and services will catch on.

*— November 2002*

# *References*

Leaders are readers. There are few original thoughts, so you need to draw from any you can get your hands on. Everyone has favorite references that they read and re-read. Here are some of mine.

On this list are books and articles that I mentioned in the columns included in this book. Because the columns were published over a time span of three decades, some of them are no longer in print. You may be able to find them at your local library or through bookstores, which have out-of-print and used books available. Other suggestions range from popular paperbacks and magazines to textbooks that continue to challenge me as I seek to add to my knowledge and explore new ideas.

## Evolution Of An Industry

*American Demographics, Consumer Trends for Business Leaders.* (800-529-7502 to subscribe.)

Ball, V. *Ball RedBook,* 16th Edition, Ball Publishing, 1998.

Dole, J.M. and Wilkins, H.F. *Floriculture Principles and Species*, Simon & Schuster, 1998.

Larson, R.A. *Introduction to Floriculture*, Academic Press, 1992.

Mastalerz, J. *The Greenhouse Environment, The Effect of Environmental Factors on Flower Crops*, Wiley, John & Sons, Inc., 1977.

Naisbitt, J. *Megatrends: Ten New Directions for Transforming Our Lives*, Warner Books, 1982.

Nelson, P. *Greenhouse Operation and Management*, Pearson Education, 2002.

USDA National Agricultural Statistics Service, *Floriculture Crops Summary,* http://usda.mannlib.cornell.edu/reports/nassr/other/zfc-bb/.

## Legends Of Floriculture

Fulghum, R. *All I Really Need to Know I Learned in Kindergarten*, Villard Books, 1988.

## Taking The Lead

Bechtell, M.L. *The Management COMPASS, Steering the Corporation Using Hoshin Planning*, AMACOM, 1997.

Buckingham, M. and Clifton, D.O. *Now, Discover Your Strengths: How to Develop Your Talents and Those of the People You Manage*, The Free Press, 2001.

Cain, H. *CEO of Self, You're in Charge*, Tapestry Press, 2001.

Canfield, J., Hansen, M., and Hewitt, L. *The Power of Focus – How to Hit Your Business, Personal and Financial Targets with Absolute Certainty*, Health Communications, Inc., 2001.

Certo, S.C. *Modern Management*, Pearson Education, 2002.

Fulghum, R. *Maybe (Maybe Not): Second Thoughts on a Secret Life*, Villard Books, 1993.

Graham, S. *You Can Make It Happen: A Nine Step Plan for Success*, Simon & Schuster, 1997.

Johnson, S. *Who Moved My Cheese?: An Amazing Way to Deal with Change in Your Work and in Your Life*, G.P. Putnam's Sons, 1998.

Jones, C.E. *Life Is Tremendous*, Tyndale House, 1981.

Ribeiro, L. *Success Is No Accident*, Urano Publishing, Inc., 2001.

### Getting Started In Business

Black, F., Kaufman, S., and Wallace, A.S. "Strategic Management for Competitive Advantage," *Harvard Business Review*, July/August 1980. (800-274-3214 to subscribe.)

Gerber, M. *E-myth Revisited: Why Most Small Businesses Don't Work and What to Do about It*, Harper Business, 1995.

Gerber, M. *Power Point*, Harper Business, 1991.

Lesonsky, R. *Start Your Own Business*, Entrepreneur Press, 2001.

### Taking Care Of Business

Collins, J.C. *Good to Great: Why Some Companies Make the Leap...and Others Don't*, HarperCollins, 2001.

Copeland, T., Koller, T., and Murrin, J. *Valuation – Measuring and Managing the Value of Companies*, Wiley, John & Sons, Inc., 2000.

*Fast Company* (Subscribe or e-mail questions or comments at www.fastcompany.com).

Flaherty, J.E. *Peter Drucker, Shaping the Managerial Mind*, Wiley, John & Sons, Inc., 2002.

*Forbes* (800-888-9896 to subscribe).

Graham, J.R. "Don't Bother with the Process; the Results Are What

Count," *Flower News, The Floral Industry's National Weekly.* (312-739-5000 to subscribe.)

Maltz, M. *Psycho-Cybernetics,* Simon & Schuster, 1970.

Wilde, S. *The Trick to Money Is Having Some,* Hay House, Inc., 1995.

## Cultivating Employees

Kiyosaki, R.T. and Lechter, S.L. *Rich Dad, Poor Dad: What the Rich Teach Their Children about Money That the Poor and Middle Class Do Not,* Warner Books, Inc., 2000.

## Connecting With Customers

Ulwick, A.W. "Turn Customer Input into Innovation," *Harvard Business Review,* January 2002.

## Marketing Your Product

Brown, S. "Torment Your Customers (They'll Love It)," *Harvard Business Review,* October 2001.

Buckingham, M. and Coffman, C. *First, Break All the Rules: What the World's Greatest Managers Do Differently,* Simon & Schuster Adult Publishing Group, 1999.

Gilmore, J.H. and Pine II, B.J. *The Experience Economy – Work Is Theater and Every Business a Stage,* Harvard Business School Publishing, 1999.

Karrass, C.L. *The Negotiating Game,* Harper Business, 1994.

Karrass, C.L. *In Business As In Life – You Don't Get What You Deserve, You Get What You Negotiate,* Stanford Street, 1996.

Lewicki, R.J., Minton, J.W., and Saunders, D.M. *Negotiation,* The McGraw-Hill Companies, Inc., 1999.

Niebenberg, G.I. *The Art of Negotiating,* Barnes & Noble, 1995.